THE
C
COMPANION

PRENTICE-HALL SOFTWARE SERIES

Brian W. Kernighan, Advisor

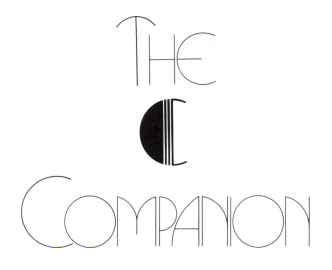

THE C COMPANION

ALLEN I. HOLUB

PRENTICE-HALL, INC., Englewood Cliffs, New Jersey 07632

Library of Congress Cataloging-in-Publication Data

Holub, Allen I.
    The C companion.

    (Prentice-Hall software series)
    Bibliography: p. 267
    Includes index.
    1. C (Computer program language)   I. Title.
II. Series.
QA76.73.C15H65   1987   005.13′3   86-25495
ISBN 0-13-109786-5

Editorial/production supervision by Margaret Rizzi
Cover design by Lundgren Graphics, Ltd.
Manufacturing buyer: Ed O'Dougherty

Printed in the United States of America

10   9   8   7   6   5

ISBN   0-13-109786-5   025

PRENTICE-HALL INTERNATIONAL (UK) LIMITED, *London*
PRENTICE-HALL OF AUSTRALIA PTY. LIMITED, *Sydney*
PRENTICE-HALL CANADA INC., *Toronto*
PRENTICE-HALL HISPANOAMERICANA, S.A., *Mexico*
PRENTICE-HALL OF INDIA PRIVATE LIMITED, *New Delhi*
PRENTICE-HALL OF JAPAN, INC., *Tokyo*
PRENTICE-HALL OF SOUTHEAST ASIA PTE. LTD., *Singapore*
EDITORA PRENTICE-HALL DO BRASIL, LTDA., *Rio de Janeiro*

CONTENTS

PREFACE

C language textbooks are usually written either for very sophisticated readers, or for very inexperienced ones. Both types of texts have a common problem, they lack technical background material. The elementary texts assume that the reader won't understand this material and the advanced texts assumes that the reader already has the required background.

To intermediate-level programmers, the basic texts are both boring and not sufficiently comprehensive. They don't cover the material in the depth the programmer requires.

The beginning C programmer has a more difficult problem. A great deal of background material is needed before you can really understand how the C language works. Trying to learn the language without that background is frustrating because the beginner won't understand what various operators do, much less how they're used. It's also very difficult to debug a C program if you don't understand the underlying structure of the computer. By not supplying this background, the "C for the beginner" sort of textbooks are actually cheating the reader. One just can't learn the language without the prerequisites.

This book corrects these problems in two ways. It provides background material useful for mastering the C language and for understanding a classic source like Kernighan and Ritchie (see Bibliography). It also looks in depth at

x

several advanced topics, such as sophisticated uses of pointers and subroutines with a variable number of arguments.

How To Use This Book

You can't learn the rudiments of C from this book. In fact, you should be studying a general textbook while using this book. You can use the book in one of two ways: You can read through it systematically, alternating chapters here with chapters in a normal textbook, or you can read the chapters more or less at random. Even the most basic chapters assume that you know a little about the language, how to declare variables, what a **while** loop is, and so on.

The book can be divided into four sections. Chapters 1 to 5 cover technical background material. Chapter 6 is an introduction to pointers. This material is included in most general textbooks but it's useful to cover it again from a different perspective. Chapters 7 to 9 are advanced applications of the C language and are thus useful for honing your understanding. A thorough knowledge of C is required for these chapters. Finally, Chapter 10 is about common debugging problems. The chapters are organized as follows:

1. Using The Compiler

This chapter discusses the various parts of a C compiler and how they work with one another. The preprocessor, compiler, linker, and librarian are all discussed as are the basic considerations of modular programming. This chapter also looks at several auxiliary programs, such as *make,* that are useful to the C programmer.

2. Basics: Binary Arithmetic

The basics of binary arithmetic are discussed here. Topics include the various bases and how to convert from one to another, how a machine represents negative numbers, how multiplication and division are done, simple Boolean algebra, and so forth. Emphasis is put on problems in C programs that are caused by the way the machine does its math.

3. Assembly Language Programming for the C Programmer

This chapter presents assembly language in a way that will help you understand why some things are done the way they are in C. Various addressing modes and simple operations are discussed, as are such topics as memory alignment.

4. Code Generation and Subroutine Linkage

This chapter discusses the code that a C compiler typically generates. It talks in depth about how a subroutine is called. Many subtle and hard-to-find bugs in C programs are the result of improper subroutine linkages. This chapter can help you find those bugs more readily. You should understand the material in Chapter 3 before reading Chapter 4.

5. Structured Programming

This chapter talks about how to design and write large C programs. It talks about formatting conventions as well.

6. Pointers

Here, the basics of pointers are discussed in depth. Pointers are the most difficult part of the C language to understand, and most texts cover them inadequately. The subject is covered from a realistic perspective; The chapter explain how various pointer operations are actually done in the machine rather than resorting to analogies such as mailboxes. You should understand the material in Chapter 3 before reading this chapter.

7. Advanced Pointers

This chapter continues where chapter 6 leaves off; It explores complex uses of pointers, multiple levels of indirection, and complex types that use both pointers and arrays. The declaration syntax for complex types is presented in depth here. Hardware interfacing is also discussed in this chapter (for example, there's a discussion of how to talk directly to the IBM-PC memory-mapped video display without using assembly language).

8. Recursion and Compiler Theory

Here we talk about recursion, exploring how it can possibly work by looking at what actually goes on in the machine as a series of recursive subroutine calls are made. We also look at a realistic use of recursion by analyzing a small compiler-like expression analyzer. You should understand the material in Chapters 4 and 6 before beginning this chapter.

9. Printf(): Subroutines with a Variable Number of Arguments

Here we discuss a complex application of C by looking at a version of *printf()*. You should understand the material in Chapters 7 and 8 before starting this chapter.

10. Debugging

This chapter discusses various complex debugging issues. It also talks about solutions to these problems.

All of the C code in this book, including the small examples and the rather strange looking stuff in the pointer chapters, was tested using the Microsoft C Compiler, version 3.0, running on an IBM PC/AT. These examples should port to Lattice version 3.x or to UNIX with no problems. I can't vouch for other compilers, but if they're standard, there should be no problems with them either.

Acknowledgments

I'd like to thank my friend and neighbor, Bill Wong, for providing invaluable comments about both early and final drafts of this book. I'm also grateful to several semesters of students, especially Tom Clement, who unwittingly found more bugs and typos in this material than I'd care to admit I made. Dale Coleman, formerly at Computerland of Albany, saved me days of watching my aged daisywheel printer chug away by graciously allowing me to print out 527 pages of manuscript on the store's laser printer. Finally, Brian Kernighan and Steve Wampler provided many useful comments and criticisms of the final drafts; I am indebted to them for their careful reviews.

THE C COMPANION

THE C COMPILER

This chapter looks at how C compilers are organized and, generally, at how to use them. It also looks at several support programs other than the compiler (such as grep and make) that are useful to the C programmer.

Though all C compilers are structurally similar, the actual details of compiling a program vary radically from compiler to compiler. You should consult your own compiler's documentation for the details of using your compiler. This chapter looks at the various pieces that compilers have in common and at how these pieces are used. We'll use the UNIX and Microsoft compilers for examples.

1.1. The Parts of a Compiler

C Compilers usually consist of one or more programs that work together in concert. The compilation process itself can be divided into several phases, each of which are included in one or more passes. A *phase* is a particular task that has to be performed before compilation can proceed. For example, the *preprocessor* phase of a compiler strips all comments from the source code and replaces all macros (such as **#define**s and **#ifdef**s) in the input. The output of the preprocessor phase is then passed to the *lexical analysis* phase of the compiler, which translates the input characters into an internal representation that the other phases can use more conveniently. A pass, on the other hand, involves the reading of an input file and the generation of an output file.

The first pass (pass one) of a compiler reads the source file and generates a temporary output file. Pass two reads this temporary file and generates its own output file in turn. The process continues until an executable program is created. Several phases of a compiler are often combined into a single pass, and most compilers are composed of at least three passes. The Microsoft C compiler is actually four passes (arranged as four programs—p0.exe, p1.exe, p2.exe, and p3.exe).

The passes of a compiler are often hidden by a driver program. The UNIX program *cc* and the Microsoft *cl* and *msc* programs are examples. A *driver* is a program that runs other programs as if they were subroutines. The subprograms communicate with each other via temporary files, and the driver communicates with the other programs using the command line. The *msc* driver executes p0.exe, p1.exe, and so on, in proper order. The driver usually deletes temporary files when they're no longer needed and does other house-keeping as well. It's useful to know what the various passes are doing, even if the operations of those passes are hidden. The various programs that make up the compiler are shown in figure 1-1.

Fig. 1-1: The Passes of a Compiler

```
Microsoft   UNIX    Function:

   cl        cc     Driver program
   p0        cpp    C preprocessor (pass 1)
   p1        c0     C compiler pass 2
   p2        c1     C compiler pass 3
   p3        c2     C optimizer (pass 4)
   masm      as     Assembler
   link      ld     Linker
   lib       ar     Librarian
```

Some versions of the UNIX compiler, *cc,* print the names of all these programs as they're executed if you specify *-v* on the command line. Figure 1-2 shows the relationships between the various passes of a compiler. The temporary files that are created by each pass are also shown.

We'll show how a driver program is used by looking at the UNIX cc driver. (The Microsoft cl driver is very similar to cc.) Cc's command line syntax is:

```
cc [options] files...
```

If a file ends in *.c*, cc assumes that it's C source code; if the file ends in *.s*, assembly language is assumed, *.o* files are assumed to be object modules. Based on the file name extension (.c, .s, or .o), cc will compile, assemble, or link the various files together as appropriate. (These operations will be discussed in greater detail momentarily.) Take the following:

```
cc hickory.c dickory.s doc.o
```

Hickory.c will be compiled (using cpp, c0, and c1), and assembled (using as). Dickory.s will only be assembled (using as). As part of this process, the object modules hickory.o and dickory.o will be created. Next hickory.o, dickory.o, and doc.o will be linked together (using ld). In addition, a *standard library* (called libc.a) is automatically linked into the program. Finally, all temporary files created by cc (including hickory.o and dickory.o) are deleted.

Cc uses several command line switches. In addition, it passes unfamiliar switches to the linker (ld). The following are some of the more useful options to cc:

-c   Compile but do not link. An object module (with a *.o* extension) is created for each *.c* or *.s* file listed on the command line, but these objects aren't linked together. This option is useful in a makefile (which will be described shortly).

-D*name*   Creates a #**define** for *name.* It's major use is for debugging. For example, debug diagnostics can be surrounded with

```
#ifdef DEBUG
    printf("This is a debug diagnostic");
#endif
```

If the program is compiled with

```
cc -DDEBUG prog.c
```

the *printf()* statement will be compiled. You can also assign a value to the macro:

```
cc -DPROCESSOR=8086 prog.c
```

creates

```
#define PROCESSOR 8086
```

inside the program.

-O   Invokes the optimizing pass of the compiler (cc2). Note that code is not optimized unless -O is specified on the command line. Since

---

Fig. 1-2: The various passes of a C compiler

```
      Notes scribbled on scraps of paper.
                         |
UNIX                     |  ↓
program                  |
name:                    |
                +-----------------+
vi              |     Editor      |
ex              +-----------------+
                         |
                         |  ASCII text comprising the C source code and
                         |  system include files like stdio.h.
                         |  Files names usually have .c or .h extensions.
                         |
                +-----------------+
cpp             |  Preprocessor   |
                +-----------------+
                         |
                         |  ASCII text. Comments have been stripped and
                         |  all # directives (#define, #include, and so on.)
                         |  have been processed. Temporary file is not always
                         |  created, but often has a .i extension if it is.
                         |
                +------------------------+
                |  Compiler:             |   Usually several programs.
c0              |     lexical analyzer   |   Temporary files with
c1              |     parser             |   indeterminate names containing
c2              |     optimizer          |   binary data are created so that
                |     code generator     |   the programs can communicate.
                +------------------------+
                         |
                         |  ASCII text. Assembly language source code.
                         |  Files usually have a .asm (CP/M or DOS)
                         |  or .s (UNIX) extension.
                         |
                +-----------------+
as              |    Assembler    |
                +-----------------+
                         |  Binary, relocatable object modules. Very close
                         |  to machine instructions, but not executable.
        Other object     |  Files usually have a .obj, .rel or, in UNIX, a
          modules        |  .o extension.
             |           |
             |           |            libc.a              ar
        +-----------------+    +---------+    +-----------+   Other
ld      |     Linker      |<----| library |<----| librarian |<--- object
        +-----------------+    +---------+    +-----------+   modules
                         |
                         |  Binary executable files, usually have the extension
                         |  .exe or .com. UNIX creates a file called a.out unless
                         |  the -o option was specified as part of the link.
                         |
                 Compilation
                 Finished.
```

---

a compile takes longer if -O is specified, it usually isn't used until the program is made to work. This option shouldn't be confused with

-o *name*   Calls the final, linked program *name* rather than *a.out.* For example:

```
cc -o reindeer dasher.c dancer.c donner.c blitzen.c
```

will call the final program *reindeer* rather than *a.out.*

-S   Generates an assembly language source file and then terminates. The file has a *.s* extension (*.asm* if you're using Microsoft).

1.1.1. The Preprocessor

The preprocessor takes as input the ASCII text that you've created with an editor. By convention, all C source code file names end with a ".c" extension (such as "program.c"), and *include files* (that are incorporated into your program via the **#include** mechanism) have ".h" as the last part of their name.

The preprocessor performs two functions: It removes all comments from the source code, and it processes all *preprocessor directives.* In C, these directives all have a # as their first character. The preprocessor directives supported by most compilers are shown in figure 1-3. To ensure portability, the # should always be in the left column, and there should be no white space (blanks, tabs, or carriage returns) following the # (even if your compiler permits these things).

Fig. 1-3: Common Preprocessor Directives

```
#define    -    Create a macro
#undef     -    Remove a macro
#include   -    Replace the current line with the contents
                of a file
#ifdef     -    Compile code if a macro has been defined with
                a previous #define
#if        -    Compile code if an expression is true
#else      -    Compiler code if a previous #if or #ifdef failed
#endif     -    Terminate a previous #if, #ifdef or #else
```

All the preprocessor directives involve some sort of text substitution: Macro invocations are replaced with the text defined with a previous **#define** directive; **#include** directives are replaced with the contents of the file specified as part of the directive; **#ifdef** causes text to be deleted (replaced with a null string), and so forth.

The preprocessor is not part of the compiler. It doesn't understand C syntax or precedence (though it does know what an identifier is). Several bugs can appear because of this lack. For example,

```
#define PRINTS(s)        printf("string is <%s>", s);
```

when invoked with

```
PRINTS( buf );
```

expands to the following:

```
printf("string is <%buf>", buf);
```

Similarly,

```
#define  SQUARE(x)        (x * x)
```

when invoked with

```
y = SQUARE( var++ );
```

expands to the following:

```
y = (var++ * var++);
```

(var is incremented twice). A third example: When SQUARE is invoked with

```
y = SQUARE(x + y);
```

it expands to the following:

```
y = (x + y * x + y)
```

Because the * operator is higher precedence than the + operator, this expression evaluates to the following:

```
y = ( x + (y * x) + y)
```

This is not what we want. This last problem can be fixed by redefining SQUARE with

```
#define  SQUARE(x)        ((x) * (x))
```

Be careful when you use macros.

Many compilers have an option that lets you see the source code after the preprocessor is finished with it, a helpful debugging aid when you're using complicated macros. For example, cc and cl both generate a preprocessor output file if "-P" is found on the command line (this output file has a .i extension with both compilers). The UNIX preprocessor (cpp) can also be run by itself, since it's an independent program. Note that cpp is in the /lib directory. If /lib isn't in your search path, you'll have to give a full path name to run the program:

```
/lib/cpp prog.c prog.i
```

1.1.2. The Compiler

The next stage of the compilation involves at least four phases: lexical analysis, parsing, optimization, and code generation. (lexical analysis and parsing are discussed in greater depth in Chapter 8.) The first two phases will, between them, generate a file consisting of *intermediate code,* a kind of generic assembly language.

The optimizer inputs the intermediate code and tries to make it take up less space and run faster. Often you can't get both of these, the code can be made smaller, or it can be made to execute faster, but not both. Cc only optimizes if -O is present on the command line so you don't have to spend time optimizing when you're debugging your program. The optimizer can also rearrange code in unexpected ways, so don't optimize if you're using an assembly language debugger (like symdeb or adb).

The optimizer outputs shuffled intermediate code. The code-generator pass translates this intermediate code into assembly language. It's possible to make a universal *front end* that does all of the compilation except the code generation. By substituting different code generators, you can create object code for various machines without having to modifying any of the rest of the compiler.

All four phases are sometimes done in one pass; more often, though, the lexical analysis and parsing phases are done by one program, optimization by a second program, and code generation by a third.

1.1.3. The Assembler

The assembler takes assembly language as its input and generates something very close to executable code as its output. Sometimes assemblers are incorporated into the code generation phase so that an assembly language intermediate file is never created. Nevertheless, most compilers incorporate some mechanism for looking at the assembly language. (In cc and cl you can compile with a -S command-line option.) Many compilers will also insert the C source code as comments into the assembly-language output.

It's important to be able to look at the assembly language generated by your compiler. You'll need it to use a debugger like adb, ddt, symdeb, or debug. In addition, it's useful to see exactly what a compiler has done with a high-level construct, especially if you're concerned about efficiency. Compilers, like most other programs, have bugs in them. This is particularly true for 8086 large-model compilations and any new release of a compiler. If you can look at the assembly language, you can see whether or not the compiler has created reasonable code (it's fairly easy to correlate C to assembly language; not so with languages like Pascal, LISP, or APL.) A final reason for looking at assembly language is hand optimization. As an alternative to writing in assembly language from scratch, it's often easier to write a program in C, compile it, and then optimize the machine-generated assembly language by hand.

The UNIX assembler (as) and the Microsoft assembler (masm) are independent programs and can be run by themselves. By convention, UNIX assembly language source file names have a *.s* extension and MS-DOS files have a *.asm* extension.

The output of an assembler is a *relocatable object module* (often just called a module). Unlike Pascal, C programs are usually written as several source files. Each of these source files are compiled independently and are then pieced together as the last stage of compilation (by the linker, which we'll look at in a moment). Though a subroutine in one file can call another subroutine that's part of a second file, the compiler can't know where the first subroutine will appear in memory when it's compiling the second subroutine (because it's in a different file). The same situation exists with global variables: A subroutine declared in one file can use a global variable that was declared in another file. Again, the compiler has no way of knowing where that global variable will end up. These sorts of objects, subroutines and variables that are part of another file, are called *external objects.*

The assembler translates as much as it can to binary machine language. Because it doesn't know where the external objects will be in memory, however, it replaces all references to them with some sort of dummy placeholder. It then creates a table that tells the linker both the location of these dummy addresses and the name of the variable associated with each dummy address.

Since a relocatable object module must be patched before it can access external objects, it is not executable. You have to run it through the linker first.

1.1.4. The Linker, or Link Editor

The linker takes as input a list of relocatable object modules resulting from the compilation process we've just described. It pieces these modules together into a single program and then replaces all the dummy addresses with real addresses. For example, the commands

```
cc -c larry.c
cc -c curly.c
cc -c moe.c
```

will compile and assemble the C source code in the files larry.c, curly.c, and moe.c, creating the three object modules larry.o, curly.o, and moe.o. The files are then merged into a single executable program using the linker:

```
ld -o /lib/crt0.o stooges larry.o curly.o moe.o -lc
```

Another possibility is

```
cc -o stooges larry.o curly.o moe.o
```

Ld creates an executable program called stooges (because of the -o). The -lc tells ld to link the three modules given on the command line with the standard library, /lib/libc.a, which contains standard I/O routines like *printf()*. The -lc isn't needed when you use cc rather than ld. The Microsoft cl driver can be used exactly as cc was just used. The Microsoft linker can also be invoked explicitly with

```
link larry.o curly.o moe.o,stooges.exe,,libc.lib
```

Here the second, comma delimited, argument is the output file name. If the third argument were present a *link map* would be created. (A link map is a table of all external objects and their actual locations in memory.) The last argument is a library that is linked into the rest of the program.

Before describing the linker's function in greater depth, we have to get technical for a moment. C (or more properly, Kernighan and Ritchie) makes a distinction between a variable or subroutine *declaration* and a *definition.* The word *declaration* means "an announcement," so a variable declaration announces a variable's existence to the compiler. The declaration doesn't allocate space, it just tells the compiler that a variable exists somewhere. The compiler assumes that the linker will find it at link time. The variable *definition* actually allocates space for the variable; actually creates the variable.

This choice of words—definition and declaration—is unfortunate because most of the literature uses the word *declaration* to refer to the place where space is allocated to a variable, which is the opposite sense in which the word is used by Kernighan and Ritchie. Consequently, I've used the two words in the more widely accepted sense throughout this book (no distinction has been made between them; both words will be used in the same sense that Kernighan and Ritchie use the word *definition*). When necessary, I'll use *allocation* and *reference* instead of *definition* and *declaration.*

The distinction is important, however. Space for a variable can be allocated in only one place. However, the same variable can be referenced in as many files as are necessary. In C, a reference is created with the **extern** keyword. That is, **extern** tells the compiler that the named variable (or subroutine) is declared in another file, but that it can be used as if it were declared in the current file (the linker will find it). No space is allocated for variables declared **extern** If the word **extern** isn't present, then space is allocated for the variable (in theory—some compilers let the linker do the allocation, as will be described in a moment.) Note that it's possible to implicitly declare an external subroutine (but not a variable) just by using it. In this case, the subroutine is assumed to return an **int**

The linker's purpose is to connect all subroutine or variable references with their declarations. Moreover, if the linker doesn't find a variable declaration (that is, if it finds only references), it usually allocates space for the variable. This can cause problems with those compilers that let the linker allocate space (rather than doing it themselves when an **extern** keyword isn't present). In these compilers, two nonstatic global variables that have the same name are assumed to be the same variable, a real maintenance headache. We'll look at ways to get around this problem in later chapters.

The object modules that the linker hooks together can take one of two forms. They can be independent object modules, like output from an assembler, or they can be libraries. A *library* is a collection of object modules that have been merged into one file (usually having a .lib extension in its name). The modules are still independent, but they've been put into one file so that a single file name, rather than a long list of module names, can be given to the linker.

An object module is indivisible. That is, when a library is scanned, if one subroutine in a particular module is needed, the entire module will be put into the final program, even if other subroutines in the same module are not needed. All subroutines and all global data that were part of the original source file will be part of the object module; thus, on the source-code level, a module is the same as a file. This relationship between source code and files does not hold for libraries, because a library is a single file that contains several object modules. A module is an indivisible chunk of code that started out as a single file, but a library is a single file that contains several modules. Modules and files are not synonymous at this level.

The linker incorporates only those parts of the library that are needed (that are referenced somewhere) into the final program. On the other hand, if an object module is not part of a library, it will always be included in the final program whether or not it's actually used.

A real advantage to using a linker is that, once a program is finished, only files that have been changed must to be recompiled (provided that the object modules for the other files in the program still exist). You can then relink the program using the new object module.

1.1.5. Librarians and Libraries

Strictly speaking, the librarian is not part of the compiler. It's a separate program used only to create and maintain libraries. Most librarians can create a library, add modules to a library, delete modules from a library, or replace a module already in a library with a new module having the same name. Some librarians also let you extract a module from a library (remove the module from the library file and put it in a .o or .obj file by itself, just as if it had never been put into the library in the first place).

Since a module that is part of a library won't be included in the final program unless subroutines or data in that module are used, libraries are usually pretty big. They often contain upwards of a hundred modules, each of which can contain several subroutines. For example, the library routines described in your compiler documentation are all individual modules and are all part of the same library file.

Many linkers only scan a library once, from front to back. Consequently the order in which modules are inserted into a library is often important. The linker maintains a table of all unresolved external references. If in scanning the library it finds a subroutine with the same name as an external reference on its list, the linker inserts the module containing this subroutine into the final program. If the newly inserted module has any external subroutine references, these new references are added to the linker's table. So, if a subroutine in a library calls an external subroutine that's also in the library, the module containing that external subroutine must follow the module that contains the calling subroutine. That is, it must have been put into the library after the subroutine that called it was inserted. The order of subroutines within a module isn't important since they all become part of the final program. Note that even those linkers that accept randomly ordered libraries will work faster when given one that's ordered linearly.

Another consideration in modules destined for a library is the number of subroutines in the module. A library module should generally have only one externally accessible subroutine. (Subroutines that are declared **static** are not externally accessible.) The other routines in the module should support the one external routine. By making the modules small, we reduce the size of the final program by not linking unused subroutines into it.

When the linker is putting a program together, it has no way of knowing whether all the capabilities of a subroutine are actually used. It only knows whether a call to that subroutine is in the already-linked code. This can cause problems with high-level functions such as *fprintf()*, the general purpose output function. *Fprintf()* can write to the screen, to a file, or to any MS-DOS device. Consequently, although you may only be using *fprintf()* to write error messages to stderr, if you call it at all, you'll end up with the entire disk interface library in your final program. The linker can't know that you're not using any of the disk-related functions in *fprintf()*; it only knows that *fprintf()* may want to write to the disk. Similarly, *fprintf()* can print a floating point number; consequently, the entire floating point math library will be part of your final program, even if you only use *fprintf()* to write integers.

There are two solutions to this problem: Either don't use the general-purpose functions, or write your own version of *fprintf()*. The first method is practical only when you're using a small part of a general-purpose routine. That is, if you're using *fprintf()* only to write strings, you can use *fputs()* instead. The second solution, writing your own *fprintf()*, is actually more practical in the long run. Many compiler manufacturers supply several, almost identical, libraries with their compilers. One of these libraries will contain a version of *fprintf()* that can't do floating point, another library will have an *fprintf()* that can't write to the disk. By choosing a particular library at link time, you can choose which of these versions of *fprintf()* to put into the final program.

There's another, related issue. All object files given to the linker explicitly (that aren't part of a library) are put into the final program. When the linker scans a library, it only looks for subroutines that it doesn't already have. If you write your own version of a library routine (one that has the same name as the library routine), and then list the module containing that routine on the linker's command line, your own routine will be made part of the final program and the linker won't even look for the subroutine with the same name that is in the library. The problem here is that other subroutines in the library may call the subroutine that you replaced. Be very careful to make your subroutine look *exactly* like the standard library routine in terms of calling syntax. That is, your routine should take the same arguments and should return the same value as the normal library routine, even if one or more of these arguments or the return value is never used.

The standard library, supplied by your compiler manufacturer, must be linked into your final program, even if you don't use any of the routines in the standard I/O library. The compiler assumes that a few small subroutines are present in the final program and will generate calls to these routines. This set of routines is called the *run-time library* and is usually put into the standard library file along with the I/O routines. Run-time library routines do things like double-precision arithmetic, process **switch** statements, and so on.

One run-time subroutine of special interest is the *root*, or *start-up*, module. The root module is the subroutine that receives control from the the operating system. Your *main()* subroutine is called from the root module, just like any other subroutine. (*Main()* is just a subroutine like any other. The only reason you need a *main()* function is that the root module calls it, so the linker requires it to be present.) The root module initializes various global variables used in the I/O library. It usually assembles the *argv* array from the command line. In operating systems such as CP/M and early versions of MS-DOS, I/O redirection is typically done in the root module as well.

This last use of the root module is of interest when you're trying to make your program as small as possible. Since redirection uses the disk, the root module will call in the entire disk I/O system if it does the redirection explicitly. You can prevent this by rewriting your root module to not perform the redirection (see the bibliography for an example of this process). You can also write a subroutine that has the same name as the root module and then link that subroutine explicitly into your own program. Because *main()* is called by the root module, you don't need a *main()* subroutine if you write your own root.

In UNIX, the standard library (/lib/libc.a) is automatically linked into your program by cc. The Microsoft linker does the same, provided that the compiler has put certain information into the object module for the linker to use. Not all compilers include this information, though. (At this writing, Microsoft does, Lattice doesn't.)

Under UNIX, several default libraries (in addition to the standard library) are also provided. (These routines are documented in section three of the UNIX manual.) These additional libraries are in the /lib and /usr/lib directories. They all have names like libm.a (the math library) and libs.a (the standard library). To use the subroutines in section three of the manual, you have to specify the library explicitly on either the cc or ld command line. The library name is part of the manual page header. For example, the header for *qsort()* looks like this:

```
QSORT(3C)              UNIX 5.0              QSORT(3C)
```

Qsort() is in libc.a (that's the *C* in the header), and you can link libc into your program by placing -lc on the ld or cc command line. The -l*X* flag is shorthand for the string /lib/lib*X*.a The expressions -lc and /lib/libc.a are treated identically. If ld can't find the library in /lib, it will look in /usr/lib, so -lm and /usr/lib/libm.a are also equivalent. If the library you're looking for isn't in the /lib or /usr/lib directories, you must spell out it's full path name on the command line. A sample cc command line for a program, sort.c, that uses the *qsort()* subroutine is

```
cc sort.c -lc
```

Note that the *-lc* must follow the names of all modules that call subroutines in *libc*. The linker doesn't know that it needs a subroutine from a library until it sees a reference to that subroutine. So, it must process all modules that reference a library function before it scans the library.

1.1.5.1. Library Maintenance

Libraries are also called *archives*. Consequently, the UNIX library manager is called *ar*. An archive is actually any collection of files that have been merged into a single file. They need not contain C object modules. MS-DOS libraries are not quite so general-purpose, though. They are created with a special utility called a *librarian*, rather than by a general-purpose archiver. (Although various archiving programs are available for use with

DOS, they can't usually be used to create libraries.)

Archives have uses other than as libraries. In a CP/M system, where there are no sub-directories, they help clean up disks. For example, all of the sources for a library can be merged into a single archive, which thereafter shows up as a single directory entry.Archives are also useful for transmitting files to another computer over a modem. You can transfer one archive file rather than many small files. The other main reason for archiving files is to save disk space. In most operating systems, all files require a minimum amount of disk space, even if that file doesn't require much space. For example, at minimum, an entire 512 byte disk sector is required to hold a file that is one character long. The problem is compounded because most operating systems don't use single disk sectors. Rather, they use a *cluster* of several sectors as their smallest *allocation unit*. Thus, if your operating system uses a four-sector cluster, then 4 * 512, or 2048, bytes are used to store a file containing 1 byte. Since archives are made up of several smaller files, the amount of wasted space is minimized.

As I said earlier, the UNIX archive maintenance utility is called *ar.* With it you can create archives, insert files into them, delete files from them, print out a file (without removing it from the archive), replace an archive file, and do other simple maintenance tasks.

Say you have four files: one.c, two.c, three.c, and four.c. You can create an archive containing these files with

```
ar rv files.arc one.c two.c three.c four.c
```

The second argument (rv) tells the archiver what to do. Here, the *r* means replace the indicated files. Since the files aren't in the archive, they'll be added to it. Note that the minus sign that usually precedes arguments to UNIX utilities isn't used here. The *v* command tells the archiver to be verbose, it tells us what it's doing as it does it. The next command-line argument, *files.arc* is the name of the archive file; the remainder of the arguments are the list of files to which the commands apply. Note that the files are copied into the archive; they aren't deleted as part of the archiving process.

An equivalent command to the Microsoft librarian (called *lib)* is:

```
lib files.lib +one.obj +two.obj +three.obj +four.obj ;
```

which creates a library called files.lib that contains the four modules: one.obj, two.obj, three.obj, and four.obj.

Moving back to UNIX, the file three.c can be examined with:

```
ar p files.arc three.c >there.c
```

The file is printed to standard output, so it must be redirected if you want to extract it from the archive. Since Microsoft libraries can only contain object modules, there's no equivalent command to lib.

```
ar tv files.arc
```

prints a table of contents for the archive. The *v* causes a long listing to be printed. Without it, only the file names are listed. The equivalent DOS command is:

```
lib files.lib,,files.ndx;
```

The empty, comma delimited, field tells *lib* that there are no operations to perform; however, the third field tells the program to create an index in the file *files.ndx*.

```
ar d files.arc three.c
```

deletes "three.c" from the archive. The equivalent Microsoft command is

```
lib files.lib -three.obj;
```

Several additional library-related programs are supported by UNIX: *lorder* and *tsort* work together with *ar* to create linearly ordered libraries. *Lorder* takes as input a collection of object modules. It determines the subroutine calling relationships between the various subroutines in the modules and outputs a set of word pairs which are passed to *tsort*. *Tsort* then orders the various object file names so that, if the modules are inserted into the library in that order, there will be no forward references.

For example, say you want to make a library consisting of three files—larry.o, curly.o, and moe.o. Each of these files consists of a single subroutine [called *larry()*, *curly()*, and *moe()*]. The subroutine *moe()* calls *larry()*, which in turn calls *curly()*. Consequently, moe.o has to be inserted into the library before either larry.o or curly.o. Similarly, larry.o has to be inserted before curly.o. The command:

```
lorder larry.o curly.o moe.o | tsort
```

generates the following list:

```
moe.o
larry.o
curly.o
```

This output is ordered so that all modules containing subroutines called by moe.o follow moe.o in the list, and so on. The output from lorder/tsort can be passed to ar with:

```
ar cr stooges 'lorder larry.o curly.o moe.o | tsort'
```

Note that we're using back-quotes here, not the usual single-quote.

The main advantage of a linear library is that it can be searched faster by the linker, thereby reducing compile time. It's not always possible to have a linearly ordered library, though. For this reason, the *ranlib* function has

been provided by UNIX. Ranlib takes as input the name of a randomly
organized library. It inserts into the library a table of contents (called
__.SYMDEF) that the linker can use to find functions as it needs them. For
example

```
ar cr stooges larry.o curly.o moe.o
ranlib stooges
```

creates a randomly ordered library called *stooges* and then modifies that
library so that the linker can access all the necessary functions.

Microsoft libraries can be randomly ordered. A linear library links faster
than a random one, however, so it's worthwhile to create libraries in a linear
fashion. Unfortunately, I don't know of an lorder or tsort that runs under
MS-DOS.

1.2. Modular Programming

Because modules are such an important part of a C program, it's worth
thinking about how a modular program should be organized. Library modules
should be as small as possible. This is not the case with program modules,
however, mostly for maintenance reasons. The subroutines in a module
should all be related functionally (you shouldn't have to go from one file to
another while you're debugging). Subroutines that are sufficiently general purpose should be put into a library rather than buried in a larger file.

An important consideration in putting your modules together is the distribution of global variables and macros. If possible, global variables should be
limited in scope to a single module; they shouldn't be used by subroutines in
other modules. (This is done primarily for maintenance reasons and is discussed in depth in Chapter 5.) The same holds for **#define**s, **typedef**s, and so
on; they should be used only in one module if possible. Sometimes, however,
this kind of organization isn't possible, and C therefore supports a **#include**
directive. The *#include <file>* statement is replaced in the source code by the
entire contents of the indicated file. The names of files so used, called *include
files,* should end in a *.h*

Include files should *never* contain executable code or variable declarations. These should be put into a .c file and compiled and linked into the final
program using the usual mechanism. Include files should contain only
#defines, **typedef**s, and **extern** statements. Although it's possible to nest
#include statements (have a **#include** statement inside a .h file) it's not generally a good idea, again for maintenance reasons. Nothing should be in an
include file unless it must be known in at least two source files. Conversely,
everything that must be known by more than one source file should be in a .h
file that's **#include**d in all the source files. It's much easier to change global
constants and the like if they are concentrated in one place instead of spread

out all over your program.

1.3. Other Useful Programs

There are several UNIX utilities that make a C programmer's life much easier. Several MS-DOS versions of these are also available.

1.3.1. Grep

Grep is a program that finds patterns in text files. The patterns can be specified by very powerful templates that enable you to locate things like "a string of characters in the range a-z, starting at the leftmost column on the page, followed by any number of spaces or tabs, followed by an open parenthesis, followed by any character at all repeated any number of times, followed by a closed parenthesis, followed by anything except a semicolon." You can use Grep to create cross-references for C programs that are spread over several files. It's also useful for finding a misspelled subroutine name that the linker thinks is an unresolved reference or for finding a subroutine declaration that's lost in one of the forty-five files that make up the operating system you're writing.

Grep looks for patterns by matching the contents of a file with a template called a *regular expression.* Regular expressions are composed of combinations of characters to match and special symbols called *metacharacters:*

^   A ^ matches the beginning of a line.

$ A $ matches the end of a line.

\   A \ followed by a single character matches that character. In this way, a * matches an asterisk, \. matches a period, and so on.

.   A . matches any character.

[ ]   A string enclosed in brackets ([ ]) specifies a *character class.* Any single character in the string is matched. For example, *[abc]* matches an *a, b,* or *c.* Ranges of ASCII character codes may be abbreviated, as in *[a-z0-9].* If the first symbol following the [is a ^, then a *negative character class* is specified. In this case, the string matches all characters except those enclosed in the brackets (in other words, *[^a-z]* matches everything except lower-case letters). Note that a negative character class must match something, even though that something can not be any of the characters listed. For example, *^$* is not the same as *^[^z]$*. The first example matches an empty line (beginning of line followed by end of line); the second example matches a beginning of line, followed by any character except a *z,* followed by end of line. In the second example, a character must be present on the line, but that character can't be a *z.* Note that * . ^ and $ are not special characters when inside a character

class.

*   A regular expression followed by a * matches zero or more matches of the regular expression.

+   A regular expression followed by a + matches one or more matches of the regular expression.

ee   Two concatenated regular expressions match a match of the first followed by a match of the second.

| Two regular expressions separated by a | or a newline match either a match for the first or a match for the second.

The order of precedence is [ ], then *, then concatenation, then | then newline. A *greedy* algorithm is used to process * and + so *a.*z* matches a string that begins with the leftmost *a* on the line and ends with the rightmost *z*. Any number of characters, including a's and z's can be in between.

Most UNIX systems have three versions of grep called *grep*, *egrep*, and *fgrep*. They all take slightly different command-line arguments so you should consult you manual for the actual details of using them. Moreover, grep itself recognizes a limited regular expression syntax (for example, it doesn't recognize the | metacharacter). Egrep recognizes all of the metacharacters described earlier. Typically *grep* is the most convenient of the three and *egrep* is the most powerful.

Let's look at some examples. The command line:

```
egrep -nf index.exp *.c
```

where the file index.exp contains:

```
^[a-zA-Z_]+.*([^;]*)[^;]*$

^#define[    ]+[a-zA-Z_]+(
```

creates a cross-reference of a large C program. The cross-reference contains both subroutine names and the names of subroutine-like macros. All files whose names end in *.c* are searched. Every output line is preceded both by the name of the file in which the line was found (this is automatic if more than one file is searched) and by the appropriate line number (the *-n* causes line numbers to be shown).

Since there are two lines in index .exp, all lines containing matches for either regular expression are printed. The regular expressions are interpreted as follows:

```
^[a-zA-Z_]+.*([^;]*)[^;]*$
```

beginning of line (ˆ), followed by any letter or underscore (*[a-zA-Z_]*) repeated at least one time (+), followed by any character repeated zero or more times (.*), followed by an open parenthesis [*(*], followed by any character except a semicolon repeated zero or more times (*[^;]**), followed by a closed parenthesis [*)*], followed any character except a semicolon repeated zero or more times (*[^;]**), followed by end of line (*$*).

```
^#define[     ]+[a-zA-Z_]+(
```

Beginning of line (^), followed by the string #*define* (*#define*), followed by at least one space or tab (*[ ]+*)—there's one space and one tab character (*^I*) between the brackets), followed by at least one letter or underscore (*[a-zA-Z_]+*), followed immediately (no intervening space) by an open parenthesis [*(*].

Grep is usually invoked with the regular expression on the command line. Be careful of using characters like * or | that are special to the shell. Either these characters must be preceded by a backslash or the entire expression must be placed in quotes. For example

```
grep "extern.*foo" *.c
```

searches all .c files for all external declarations of foo. The * in the expression won't be expanded by the shell because of the quotes. The * in *.c is expanded by the shell, however. Our earlier example can be executed from the command line with

```
egrep "^[a-zA-Z_]+.*([^;]*)[^;]*$|^#define[     ]+[a-zA-Z_]+(."   *.c
```

Here, the | has the same function as the newline in the original file.

1.3.2. Lint

Lint is a C syntax checker that is much more rigorous than most compilers in hunting down potential problems. It finds things like the wrong number of parameters passed to subroutines (or parameters of the wrong type), or the return value of a subroutine that is not assigned to a variable of the correct type. Lint also flags as potential errors unusual uses of operators (= in an test instead of ==), unreachable code, truncation caused by implicit type conversion, and so on. It can be quite useful in finding simple errors. On the other hand, it often generates error messages or warnings for perfectly reasonable code, so it's not all that useful for some applications.

Lint is actually a version of the compiler. It generates error messages as output rather than code. Consequently, it is used in much the same way as a compiler would be used. The one difference is that lint is operating on source code so there is no equivalent to a linker. If you don't want to run all the modules in your program through lint at once, you can give lint special files that contain dummy subroutine definitions like:

```
long  foo(a,b) int a; long b; { return 0L; }
```

instead of the real files. This dummy definition tells lint everything it needs to

know to do error checking, but it is processed much faster than a complete
subroutine.

1.3.3. Make

Make is one of those utilities where you can't figure out why anyone
would bother to use it until you actually do use it; then you can't figure out
how you got along without it. Make is an automated program compilation
utility. It determines (from a set of rules that you supply) which of the 47
modules that make up the giant program you're working on need to be
recompiled, and then recompiles only those modules. It can also tell what
needs to be recompiled when you change an include file. It does all this by
keeping a list of *dependencies.* You tell it that a particular file must be recompiled if a certain include file has been modified more recently than has the
C source file (or if the C source has been modified more recently than its
object file). Make is an invaluable aid for maintaining large programs that
have been broken up into several files. Fortunately, several MS-DOS versions
of make are available, so you don't need UNIX to use make.

Make takes as input a *makefile*— a file that describes all the modules in
a large program and the relationships between these modules. Using the
makefile, *make* determines what modules need to be recompiled at any given
moment, and then compiles them (and only them). It is like an intelligent
batch utility that knows how C programs and C compilers work and performs
only absolutely necessary actions.

The best way to explain make is with an example. You want to create an
executable program called *farm.* The original source is split up into three files:
cow.c, pig.c, and farm.c. All three files contain a *#include <stdio.h>* statement. In addition, cow.c and pig.c have a *#include "animals.h"* statement.
Now, if you change something in cow.c, you'll have to recompile cow.c and
then relink the new cow.obj into farm.exe. If you change something in
animals.h, you must recompile both cow.c and pig.c and relink. If you change
stdio.h, you'll need to recompile everything. Make describes the relationships
between these files as *dependencies.* The makefile is a list of these dependencies. A makefile for the program just described is shown in figure 1-4.

The # designates a comment line. Farm.exe "depends on" cow.o, pig.o,
and farm.o. Therefore, if any of the files cow.o, pig.o, or farm.o have been
changed more recently than farm, then farm has to be remade. This remaking
is accomplished by executing the line *cc -o farm cow.o pig.o farm.o.* Similarly,
if any of the files pig.c, stdio.h, or animals.h have been changed more recently
than pig.o, then pig.o needs to be remade using the command *cc -c pig.c.* The
-c causes an object module to be created without a link being attempted. The
actions associated with each set of dependencies can extend to several lines.
To activate the process, just type the command *make.* Make reads in the

---

Fig. 1-4: A Simple Makefile

```
#
# Make farm using cc
#
farm:     cow.o pig.o farm.o
          cc -o farm cow.o pig.o farm.o

cow.o:    cow.c  stdio.h animals.h
          cc -c cow.c

pig.o:    pig.c  stdio.h animals.h
          cc -c pig.c

farm.o:  farm.c stdio.h
          cc -c farm.c
```

---

makefile, and, using the information found there, figures out what to do and does it.

Were we using an MS-DOS compiler such as the Microsoft compiler, *farm* would be called *farm.exe* in the example just cited. Similarly, all the *.o* files would be named *.obj.* Finally the program name *cc,* should be changed to *cl,* the name of the Microsoft driver program. Otherwise the makefile would look the same.

Make supports several options that make your life a little easier. Macros may be used to save some typing. A macro is defined by:

```
                  name = stuff
```

where *name* is the macro name and *stuff* is the text to be expanded. The macro is expanded by *$(name).* Our original makefile, redefined using macros, is shown in figure 1-5

The makefile can be simplified even further. Note that all .c files are converted to .o files with the same set of actions. Make provides a mechanism, called a *generic dependency,* for doing this sort of repetitive action. Consider the makefile shown in figure 1-6.

Fig. 1-5: A Makefile with Macros

```
INCLUDES = stdio.h animals.h
OBJECTS  = cow.o pig.o farm.o
COMPILE  = cc -c

farm:    $(OBJECTS)
         cc -o farm $(OBJECTS)

cow.o:   $(INCLUDES) cow.c
         $(COMPILE)  cow

pig.o:   $(INCLUDES) pig.c
         $(COMPILE)  pig

farm.o:  stdio.h     farm.c
         $(COMPILE)  farm
```

Fig. 1-6: A Generic Makefile

```
#
# Make farm using the Lattice C compiler.
#

INCLUDES = stdio.h animals.h
OBJECTS  = cow.o pig.o farm.o

.c.o:
         cc -c $*.c

farm:    $(OBJECTS)
         cc -o farm cow.o pig.o farm.o

cow.o:   $(INCLUDES)
pig.o:   $(INCLUDES)
farm.o:  stdio.h
```

The lines

```
.c.o:
         cc -c $*.c
```

say the following: To turn a .c file into a .o file execute the line:

```
cc -c $*.c
```

$* is a predefined macro that evaluates to the root portion of the file being made (the one to the left of the colon on the dependency line). That is, given the following dependency line:

```
foo.o: foo.c rat.h
```

$* evaluates to the string: *foo.* In the case of this generic dependency, make assumes that all .o files depend on a .c file having the same root name. That is, when foo.obj is being made, a dependency on foo.c is assumed and need not be listed on the dependency line.

To start the whole compilation process, just type *make.* The dependencies are examined by make and the appropriate actions taken. Make can also recompile a single object by specifying the target name on the command line. For example,

```
make pig.o
```

recompiles pig.c only (provided that pig.o needs to be remade).

Two command-line options are particularly useful. The *-t* (for "touch") option causes all the last-modified times to be changed as if the program had been recompiled. The actual compilation isn't carried out, though. This option is useful when you change a comment in a header file and don't want to recompile the entire program. The *-i* option tells make to ignore any error conditions returned from subprograms. Normally, if the compiler returns an error to make, the program terminates. If -i is specified on the command line, make just keeps working. This option is useful if you want to start a long compilation and then go to lunch. The compilation continues even if there are errors. Be sure to redirect the output of make to a file (in other words, *make -i >& err*), or error messages will just roll off the screen and you'll never see them.

1.4. Exercises

1-1 Write a program that reads in a line of text using *getchar()*, and then prints that line using *putchar()*. Put the program in three separate files, one containing the input routine, one containing *main()*, and a third containing the output routine. Compile the files separately and link them together.

1-2 Using the librarian supplied with your compiler, Create a library containing the input and output routines written for exercise 1-1. Link it with the module containing *main()* to make a complete program.

1-3 Write a makefile that does everything in exercises 1-1 and 1-2. Then do the exercises again, this time using make.

1-4 Run all your source files through lint. What kind of output does it generate? Add a few errors to your code (declare a variable that isn't used and call a subroutine with the wrong number of arguments of the wrong type) and resubmit it to lint. Now what does lint do?

1-5   Write a grep command line that searches a C program for all nonstatic
      global variable declarations. That is, it should find

```
                        int      Jack ;
                        long     Jill ;
                        char     *hill[20];
```

      but not

```
                        int      Alice ( )        /* no ; */
                        int      Humpty ( ) ;
                        static   int  Tweedledum;
                        extern   long Tweedledee( );
```

BINARY ARITHMETIC

This chapter explores low-level binary arithmetic and problems you may encounter that are caused by the way that numbers are represented in a machine. On the way we'll talk about the C operators.

2.1. Bases and Powers

For the most part, operations in the binary number system are performed identically to those in the decimal system. If you keep this fact firmly in mind you'll avoid a lot of potential confusion. You may remember from the third grade (we're going to talk a lot about third-grade arithmetic in this chapter) that numbers in any base consist of the sum of a series of digits whose position in the number determine their exact value. In addition, no single digit in a number can be greater than or equal to that number's base. For example, all digits in an octal (base eight) number are in the range zero to seven; binary (base two) numbers are made of ones and zeros; base sixteen numbers require special symbols for digits whose values are greater than nine (the letters A–F are used).

The value of an entire number is the sum of the values of the digits after they have been multiplied by the base raised to a power determined by the digit's position in the actual number. The decimal number 418 is actually the sum of

$$400 + 10 + 8$$

Expressed another way,

$$(4 * 10^2) + (1 * 10^1) + (8 * 10^0)$$

(As is the case in C, * here means "multiply.") Binary (base two) numbers are just like decimal numbers except that powers of two are used to interpret the digits rather than powers of ten. For example, the binary number 1101 has the value:

```
(1 * 2³) + (1 * 2²) + (0 * 2¹) + (1 * 2⁰) =
(1 * 8) + (1 * 4) + (0 * 2) + (1 * 1) =
     8  +      4  +      0  +      1  =   13
```

The only difference between binary and decimal is the multiplier used for each digit. The process is illustrated in figure 2-1. The powers of two are shown in figure 2-2. The letter K (for kilo) is used to represent 2^{10} (10K bytes = 10 * 1024 = 10240 bytes).

Fig. 2-1: Decimal and Binary Number Systems

```
     A decimal (base ten)                    A binary (base two)
        number: 1985                            number: 1010


   1 * 1000  = 1 * 10³                     1 * 8  = 1 * 2³
   9 * 100   = 9 * 10²                     0 * 4  = 0 * 2²
   8 * 10    = 8 * 10¹                     1 * 2  = 1 * 2¹
   5 * 1     = 5 * 10⁰                     0 * 1  = 0 * 2⁰
```

Although, strictly speaking, hexadecimal (usually just called "hex") and octal numbers are base sixteen and base eight numbers, they are used in practice as a sort of shorthand when talking about what are really binary operations. In C, all numbers with a leading *0x* are hex, and octal numbers have a leading *0* (no *x*). Figure 2-3 shows correspondences between the decimal, binary, hex and octal numbering systems.

2.2. Converting Bases

Both hex and octal numbers are easily formed by splitting up a binary number in different ways. An octal digit is formed from three binary digits. For example

---

Fig. 2-2: Powers of Two

2^0 =	1	2^7 =	128	2^{14} =	16,384
2^1 =	2	2^8 =	256	2^{15} =	32,768
2^2 =	4	2^9 =	512	2^{16} =	65,536
2^3 =	8	2^{10} =	1,024	2^{17} =	131,072
2^4 =	16	2^{11} =	2,048	2^{18} =	262,144
2^5 =	32	2^{12} =	4,096	2^{19} =	524,288
2^6 =	64	2^{13} =	8,192	2^{20} =	1,048,576

Fig. 2-3: Numbers

```
dec:   binary:  hex:  octal: |  dec:   binary:   hex:  octal:
                              |
  0    00000    0x0   000     |   16    10000     0x10   020
  1    00001    0x1   001     |   17    10001     0x11   021
  2    00010    0x2   002     |   18    10010     0x12   022
  3    00011    0x3   003     |   19    10011     0x13   023
  4    00100    0x4   004     |   20    10100     0x14   024
  5    00101    0x5   005     |   21    10101     0x15   025
  6    00110    0x6   006     |   22    10110     0x16   026
  7    00111    0x7   007     |   23    10111     0x17   027
  8    01000    0x8   010     |   24    11000     0x18   030
  9    01001    0x9   011     |   25    11001     0x19   031
 10    01010    0xa   012     |   26    11010     0x1a   032
 11    01011    0xb   013     |   27    11011     0x1b   033
 12    01100    0xc   014     |   28    11100     0x1c   034
 13    01101    0xd   015     |   29    11101     0x1d   035
 14    01110    0xe   016     |   30    11110     0x1e   036
 15    01111    0xf   017     |   31    11111     0x1f   037
```

```
10110011 = 10,110,011  = 0263 (octal)

 10 binary is 2 in octal
110 binary is 6 in octal
011 binary is 3 in octal
```

The process is the same for hex numbers, except that groups of four are used:

```
10110011 = 1011,0011  = 0xb3 (hex)

1011 binary is b in hex
0011 binary is 3 in hex
```

Binary-to-decimal conversion is performed by multiplying the various digits out by hand and then adding the resulting numbers together. Hex to decimal is done the same way but the multipliers are different. The process is illustrated in figure 2-4.

Fig. 2-4: Binary/Hex to Decimal Conversion

```
_____ 1 * 8 =   8        _____ (a * 16³) = (10 * 4096)  = 40960
|_____ 0 * 4 =   0        |_____ (6 * 16²) = ( 6 *  256)  =  1536
||____ 1 * 2 =   2        ||____ (f * 16¹) = (15 *   16)  =   240
|||___ 0 * 1 = + 0        |||___ (2 * 16⁰) = ( 2 *    1)  =     2
||||         -----        ||||                             -------
||||            10        ||||                             42738
1010                      a6f2
```

Decimal-to-binary conversion is more difficult. There are two ways to do the conversion; both are useful, but in different applications. Method 1 is better for a routine that's printing the converted number to the screen or putting it into an array, method 2 is better for most other applications. In both algorithms, the binary digits are arranged:

```
        D15, D14, ... , D1, D0.
```

D15 is the most-significant bit, *D0* is the least significant.

```
Method 1:

    (1) D15 = Number / 2¹⁵
    (2) D14 = (Remainder from divide in step 1) / 2¹⁴
    (3) D13 = (Remainder from divide in step 2) / 2¹³
    (4) continue as above until you reach D0.

Method 2:

    (1) if number is odd, D0 = 1, else D0 = 0;
    (2) number = number/2 ;
    (3) If number is odd D1 = 1, else D1 = 0;
    (4) number = number/2 ;
    (5) Continue as above until you reach D15.
```

In this algorithm, / is an integer divide. The fractional part of the quotient is discarded. $1/4 = 0$ ($1/4=0.25$, but the fraction [.25] is discarded). $5/2=2$ (2.5, but discard the .5). The *remainder* is the fractional part of the quotient, represented in terms of the divisor. That is, $7/5 = 1 + 2/5$; 1 is the integer quotient, and the remainder is 2 (from the 2/5). Another example: 17/6 = 2 + 5/6 (2 is the quotient, 5 is the remainder). The *modulus* operator (often abbreviated *MOD*) yields the remainder of an integer division. In C, % is used to represent the modulus operation. Thus, 17 / 6 = 2 and 17 % 6 = 5.

2.3. Addition and Subtraction

As noted earlier, binary operations are performed like the decimal operations. Decimal numbers are added as follows:

(0) Add the right-hand column.

(1) If the result is greater than nine, carry the excess digit to the next column.

(2) Add the next column (including the carry).

(3) Continue in this way until you reach the left-hand column.

Binary addition is done the same way:

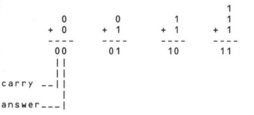

0+0 is 0 with a 0 carry, 0+1 is 1 with a 0 carry, 1+1 is 0 with a 1 carry, and 1+1+1 is 1 with a 1 carry. Two, more realistic, addition examples are shown in figure 2-5. To subtract, make one number negative (see the next section) and add.

Fig. 2-5: Addition

```
carry:   1     1                carry:    111111
         00101001  = 41                   00101111  = 47
        +00100101  = 37                  +00011101  = 29
        ----------  ----                 ---------  ----
         01001110    78                   01001100    76
```

When addition is performed in C, the carry-out from the most significant bit is silently discarded. This can cause problems. For example, the 8-bit unsigned number 255 can be stored in a **char**-sized variable (it has the value 0xff). But:

```
unsigned char   x ;

x = 255;
z = x + 1 ;
```

yields the number 0 as the result of the addition. You can see why by looking at the following binary operation:

```
carry: 1 1111 111
         1111 1111 = 255
       + 0000 0001 =   1
       ------------   ---
       1 0000 0000     0
```

The leftmost bit is discarded because it won't fit into an 8-bit number.

2.4. Negative Numbers

The concept of a negative number has meaning only in the decimal number system. You can use a binary, hex, or octal number to *represent* a negative decimal number, but the binary number itself is not negative. That is, even though 0x1a2 is 418 in decimal, -0x1a2 is meaningless. 0xfe5e *represents* the decimal number -418 in a 16-bit machine. Negative numbers are represented in most computers by a method known as *two's complement*. To form a two's complement negative number, invert all the bits in a positive number (turn the ones to zeros and the zeros to ones) and add one to the result. If the carry overflows the word width, discard it. The process is illustrated in figure 2-6.

Fig. 2-6: Forming a Negative Number

```
                 1 = 00000001        27 = 00011011       88 = 01011000

    invert:        11111110              11100100             10100111
    add 1:       + 00000001            + 00000001           + 00000001
                 ----------            ----------           ----------
                -1 = 11111111       -27 = 11100101       -88 = 10101000
```

Two's complement numbers have several interesting properties. You can negate a negative number to turn it into a positive number. More important, all the various arithmetic operations still work (that is, negative and positive numbers can be added or subtracted and yield a result with the correct sign; multiplying a negative by a positive number yields a negative result, and so on).

It is also important to note that the leftmost bit of a negative number is always 1. (It's always 0 in a positive number.) For this reason, the high-order bit of a binary number is often called the *sign bit*. Several bugs can pop up because of the sign bit. The following is an example from an 8-bit machine:

```
carry: 11
         00101000  =    40
       + 01100100  =   100
       ----------      ----
         10001100  =  -116
         |
         |
         |___ The high bit is 1
              so the number is
              negative.
```

which isn't what we wanted. Note that this error wouldn't have happened if we had used 16-bit, rather than 8-bit, arithmetic:

```
carry:            11
        0000000000101000  =   40
      + 0000000001100100  =  100
        ----------------      ----
        0000000010001100  =  140
```

Note that when negative numbers are a possibility, binary numbers have to be shown padded to the full word width of the machine.

An important side effect of the way that negative numbers are represented is *sign extension*. Whenever a number is converted to a wider type (for example, 8 to 16 bits), the sign of the original number must be maintained. This is done by duplicating the sign bit of the smaller number in the newly added high bits. Consider the number -27 in both 8 and 16 bit formats:

```
-27 =          11100101  ( 8 bits)
-27 = 1111111111100101  (16 bits)
```

When the 8-bit number is made wider, the leftmost bit of the smaller number is duplicated in every bit of the leftmost byte of the larger number. The sign bit of the low byte is *extended* into the high byte. Sign extension can produce several hard-to-find bugs in C programs that we'll look at later on in this chapter and in Chapter 10.

2.5. Shifts, Multiplication and Division

2.5.1. Shifting

In decimal arithmetic, a multiplication by 10 can be done with a left shift. Move all the digits one place to the left, and then put a 0 into the rightmost digit (60 shifted left one digit is 600). Similarly, a decimal number can be divided by 10 by shifting to the right (60 shifted right one digit is 6). This process can be generalized to any base: shift left one digit to multiply by the base. To divide by the base, shift right. Since a computer is a binary animal, a left shift is a multiply by 2 and a right shift is a divide by 2. In C, the operators $<<$ and $>>$ are used to represent left and right shifts. (Be careful not to confuse them with the less-than and greater-than operators, $<$ and $>$.) N$<<$2 evaluates to N shifted left by two binary digits (multiplied by 4), N$>>$X is N shifted right X bits (divides by 2^x). Note here that the $>>$ or $<<$ operator doesn't modify either operand (any more than +, -, or any other binary operator does). To actually modify N in the above example, an $=$ sign is required (in other words, N $>>= $ X or N $= $ N $<<$ 2). The least significant bit is filled with a 0 when a number is shifted to the left. The high bit is usually *duplicated* in a right shift (to maintain the sign of the shifted number). For example, the 8-bit binary number 10001101 shifted left one bit is 00011010; 10001101 shifted right one bit is 11000110. In theory, sign extension on a right shift is not guaranteed, but just about every compiler does it.

2.5.2. Multiplication

A good rule of thumb is that computers are remarkably stupid. Most computers are essentially glorified adding machines: All they can do is very simple arithmetic and memory move operations. Several computers (the 8080/Z-80 family is a case in point) can't multiply, but like old-fashioned adding machines, they can add and shift.

Two numbers can be multiplied together by adding one number to itself several times; in fact, it's sometimes quicker to use $X+X+X$ rather than $X*3$. Some compilers do generate repetitive additions (or some combination of adds and shifts) to perform multiplication when the operands are small enough. However, once the multiplier gets larger than the word width (about 16), successive addition gets pretty slow. If all we ever wanted to do is multiply by 2, we could just shift the number. (It's usually more efficient to use shifts if you can, rather than multiplies and divides.) Multiplying by other numbers requires a little more sophistication. You probably use an algorithm something like the following to multiply two decimal numbers:

(0)   Returning to the third grade: The number being multiplied is the *multiplicand*; the *multiplier* is the number by which the multiplicand is being multiplied; the resultant number is the *product*. (In the expression 2*3=6, 2 is the multiplicand, 3 is the multiplier, and 6 is the product.)

(1)   Multiply the multiplicand by the rightmost digit of the multiplier, forming a *partial product*.

(2)   Multiply the multiplicand by the next digit of the multiplier (the one immediately to the left of the one in the previous step). Shift the result of the multiplication one digit to the left, and add the resulting number to the partial product produced in step 1.

(3)   Continue in this manner until you've gone through the entire multiplier.

The process can be expressed more formally as follows:

(0)   The least significant digit is numbered 0; the most significant digit is numbered 1.

(1)   N = 0; product = 0.

(2)   If the multiplier equals 0, stop.

(3)   Multiply the multiplicand by the rightmost digit of the multiplier. Shift the result of this multiplication N digits to the left and add the resulting number to the product.

(4)   Shift the multiplier one digit to the right, discarding the rightmost digit.

(5)   N = N + 1.

(6)   Go to step 2.

This algorithm can be used for binary multiplication, too; just replace the word *digit* with *bit*. A problem with this algorithm is that it's defined recursively. Although the algorithm is telling you how to multiply, it requires you to multiply in step 3. That is, multiplication is being defined in terms of multiplication. Fortunately, if we apply the algorithm to binary numbers, we're always multiplying by either 1 or 0. This degraded case isn't really multiplication at all. Rather, it's deciding whether to move a number from one place to another, or to move 0 rather than the number. The process of binary multiplication is illustrated in figure 2-7.

Fig. 2-7: Binary Multiplication

```
          00110 =   6
    ×     01010 =  10
    -----------
          00000          (0110 * 0 shifted left 0 bits)
          00110          (0110 * 1 shifted left 1 bits)
         00000           (0110 * 0 shifted left 2 bits)
        00110            (0110 * 1 shifted left 3 bits)
    -----------
      00111100 = 60      (the sum of all 4 partial products)
```

If you prefer, the partial products can be added two at a time rather than all at once:

```
      00000      (first  partial product)
    + 00110      (second partial product)
    ---------
     001100      (first + second)
   + 00000       (third  partial product)
   ---------
    0001100      (first + second + third)
  + 00110        (fourth partial product)
  ---------
   00111100      (first + second + third + fourth)
```

Sign extension is also a problem in binary multiplication. If a partial product is negative, we have to sign extend it out to the full word width of the product (16 bits when two 8-bit numbers are being multiplied). This situation is illustrated in figure 2-8.

Fig. 2-8: Multiplying Numbers with Different Signs

```
Multiplication of two 4-bit numbers, one negative, yielding an
8-bit result. All but the rightmost 4 digits in the partial
              products are caused by sign extension.

                        1010 = -6
                        0011 =  3
                    -----------
                    111111010
                    11111010
                   0 0000000
                  00 000000
                    -------------
                    11101110   = -18
```

Note that the result *must* be truncated to 8 bits. If we hadn't truncated, we would have ended up with 0111101110 = 494. Also note that the negative operand must be on top for this method to work. (Otherwise there will never be a sign extension.) Some multiplication algorithms avoid the sign-extension problem by making both the multiplicand and multiplier positive and then adjusting the sign of the product. There are other, more efficient ways to do things but they're beyond the scope of this book.

2.5.3. Division

Binary division is also modeled after decimal arithmetic, so it's worthwhile to look at the decimal process first. Consider the following problem:

```
                              __014_      <--quotient
            divisor --> 11 )  156        <- dividend
                               11
                              -----
                               46
                               44
                              -----
                                2         <- remainder
```

The long-division process can be described as follows:

(0)   In the expression A/B = C, A is the *dividend*, B is the *divisor*, and C is the *quotient*.

(1)   Try to divide 1 (the leftmost digit of 156) by 11 (the divisor). It "doesn't go," so put a 0 into the quotient.

(3)   Try to divide 15 (the left two digits of 156) by 11, It goes 1 time, so put a 1 in the quotient and then subtract 11 (1*11) from 15, yielding 4. Now, "bring down" the 6 from the dividend, forming the number 46.

4)   Try to divide 46 by 11. It goes 4 times, so put a 4 into the quotient and subtract 44 (4*11) from 46, yielding 2.

5)   There are no more digits to "bring down," so the process is finished. The remainder is 2.

This algorithm presents us with several problems: It's worthwhile to notice that the operations themselves are quite complex. What do "bring down" and "doesn't go" really mean? In a normal situation, we don't even think about the leading 0's, in binary division we have to. Note that the divisor must constantly be repositioned relative to the dividend. Moreover, the dividend itself changes as the algorithm progresses. (When we subtract, we're actually creating a new dividend.) Finally, note that we never look at the entire dividend; we only look at a small portion of it.

Now, lets take a binary example. The following shows the division in a familiar format:

```
              _____101_
        110 ) 100010       (34 / 6 = 5)
              110
              -----
              101
              000
              -----
              1010
              110
              -----
              100          Remainder = 4
```

Note that we're always subtracting either the divisor or 0 from the remainder. Also note that at no point are we looking at more than 4 bits of the dividend.

It turns out to be easier to shift the dividend left than to shift the divisor right. We won't operate on the entire dividend, but rather on a 4-bit window into the dividend. The algorithm shifts the dividend through that window as it progresses. Digits shifted out of the window (to the left of it) are discarded. The window is initialized to hold a 0 bit, followed by the top three bits of the dividend.

This algorithm produces an N-bit-wide quotient by dividing a 2N-bit dividend by an N-bit divisor. The *window* is the contents of an N+1-bit-wide number formed from the top 4 bits of the dividend. Both the divisor and the dividend are assumed to be unsigned numbers. The division is performed as follows:

```
(1)    If( divisor <= window contents )
           The quotient will overflow (it will
           be larger than N bits).
           *** ERROR ***

(2)    Repeat N times:
       {
              If( divisor <= window contents )
              {
                     window = window - divisor;
                     Rightmost bit of quotient = 1;
              }
              shift dividend and quotient 1 bit left
       }

(3)    If( divisor <= window contents )
       {
              window = window - divisor;
              Rightmost bit of quotient = 1;
       }

(4)    STOP: the window holds the remainder and
             the quotient the quotient.
```

The foregoing is easier to understand if you look at a concrete example. We'll divide a 6-bit number (100010 = 34) by a 3-bit number (110 = 6), yielding a 3-bit quotient (101 = 5) and a 3-bit remainder (100 = 4). All four are unsigned (A leading 1 won't signify a negative number.) The *window* is shown as a box around part of the dividend. Any digits to the left of this box have been discarded.

```
                        Initial values:

     000           quotient = 0
    +------+
    | 0100 | 010 dividend = 34
    +------+
     110           divisor  = 6
```

Step 1:
    The divisor > window contents; no overflow.

Step 2 (iteration 1):
    Divisor > window contents; don't subtract.
    Shift divisor and quotient left.

```
     000           quotient
    +------+
  0 | 1000 | 10 dividend
    +------+
     110           divisor
```

Step 2 (iteration 2):
    The divisor <= window contents: subtract
    the divisor from the window contents
    putting the result into the window.
    (1000 - 110 = 0010). Put a 1 into
    the low bit of the quotient. Shift
    quotient and dividend one bit left.

```
  subtract ..... and then ...... shift:
     001           quotient          010
    +------+                        +------+
  0 | 0010 | 10 dividend    00 | 0101 | 0
    +------+                        +------+
     110           divisor          110
```

Step 2 (iteration 3):
    The divisor > window. Don't subtract but
    shift quotient and dividend to left.

```
     100           quotient
    +------+
  000 | 1010 |     dividend
    +------+
     110           divisor
```

Step 3: The divisor <= window contents;
    subtract, putting the result into
    the window. (1010 - 110 = 0100).
    Bottom bit of quotient = 1;
    (no shift).

```
        101        quotient
      +------+
001  | 0100 |      dividend
      +------+
        110        divisor
```

> Step 4: Done, the window now holds the
> remainder (0100 = 4). The quotient
> is 101 = 5.

2.5.4. Truncation, Overflow and Speed

A major multiplication-and-division-related problem is the accuracy of the result. When you shift a number to the right, the rightmost digits are discarded. They won't be replaced in a subsequent left shift. Consequently, when a division (which implies a right shift), is followed by a multiplication (which implies a left shift) you can loose some accuracy (because you discard some of the significant digits when you divide). If you do the multiplication first, you won't lose any accuracy, but you may overflow the word size of your machine (the result may be too large to represent in the available bits). Of course, if the word width of the product is twice that of both the multiplier and the multiplicand, there won't be an overflow problem, but this isn't always possible (if, for example, you have to multiply two **doubles** together).

There are related problems. For example, -1/4 can yield -1 rather than 0. Here, -1 has the value 0xffff. The divide-by-four does a right shift, but the high bit is sign extended as part of the shift. Consequently, -1/4 does nothing (0xffff shifted right 2 bits is 0xffff). A related problem is a side-effect of the division algorithm used. Because our *window* register is a different size from the operands, the high bit of a number can be truncated incorrectly. For example, 49152/-1 can yield 16384. You can see why by looking at the hex versions of the same numbers: 0xc000/-1 == 0x4000. The high bit has been incorrectly truncated.

Truncation and overflow problems are especially marked in floating-point arithmetic, in which you can lose all your precision if you divide and multiply in the wrong order. More to the point, it's the programmer who has to worry about overflow problems. The C language has no provisions for dealing with overflow. It's up to you to check that the two operands are in range before performing any operation (including addition and subtraction).

Another problem with multiplies and divides is speed. Multiplies and divides are expensive operations (as compared to shifts or even, at times, to a series of additions or subtractions). Floating-point operations are even more expensive than integer ones. If efficiency is important, be judicious about your math. It's worthwhile to develop algorithms that minimize multiplies and divides.

Another problem: Type conversion takes time, and expression evaluation often involves an implicit type conversion. For example, expressions involving **char**s take longer to evaluate than expressions made only of **int**s because the automatic type-conversion rules force all **char**s to be converted to **int**s before they're used. The same automatic type-conversion rules also apply to **float**s and **double**s; that is, all **float**s are converted to **double**s before they're used. Consequently, it takes longer to perform an operation on two **float**s than it does to do the same operation on two **double**s, even though the **float**s are shorter. The moral is: Use **int**s to store numbers rather than **char**s, **double**s rather than **float**s. Any illusory space savings you get from putting variables into **char**s is counter-balanced by the extra code you need to do type conversions. With **float**s and **double**s, the space savings may be real but you may have speed problems if you use **float**s. If speed is important, try to minimize type conversion by storing all numbers in the worst-case type. If any operand is a **double**, store all operands in **double**s, even if they could be integers. Since C dynamically recycles local memory from procedure to procedure, no space is wasted by assuming the worst. (We'll look at how this recycling happens in Chapter 4.)

2.6. Boolean Algebra

2.6.1. The Logical Operators

C supports various logical operators, the simplest of which are the comparison operators. When A and B are any expression,

```
A >  B        is true if A is greater than B
A <  B        is true if A is less than B
A >= B        is true if A is greater than or equal to B
A <= B        is true if A is less than or equal to B
A == B        is true if A is equal to B
A != B        is true if A is not equal to B
```

Note that "equal to" is represented by a double equal sign (==). A single equal sign represents assignment ($a = b$ puts the contents of b into a and evaluates to the contents of b). Be careful not to confuse the two.

In C, the number 0 signifies false and any non-zero quantity (including a negative number) signifies true. The logical operators evaluate to numbers (1 if they're true, 0 if false) and they behave like any other operator. The expression:

```
X + (A > B)
```

is perfectly legal. It evaluates to (X + 1) if A is greater than B and (X + 0) if A isn't greater than B.

There are three Boolean logical operators in C: AND (&&), OR (||), and NOT (!). Again, note that the & and the | are doubled; be careful not to confuse them with the equivalent bit-wise operators & and | (more on these in a moment). AND, OR, and NOT use the following truth tables:

```
NOT  !              AND  &&                    OR  ||

A  |  !A        A  |  B  |  A && B         A  |  B  |  A || B
---|----        ---|---|--------          ---|---|--------
F  |  1         F  |  F  |    0            F  |  F  |    0
T  |  0         F  |  T  |    0            F  |  T  |    1
                T  |  F  |    0            T  |  F  |    1
                T  |  T  |    1            T  |  T  |    1

T  ==  TRUE   (non-zero)
F  ==  FALSE  (zero)
```

A truth table works something like a multiplication table. A and B are the two numbers in the expression. The rightmost column represents the result of the indicated operation, given the specified values of A and B. A multiplication table arranged like a truth table would look like this:

```
A  |  B  |   A * B
---|---|--------
1  |  1  |     1
2  |  3  |     6
4  |  5  |    20
        etc.
```

1 * 1 == 1, 2 * 3 == 6, and so on. In a similar way T || F == 1 (if the left operand is non-zero and the right operand is zero, the entire expression evaluates to 1). It's worth memorizing the truth tables for AND, OR, and NOT. (Just remember that (A && B) is true only if both A and B are true. (A || B) is true if either A or B [or both] are true).

&& and || have a unique property. The order of evaluation in expressions that use && and || is guaranteed to be left-to-right (unless parentheses force it to go otherwise) and the evaluation is guaranteed to terminate when the truth or falsity of the expression can be determined. So, in the expression

```
if( x && spot( ) )
```

spot() won't be called if *x* is false (zero) (because the expression can't possibly evaluate to true if *x* is false). Similarly, in

```
if( x || dog( ) )
```

dog() won't be called if *x* is true (because the expression evaluates to true regardless of the subroutine's return value.

2.7. Simple Identities

The logical operators are most often used to control loops and **if** statements. Since, in terms of efficiency, these are often the most critical parts of a program (the parts that are executed most often), it's a good idea to optimize logical expressions if at all possible. Some C compilers do some optimization for you, but you can't count on it. This section presents various simple ways to optimize expressions.

2.7.0.1. Inverting Expressions and DeMorgan's Theorem

The simplest logical operator is NOT (!). *!A* evaluates to one if *A* is FALSE (zero); it evaluates to zero if a is TRUE (non-zero). Combining the ! operator with other operators can be tricky. In particular,

```
!( A == B )      ==      ( A != B )
!( A != B )      ==      ( A == B )
!( A >  B )      ==      ( A <= B )
!( A <  B )      ==      ( A >= B )
!( A >= B )      ==      ( A <  B )
!( A <= B )      ==      ( A >  B )
```

The first two equivalences are obvious, but the others require some thought.

The ! operator can also be used with the AND and OR operators:

```
!( A && B )      ==      ( !A || !B )
!( A || B )      ==      ( !A && !B )
```

These two identities are know as *DeMorgan's Theorem*. The important thing to note is that *(!A || !B)* represents three operations to the computer. *!A*, *!B*, and the || have to be computed separately. On the other hand, *!(A && B)* is only two operations (one && and one !), so you reduce the evaluation time by one-third by going from one form to the other. The other side of this issue is readability. Sometimes it's worthwhile to keep an expression inefficient in order to improve the overall readability of the program. The decision whether or not to do algebraic reduction has to be made on a case-by-case basis.

2.7.0.2. Boolean Algebraic Simplification

In addition to DeMorgan's theorem, there are several other useful logical identities. Those used most often are listed in figure 2-9.

Fig. 2-9: Logical Identities

```
    OR Expressions:                        |    AND Expressions:
--------------------------------------------|------------------------------------------
1.  !(!A)        == A                       |
                                            |
2.  !(A  ||    B) == (!A && !B)             |  !(A &&   B) == (!A || !B)
3.   (A  ||    0) == A                      |   (A &&   1) == A
4.   (A  ||    1) == 1                      |   (A &&   0) == 0
5.   (A  ||    A) == A                      |   (A &&   A) == A
6.   (A  ||   !A) == 1                      |   (A &&  !A) == 0
                                            |
7.  (A||B)         == (B || A)             |   (A&&B)         == (B && A)
8.  ((A||B) || C) == (A || (B || C))       |  ((A&&B) && C) == (A && (B && C))
9.  ((A||B) && C) == (A&&C) || (B&&C)       |  ((A&&B) || C) == (A||C) && (B||C)
                                            |
10. (A && B)  || (A && !B) ==   A          |  (A || B) && (A || !B) ==   A
11.      A    || (A && B) ==   A           |       A   && (A ||  B) ==   A
12.      B    || (A && !B) == (A || B)      |       B   && (A || !B) == (A && B)
                                            |
```

2.8. Bit-wise Operators and Masks

2.8.1. AND, OR, XOR, NOT

In addition to the normal logical operators, C supports several bit-wise operators. A bit-wise operator follows the same truth table as a normal logical operator does, but it operates on numbers 1 bit (or column) at a time. For example, if we were doing a bit-wise AND of the number 101 and 011, the rightmost bits are ANDed together and the rightmost bit of the answer is set to the result (1 AND 1 == 1). The 2 middle bits are ANDed together, and the middle bit of the answer is set to the result (1 AND 0 == 0). The leftmost bits are processed in the same way. Examples are given in figure 2-10.

C provides four bit-wise operators: & (AND), | (OR), ˜ (NOT), and ˆ (XOR). Note that the bit-wise AND and bit-wise OR use a single & and |, unlike logical AND (&&) and logical OR (||). These operators do very different things; don't confuse them. The bit-wise NOT (˜) evaluates to the operand with all bits inverted (the ones turned to zeros and the zeros to one). The operand itself isn't affected. (Don't confuse this with the logical NOT (!), which evaluates to zero if the operand is non-zero, to one otherwise). The XOR (or eXclusive OR) operator follows this truth table:

Fig. 2-10: Bit-wise Operations

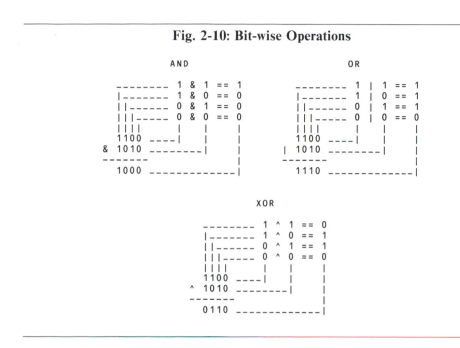

```
        AND                                    OR

-------- 1 & 1 == 1                 -------- 1 | 1 == 1
|------- 1 & 0 == 0                 |------- 1 | 0 == 1
||------ 0 & 1 == 0                 ||------ 0 | 1 == 1
|||----- 0 & 0 == 0                 |||----- 0 | 0 == 0
||||      |    |     |              ||||      |    |     |
1100 ----|    |     |               1100 ----|    |     |
& 1010 --------|     |              | 1010 --------|     |
-------              |              -------              |
  1000 --------------|                1110 -------------|


        XOR

-------- 1 ^ 1 == 0
|------- 1 ^ 0 == 1
||------ 0 ^ 1 == 1
|||----- 0 ^ 0 == 0
||||      |    |     |
1100 ----|    |     |
^ 1010 --------|     |
-------              |
  0110 --------------|
```

A	B	A ^ B
0	0	0
0	1	1
1	0	1
1	1	0

Exclusive OR can be viewed as a bit-wise not-equal operator. It evaluates to one only if the operands are different. That is, it's TRUE if either operand (but not both) is TRUE.

2.8.2. Masks

An interesting property of the bit-wise operators emerges in figure 2-10. Look at the bottom operand as if it were a sort of filter through which the top operand is being processed to reach the answer. This bottom operand is called a *mask*. If you look at the AND operation, you'll note that everywhere there's a one in the mask, the top operand passes through to the answer unmolested. Everywhere there's a zero in the mask, however, there's also a zero in the answer. AND masks are used to selectively clear (set to 0) or test any single bit of a number. For example, the expression $c = c$ & $0x7f$ clears all but the bottom 7 bits of the variable c. (This is especially useful for stripping the parity bit from a raw input character.) In the expression

```
if( A & 0x03 )
        do_something( );
```

do_something is executed only if one of the bottom two bits of *A* are set.

The OR mask works in a similar way, but here the top operand passes through to the answer unmodified everywhere there's a 0 in the mask. If there's a 1 in the OR mask, the corresponding bit in the answer is set (to 1). OR masks are used to set individual bits in a word. For example, $x = x \mid 1$ forces the bottom bit of x to be 1.

Finally, the XOR mask can be used to selectively invert bits. Everywhere there's a 0 in the XOR mask, the top operand passes through to the answer unmodified. Everywhere there's a 1 in the XOR mask, the sense of the corresponding bit in the top operand is inverted in the answer (each 1 becomes a 0 and vice versa). XOR masks are useful in graphics applications when you want to invert a single dot on a bit-mapped display. They're also used to invert the sense of a single bit in a hardware register (in other words, if every bit in a register except one is set to 0 on success and 1 on error, and that single bit has the opposite sense, an XOR mask can be used to invert the sense of the recalcitrant bit so that you can test the whole register for 0 on success).

2.9. The Comma, Equals, and Conditional Operators

Two of the operators supported by the C language are strange enough to deserve some comment. These are the comma (,) and conditional (?:) operators. In addition the assignment operator (=) is treated differently in C than it is in most languages.

First, don't confuse a test for equality (==) with assignment (=). The expression

```
x == y
```

does not modify *x* or *y*. The statement evaluates to 1 if *x* and *y* have the same value, to 0 if they're different. The statement

```
x = y
```

modifies *x* to hold the contents of *y*. This second expression evaluates to the contents of *x* after the assignment is made.

It's important to note that both == and = are operators, and expressions that use them evaluate to something. (All expressions evaluate to something.) The assignment operator is an operator like any other and can be part of an arithmetic expression, just like any other operator. For example

```
x = 5 + (y = z);
```

is a perfectly valid statement. The contents of z are copied to y (this subexpression evaluates to the contents of y after the assignment); then the contents of y are added to 5, and the result is put into x. Be careful of the low precedence of =. The expression

```
x = a + b = z + 5 ;
```

Has implied parenthesis:

```
x = (a + b) = (z + 5);
```

Since you can't assign a value to an expression, the compiler will print an error message when it sees this.

The comma, like many symbols in C, has different functions depending on its context. It is used both for separating function arguments from each other and as an actual operator. Don't confuse these uses; the comma in a function's argument list is not an arithmetic operator.

The main purpose of the comma operator is to provide for multiple expressions in a **for** statement. For example, in the loop

```
for( i = 0, j = size ;   i <= j ; i++, j-- )
```

both i and j are initialized in the left part of the **for** statement, and they are both modified in the right part of the statement.

Since the purpose of a **for** loop is the concentration of loop control into one place, it's considered bad style to include operations that have nothing to do with loop control in a **for** statement. The comma operator is often abused in this way; it's used to move an expression into a **for** statement that has no business being there (because it has nothing to do with controlling the loop). For example, in

```
for( x += 7, y = 1; y < 10; y++ )
    body( );
```

the statement involving x doesn't belong in the loop because it's not used for purposes of control. This statement should be restated as follows

```
x += 7;

for( y = 1; y < 10; y++ )
    body( )
```

The comma operator is actually an operator that can be used in any expression. You can look at it as an assignment operator that doesn't do an assignment. That is, the expression:

```
x = ((y += 1), (z += 1));
```

increments both y and z. The statement evaluates to the contents of the expression to the right of the comma, in a manner analogous to the assignment operator (=). That is, the value of z (after the increment) is added to x. Be careful of precedence here. The comma has the lowest precedence of any operator, including assigment. For example,

```
x = ( 1, 2 );
```

evaluates to *2* because of the comma operator. The expression

```
x = 1 , 2;
```

evaluates to 1, however, because the compiler parenthesizes it as:

```
(x = 1) , 2;
```

The comma operator is occasionally useful in a macro. It's so hard to read, however, that it usually should be shunned. The foregoing expression should be written as follows

```
z += 1;
x = (y += 1);
```

The third operator of interest is the conditional operator (?:), The conditional is a ternary operator, that is, it has three, rather than two, parts. In

```
x + y
```

the binary operator (+) has two parts, and it evaluates to one result (the sum). The ternary expression

```
x ? y : z
```

has three parts, but it still evaluates to one result. It evaluates to y if x is true, and to z if x is false. If either operand is a subroutine call, as in

```
x ? sam( ) : dave( )
```

only one of the subroutines will be called. The conditional is an operator so it can be used in an expression:

```
a = x ? y : z;
```

assigns the contents of either y or z to a, depending on whether x is true of not. In this example, the conditional is preferable to the equivalent

```
if( x )
        a = y;
else
        a = z;
```

because the code generated by the conditional is more efficient (the address of a only needs to be computed once rather than twice).

The conditional can also be used in other ways. For example

```
printf( "x is %s", x ? "TRUE" : "FALSE" );
```

prints either "x is TRUE" if x is non-zero or "x is FALSE" if x is zero. Here the conditional evaluates to one or the other of the strings. The equivalent code:

```
if( x )
        printf( "x is TRUE" );
else
        printf( "x is FALSE" );
```

is, again, less efficient. Here we need to store more characters in the two strings and, more important, we need to generate the code for two, rather than one, subroutine calls.

Conditional operators can also be nested. For example:

```
#define YES     0
#define NO      1
#define MAYBE   2


printf("x = %s",   x == YES  ?  "YES"  :
                   x == NO   ?  "NO"   :
                                "MAYBE" );
```

It's important to format nested conditionals in a way that makes the order of evaluation clear. To my mind:

```
printf("x = %s",   x == YES ? "YES" : x == NO ? "NO" : "MAYBE" );
```

is harder to read than the earlier example.

2.10. Bugs

There are several bugs that can pop up as a result of unexpected sign extension or numeric truncation. For example, a **char** is a signed number in most compilers. (You can declare a variable as **unsigned char**, however.) All ASCII characters are represented by the bottom 7 bits of the number. However, some machines (such as the IBM-PC) use the eighth bit to represent special keys. For example, when you hit an auxiliary key such as F1 on the IBM keyboard, the ROM-BIOS passes a 2-byte code to the software. The first byte is always 0 and the second byte is a special non-ASCII code. Since it's inconvenient for a single-character input routine to return 2 bytes, the second byte is often returned with the high bit set to indicate a special code. Hitting F1 transmits the 2-character sequence 0x00 0x3b (00000000 00111011 in binary) which is then mapped into 0xbb (10111011).

This mapping is done in the following subroutine: *getkb()*, that calls *scan()* to get a single character from the hardware and maps two-character sequences into a single character:

```
getkb( )
{
        char x;

        if( (x = scan( )) == 0 )
                x = scan( ) | 0x80 ;

        return x;
}
```

Getkb() returns an **int**, as do most character-input routines. In every expression, all variables of type **char** are converted to type **int** before the expression is evaluated. The **return** keyword takes an expression as its argument, so x is treated as if it were an expression and a type conversion is done. If x contains 0xbb, this number is converted to 0xffbb when the **char** is converted to **int** (0xbb is a negative number, sign extension is performed resulting in 0xffbb). Consequently, the test

```
if( getkb( ) == 0xbb )
```

fails because 0xffbb, not 0xbb, is returned from *getkb()*. The problem can be corrected as follows:

```
if( (getkb( ) & 0xff) == 0xbb )
```

Saying

```
return( x & 0xff );
```

inside *getkb()* would also work, but only because x is converted to **int** before the AND operation is performed.

A related problem shows up in interfaces to communications hardware. Most of this hardware supports an error-detection mechanism called *parity checking.* If *even parity* is used, then all characters have an even number of bits set (the binary number 101 has an even number [2] of set bits; 010 has an odd number [1]). Since not all ASCII codes have an even number of bits, the parity bit is used to fill out the number so that it will have an even number of bits. For example, an ASCII *a* has the numeric value 0x61 (01010001 in binary). This number has an odd number of bits set to 1. Consequently, if an ASCII *a* is sent over a modem that's using even parity, the high bit is set to 1 so that the number will contain an even number of bits. That is, the number 0x61 (01010001) is converted to 0xd1 (11010001), which is a negative number in an 8-bit signed **char**. If this character is read directly from the hardware, and then stored in an **int**-sized variable, sign extension is performed: 0xd1 (11010001) is converted to 0xffd1 (1111111111010001).

Some older compilers, such as Lattice C, treated all **char**s as unsigned quantities by default. Consequently, these sign-extension problems may not show up until you port a program to a newer compiler that assumes that **char**s are signed numbers.

Automatic type conversion and sign extension can work together in other unexpected ways. For example, when using an 8-bit **int**, the expression

```
(64 * 2) / 2
```

evaluates to -64. 64 has the hex value 0x40. Multiplying it by 2 yields 0x80, which is a negative number in an 8-bit machine (it has the value -128). Dividing that number by 2 yields the hex number 0xc0 (a right shift with a sign extension), or -64.

Overflow is also a problem.

```
(64 * 32) / 16
```

evaluates to 0 if we have an 8-bit **int**. A multiply by 32 is a left shift of 5 bits. However, if we shift 64 by 5 bits, we'll shift the only significant digit clear off the left end of the number. That is, 01000000 shifted left 5 bits is 0100000000000 but since there are only 8 bits of precision, all but the bottom 8 bits are discarded, leaving us with 0.

We'll look at these problems again in Chapter 10.

2.11. Exercises

2-1   Convert the decimal numbers 93 and -56 to binary, hex, and octal. Use an 8-bit word.

2-2   Convert the decimal numbers 17 and -11 to binary and multiply them together in binary, showing all intermediate stages of the multiplication process (as in figure 2-7). Use 6-bit operands and generate a 12-bit result.

2-3   Divide 21 by 3 in binary, showing all intermediate stages of the division process. Assume a 6-bit unsigned dividend and a 3-bit unsigned divisor and quotient. What is the remainder?

2-4   To what do the following expressions evaluate? Show your work and give the answers in both decimal and hex. Assume that all operands and answers are 8-bit numbers. C syntax is used to identify the number's radix.

```
a.   (111 & 011) ^ 0xa5
b.   -(0x55 + 0252)
c.   127 * 3
d.   (0x62 << 1) / 2
e.   17 | 36
f.   64 * (32 / 16)
g.   (17 < 11) + ((93 && 66) || 56)
```

2-5   What does the following expression do? Prove your answer with a few concrete examples.

```
                              a ^= b ^= a ^= b;
```

2-6   It's sometimes necessary to manipulate numbers that are larger than can
      be put in an int or long. Several *large integer* manipulation packages are
      available that can do arithmetic on these large numbers. The numbers
      themselves are stored in arrays. Write the following large integer rou-
      tines:

```
#define NUMBYTES 8

typedef char    BIGINT[ NUMBYTES ]    /* 64 bit wide integer */

b_atoi( str, num )
char    str[ ];
BIGINT  num;

mult(  multiplicand, multiplier, product )
BIGINT multiplicand, multiplier, product;

add(     num1, num2, sum )
BIGINT   num1, num2, sum ;

negate( num );
BIGINT  num;

print_hex( num );
BIGINT     num;
```

b_atoi(str, num) takes as input an ASCII string containing a hexadecimal
representation of a large integer and converts that number to binary,
storing the binary representation in the indicated *num*. For example, a
call to

```
BIGINT  num;
b_atoi( "0x123456789a", num );
```

initializes the *num* array as follows:

```
                num[0] == 0x9a    <-- LSB
                num[1] == 0x78
                num[2] == 0x56
                num[3] == 0x34
                num[4] == 0x12
                num[5] == 0x00
                num[6] == 0x00
                num[7] == 0x00
```

mult(multiplicand, multiplier, product) multiplies the multiplier by the
multiplicand and puts the result in product. It returns 0 if the result was
too large to be stored in a *BIGINT*, otherwise it returns 1. **add(num1,
num2, sum)** adds num1 to num2 and puts the result in sum.
negate(num) negates num, using a two's complement negation.
print_h(num); prints the number in hex.

Your code should be written so that the word width (#**defined** as *NUM-
BYTES* above) can be changed by modifying *NUMBYTES* only. That is,

to change the word width, all you should have to do is modify *NUM-BYTES* and recompile. None of the code itself should need to be modified in this case. Your code should work with *NUMBYTES* set to any positive integer (within reason).

All the routines should work properly with negative and zero operands. Moreover, the two operands should not be modified unless one of the operands is also a target (sum, product, and so on). All three arguments to *mult()* or *add()* can be the same. For example

```
BIGINT   num;
b_atoi( "10", num );

add( num, num, num );
```

should work. When *add()* returns, *num* should contain 20. You should devise your own test data. Nonetheless, include the following numbers in your tests:

```
n1         = 12345678            (decimal)
n1         = 0000000000bc614e    (hex)
n2         = -87654321           (decimal)
n2         = ffffffffffac6804f   (hex)
-n1        = fffffffffff439eb2
n1 + n2    = fffffffffb82e19d
n1 - n2    = 0000000005f5e0ff
n1 * n2    = fffc27c9d91d0712
n1 / n2    = 0000000000000000  (R 0000000000bc614e)

n1         = 123456789012345678 (decimal)
n1         = 01b69b4ba630f34e    (hex)
n2         = 123456789012345678 (decimal)
n2         = 01b69b4ba630f34e    (hex)
-n1        = fe4964b459cf0cb2
n1 + n2    = 036d36974c61e69c
n1 - n2    = 0000000000000000
n1 * n2    = (invalid)
n1 / n2    = 0000000000000001 (R 0000000000000000)
```

2-6   Add the routine

```
div( dividend, divisor, quotient, remainder )
BIGINT dividend, divisor, quotient, remainder)
```

to your *BIGINT* package. The routine divides the *dividend* by the *divisor* and puts the resulting numbers in *quotient* and *remainder*. Your routine must be able to handle the following:

```
123456789012345678/123456789012345678
```

and get a quotient of 1 and a remainder of 0. Be sure that the remainder has the correct sign. The following formula should hold:

```
((dividend/divisor) * divisor) + remainder == dividend
```

2-7   Modify *b_atoi()* so that it can take as input a string representing either a
       decimal or hex number. It should check for a leading 0x and treat the
       number as hex if it's there and as decimal if it's not. Write the routine
       print_d(num) that outputs the *BIGINT num* in decimal.

ASSEMBLY LANGUAGE

There are several reasons for the C programmer to know the basics of assembly language. For a high-level language, C is remarkably close to assembly language. Many tasks usually done in assembler (low-level math routines, interrupt service routines, and so on) can be done in C. In order to exploit this part of the C language, however, you need to know the basics of assembly language. Similarly, many of the operators in C (bit-wise Boolean operators, shift operators, and the like) are analogs of assembly language instructions. Knowing assembly language can help in understanding C itself. Many assembly language concepts (such as indirection) are reflected in C concepts (such as pointers). Learning the underlying language helps you understand these higher-level constructs. But perhaps the most important reason for knowing assembly language is debugging. In the next chapter we'll look in depth at code-generation techniques used by C compilers. Knowing how a compiler calls a subroutine, and knowing how variables are stored in memory, can help a great deal in tracking down hard-to-find bugs. We can't look at these issues without some assembler.

In this chapter we'll look at how a computer is organized from a programmer's perspective, and we'll look at the basic assembly language instructions needed to manipulate this machine. The language and the machine described here aren't real (though they borrow heavily on the 68000 and the PDP-11). Our demo machine is much easier to program than most real computers, and many of the common problems of real assembly language programming aren't even mentioned here. Moreover, our language has been designed to help look at C-related issues. Since we're learning concepts, it's pointless to complicate things with needless details.

There are several flavors of assembly language. If you already know 8080 or Z–80 assembler, but don't know any other, you should read the sections on addressing modes very carefully. Neither machine supports extensive addressing modes. The other truly important concepts in this chapter are in the "Subroutine Calls and Stacks" section (3.5.4), which you should review before going on to the next chapter.

3.1. What is Assembler?

Assembly language (or *assembler*) is a programming language in which each instruction translates directly into a machine-level op-code. That is, you can translate an assembly language program directly into the binary codes that the machine itself uses. One assembly language instruction translates directly into one machine instruction. On this level, a computer is essentially an elaborate adding machine. It can do only simple operations like moving the contents of one memory cell to another or adding together two numbers. Most calculators have a more powerful instruction set than most computers (but the computers are faster). A high-level language like C can do, in one statement, an action that requires several assembly language instructions to accomplish. In fact, a compiler can be seen as a high-level language to assembly language translator.

3.2. Memory Organization and Alignment

Memory in a computer is composed of a series of *cells*, each having a unique *address*. A good analogy is a book whose text consists of one number on each page. The physical size of a page restricts the number of digits that can be held on the page. If a number is larger than this number of digits, then it has to overflow to the next page. In this analogy, each page is a single cell and the page number is that cell's address. The number of digits that can fit on the page is the machine's *word width* (that is, the number of binary digits [bits] comprised by one cell of memory). There's one further restriction. Numbers that are large enough to take up two pages must use facing pages. You can't turn a page to get to the second half of a large number. This last restriction is called *alignment*. The first page in the book is numbered 0 (0 is an even number) and, in fact, all left page numbers are even. Our demo machine uses a 16-bit *word*. Each word can be broken up into two 8-bit *bytes*, and each byte has a unique address. That is, since 2 bytes are required to hold a word, then each word takes up two addresses. In our machine, byte and word operations are handled differently. A byte operation can manipulate any byte in the machine. However, a word operation (like a 16-bit add) always requires the least significant byte of the operands to be at an even address, and the corresponding most significant byte to be at the next largest address. This requirement is called *word alignment* because the words have to be lined up on an even address. Some machines impose more involved alignment restrictions. For example, the segment registers in an 8086 have to be aligned on 16-byte (*paragraph*) boundaries.

The alignment on our demo machine is illustrated in figure 3-1. *MSB* stands for "Most Significant Byte" and *LSB* for "Least Significant Byte." A decimal analogy is: Given the 2-digit number 56, 5 is the most significant digit and 6 is the least significant.

Fig. 3-1: Memory Organization

```
                          Bit position

                       15      8 7       0
                       |-------|-------|
         Address   1 |  MSB  |  LSB  | 0
                       |-------|-------|
                   3 |  MSB  |  LSB  | 2
                       |-------|-------|
                   5 |  MSB  |  LSB  | 4
                       |-------|-------|
                     |       etc.      |
```

All the instructions given in this chapter operate on single bytes unless a *W* follows the actual instruction. For example, the *MOV* instruction moves a byte from one place to another. The instruction *MOV.W* moves a word-sized object (2 bytes).

Code and data share the same memory space, and the computer cannot tell whether a cell contains an instruction or data. On most microcomputers, it's possible for a C program to accidentally modify the code that's being executed, while it's being executed—a disastrous event indeed. It's also possible to accidentally start executing data, another catastrophe.

3.3. Registers and Machine Organization

To understand how an assembly language works, we must first look at the machine upon which it works. Most computers can be split up into two distinct parts—the *central processing unit* (or *CPU*) and the *memory*. The CPU talks to the memory over a collection of wires known as a *bus*. In addition to the main memory, all CPUs have a small number of memory locations, called *registers*, actually built into them. Because of various constraints placed on the CPU by the hardware, it takes much longer to access the main memory store than it does to access an internal register. Consequently, a good C compiler makes extensive use of registers in the code that it generates. The C keyword **register** causes a register to be used to store a variable, provided that a register is available. (There are a limited number, and the compiler uses some of them for its own run-time scratch space.) A memory location's address is actually a way of representing a set of voltages that the CPU puts onto the bus to access that memory location. Since the CPU doesn't need to talk to the bus to access a register, registers don't have addresses; rather, they have names.

A simple calculator has one register (the contents of which are displayed in a little window on the face of the calculator) called the *accumulator* because the ongoing result of all operations are accumulated there. All instructions affect the accumulator. Most calculators have a few additional registers where the current contents of the accumulator can be stored and then retrieved at a later date, but only certain instructions (store and recall) apply to these additional registers. A computer has a similar structure, but the registers are usually named A, B, C, and so on, rather than *accumulator.* Similarly, some instructions can only access registers, while others can also access memory.

Our demo machine has a total of eight registers named A, B, C, D, SP, PC, FP, and FL. They are shown in figure 3-2.

Fig. 3-2: Demo Machine Register Set

```
15      8   7      0        15                0
|-------+-------|          |-----------------|
|       A       |          |       SP        |  (stack pointer)
|-------+-------|          |-----------------|
|       B       |          |       PC     |0|  (program counter)
|-------+-------|          |-----------------|
|       C       |          |       FP        |  (frame pointer)
|-------+-------|          |-----------------|
|       D       |          | FL:   |V|Z|P|N|  (flag register)
|-------+-------|          |-----------------|
```

All registers are 16 bits wide (2 bytes). The A, B, C, and D registers are general-purpose registers; we can use them as accumulators. The other registers are special-purpose, and we'll see how they are used as we describe the instructions that affect them (though we won't look at the frame pointer (FP) until the next chapter). The one special-purpose register we'll look at now is

the *program counter*, or *PC*. The PC always holds the address of the instruction currently being executed. It is automatically updated as each instruction
is executed to hold the address of the next instruction to be executed. In our
demo machine, all instructions occupy exactly 2 bytes, so the PC is normally
incremented by 2 with every instruction. The important concept here is that
the PC holds the *address* of the next instruction, not the instruction itself.
When an instruction is executed, the machine first fetches the actual instruction from the indicated address, and then executes it.

3.4. Addressing Modes

All of the machine's instructions access either a memory location or a
register in the course of their execution. Unlike most real computers (and
most calculators for that matter), every instruction can be applied to any
register. For example, an ADD instruction can be used to add a number to
any of the eight registers. Many computers limit the registers to which certain
instructions can be applied. For example, in our calculator analogy, the + key
can only affect the accumulator. (It can't be used to modify an additional
storage register.) To modify a storage register, you have to move its contents
into the accumulator, then modify the accumulator, then move the result back
into storage.

Register and memory accessing can be done in one of several ways. For
example, we can access a memory location or register directly, we can access a
memory location that is at some offset from a certain address, or we can
access a memory location whose address is held in a register. The various
ways in which addresses can be used are called *addressing modes*.

In the instruction descriptions that follow, we use the notation *rN* to
represent an address or register. Since this address or register can be used in
various addressing modes, we won't list all possibilities in the actual descriptions; rather, you can replace the rN notation with any of the following.

3.4.1. Register Direct Addressing

When *rN* is replaced by a register name, it refers to the contents of that
register. This mode is called *register direct addressing*. The instruction
MOV A,B moves the contents of the A register into the B register. The previous contents of the B register are destroyed, and the A register isn't modified.
Since this is a byte-move instruction (there's no *.W* attached to the *MOV*),
only the least significant bytes of the A and B registers are used. The high
byte (bits 8–15) remains unmodified. The instruction *MOV.W A,B* transfers
both the high and low bytes of register A into B.

Fig. 3-3: Register Direct Addressing

```
        Before:            MOV.W A,B              After:

        |---------------|                    |---------------|
  A:    |       3       |              A:    |       3       |
        |---------------|                    |---------------|
  B:    |       4       |              B:    |       3       |
        |---------------|                    |---------------|
```

An equivalent operation in C is $x = y$; where both x and y are register variables:

```
register    int    x,y;
x = y;
```

3.4.2. Memory Direct Addressing

When *rN* is replaced by an explicit number, the contents of the memory cell whose address is that number is accessed. The instruction *MOV 100,200* moves the contents of memory location 100 into memory location 200. Location 100 isn't modified but the previous contents of location 200 are destroyed. The equivalent word-move instruction *MOV.W 100,200* moves the contents of memory location 100 into memory location 200, and the contents of location 101 into 201. *MOV.W 100,A* moves the contents of location 100 to the low byte of the A register and the contents of location 101 to the high byte of the A register. It's an error to try to move a word-sized object to or from an odd address (that is, *MOV.W 101,A* is an illegal instruction).

Fig. 3-4: Direct Addressing

```
        Before:            MOV.W 100,200            After:

        |---------------|                      |---------------|
100:    |      999      |              100:    |      999      |
        |---------------|                      |---------------|
102:    |       .       |              102:    |       .       |
                .                                      .
198:    |       .       |              198:    |       .       |
        |---------------|                      |---------------|
200:    |       0       |              200:    |      999      |
        |---------------|                      |---------------|
```

Here the C analogy is still $x = y$; but now both variables have been declared static:

```
static   int      x,y;
x = y;
```

Remember that a memory access takes longer than a register access. Similarly, in most machines a memory access requires a physically larger instruction (for example, two words instead of one).

3.4.3. Immediate Addressing

If the number is preceded by a #, then the number itself is referenced, rather than the contents of the cell with the indicated address. The instruction *MOV #100,200* puts the number 100 into memory location 200. *MOV.W #999,A* loads the A register with the number 999. Immediate instructions on registers are, again, faster than those that modify memory. However, they are all faster than memory-to-memory moves. The following are equivalent statements in C:

```
register int  x;   /* Use the A register    */
static    int  y;   /* Use memory location 200 */

x = '*';        /* generates a    MOV.W #42,A */
y =  3 ;        /* generates a    MOV.W #3,200 */
```

The 42 in the first assignment derives from the '*'. In C, a character surrounded by single quotes evaluates to the ASCII code for that character. '*' in ASCII is 0x2a, or 42 decimal.

3.4.4. Indirect Addressing

The notation *(rN)* is used for indirect addressing. In this mode, the contents of the memory cell whose *address* is in the indicated register or memory location is accessed. For example, if the A register contains the number 100, the instruction *MOV (A),B* moves the contents of memory location 100 into the B register. This example is shown in figure 3-5.

Another example: If the A register is set to 100 and the B register contains the number 200 then a *MOV (A),(B)* instruction transfers the contents of memory location 100 to memory location 200. Neither register is modified.

One final example: A *MOV.W (100),(200)* moves the contents of the cell whose address is stored at location 100 into the cell whose address is stored at location 200. It moves a word-sized object. This example is illustrated in figure 3-6.

Indirect addressing is an important concept. The register contains the *address* of the memory location to be manipulated, and the register itself is not modified. The cell whose address is contained in the register is the one that is affected. The expression *points to* is used to express this relationship.

Fig. 3-5: Register Indirect Addressing

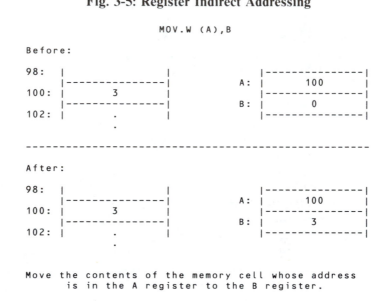

```
                           MOV.W (A),B

        Before:

        98:  |                |          |----------------|
             |----------------|      A:  |      100       |
        100: |       3        |          |----------------|
             |----------------|      B:  |       0        |
        102: |       .        |          |----------------|
                     .

        --------------------------------------------------

        After:

        98:  |                |          |----------------|
             |----------------|      A:  |      100       |
        100: |       3        |          |----------------|
             |----------------|      B:  |       3        |
        102: |       .        |          |----------------|
                     .
```

Move the contents of the memory cell whose address
is in the A register to the B register.

In the examples just cited, the A register points to memory location 100. That is, it holds the address 100, which is being *pointed at* by the A register.

C uses indirect addressing to access all automatic variables (local variables that are not explicitly declared **static**). We'll see why in the next chapter. Indirect addressing is also used for pointer operations. For example—

```
register int    *p;      /* Use the A register       */
int             x;       /* Use memory location 200 */
int             y;       /* Use memory location 202 */

p = &x;                  /* Put the address of x into p. This    */
                         /* generates a "MOV.W #200,A"           */

*p = 5;                  /* Generates a "MOV.W #5,(A)" that puts  */
                         /* the number 5 into memory location 200 */

y = *p;                  /* Generate a "MOV.W (A),202" The        */
                         /* contents of memory location 200 and   */
                         /* 201 are copied to location 202 and 203.*/
```

Fig. 3-6: Memory Indirect Addressing

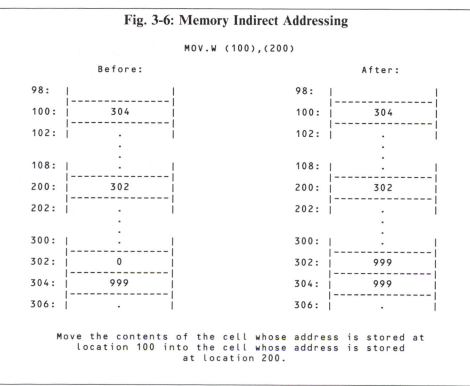

```
                        MOV.W (100),(200)

           Before:                                  After:

 98:  |               |              98:  |               |
      |---------------|                   |---------------|
100:  |      304      |             100:  |      304      |
      |---------------|                   |---------------|
102:  |       .       |             102:  |       .       |
              .                                   .
              .                                   .
108:  |       .       |             108:  |       .       |
      |---------------|                   |---------------|
200:  |      302      |             200:  |      302      |
      |---------------|                   |---------------|
202:  |       .       |             202:  |       .       |
              .                                   .
              .                                   .
300:  |       .       |             300:  |       .       |
      |---------------|                   |---------------|
302:  |       0       |             302:  |      999      |
      |---------------|                   |---------------|
304:  |      999      |             304:  |      999      |
      |---------------|                   |---------------|
306:  |       .       |             306:  |       .       |
```

Move the contents of the cell whose address is stored at
location 100 into the cell whose address is stored
at location 200.

3.4.5. Indirect Addressing with Auto-postincrement

The notation *(rN)+* is used for this mode. The action performed is similar to indirect addressing in that rN holds the address of the cell to be accessed. However, now the register itself is modified after the contents of the memory cell whose address is in rN is accessed. The number 1 is added to rN if the instruction operates on a byte-sized object; 2 is added if the instruction operates on a word-sized object. The process is identical to a trailing ++ operator in C. To give an example, if A holds the number 100, then the instruction *MOV (A)+,B* transfers the contents of memory location 100 to the B register; the A register is then automatically incremented to 101 (remember, this is a byte move). Both the A and B registers are modified, but memory location 100 remains unchanged. *MOV.W (A)+,B* moves the contents of cells 100 and 101 into the B register and then adds two to the contents of the A register. The important concept here is that the amount of the increment varies with the type of object being moved. When a byte is moved, the register is incremented by one; when a word is moved, the register is incremented by two.

Fig. 3-7: Indirect Addressing with Auto-Postincrement

```
                              MOV.W  (A)+,B

      Before:

      99:  |               | :98        |---------------|
           |---------------|        A: |      100      |
      101: |      99       | :100       |---------------|
           |---------------|        B: |       0       |
      103: |       .       | :102       |---------------|
                   .


      -----------------------------------------------------------


      After:

      99:  |               | :98        |---------------|
           |---------------|        A: |  400     102  |
      101: |      99       | :100       |---------------|
           |---------------|        B: |   0       99  |
      103: |       .       | :102       |---------------|
                   .
```

Move the contents of the cell whose address
is in the A register to the B register. Then increment
increment the B register by the size of a word.

The major uses of auto-increment in C is array accessing via a pointer.

```
static    int    x[20] ;  /*  Use memory locations 200-239 */
register int     *xp   ;  /*  Use A register.              */

xp = x;          /*      MOV.W  #200,A           */
*xp++ = 'c';     /*      MOV.W  #99,(A)+         */
```

This example is complex enough to require some explanation. (This material is covered in greater depth in Chapters 7 and 8, so you may want to skip this until after you've read these chapters.) Since x is an integer array, and an **int** uses 2 bytes, 40 memory locations are needed for it. The first cell in the array ($x[0]$) is at location 200 and 201, the next cell at 202 and 203, and so on. In C, an array name by itself (without an adjacent * or []) evaluates to the address of the first element of the array (200). The expression $xp = x$ initializes the pointer itself (the A register in this example) to point at the array. That is, A is loaded with the address of the first element of x.

Now we come to the *xp++ = 'c'*. The A register contains the number 200 (the address of *x*). Since indirect addressing is being used, contents of the cell whose address is 200 is modified, so the number 99 (the ASCII code for 'c') is moved into memory locations 200 and 201 (this is a word move). Then the pointer itself (the A register) is incremented. Since this is a word move, two is added, so A contains the number 202—the address of the second element of the array. Interestingly, almost identical code is used for character arrays:

```
static    char    x[20]  ;  /*  Use memory locations 200-219 */
register  char    *xp    ;  /*  Use A register.               */

xp = x;           /*     MOV.W   #200,A           */
*xp++ = 'c';      /*     MOV     #99,(A)+          */
```

First note that a *MOV.W* is still needed to initialize the pointer. All pointers are the same size, regardless of what they point at. (Remember that a pointer is a variable that holds the *address* of another variable, so the size of a pointer is the number of bytes required to hold an address on a particular machine.) Because we are working with a character array, (which occupies 20 bytes), we use *MOV*, rather than *MOV.W*, to access it, and one, rather than two, is added to the pointer (because we're using a byte rather than a word move). After the *MOV* is executed, memory location 200 contains the number 99; the A register contains the number 201.

3.4.6. Indirect Addressing with Auto-predecrement

The notation *-(rN)* is used in this mode. The action is similar to auto-postincrement mode except that the register contents are decremented before the fetch. For example, if A holds the number 100, the instruction *MOV-(A),B* decrements the A register to 99, and then moves the contents of memory location 99 to the B register. As with the auto-postincrement mode, the amount the register is modified depends on the size of the object being moved. Again, assuming that the A register holds the number 100, *MOV.W -(A),B* decrements the A register by two (this is a word move) yielding 98. The contents of memory cells 98 and 99 are then transferred into the low and high bytes of the B register.

Fig. 3-8: Indirect Addressing with Auto-Predecrement

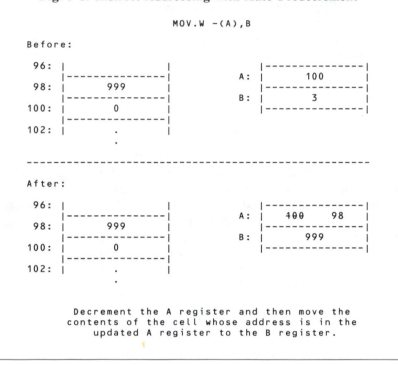

```
                            MOV.W  -(A),B

  Before:

   96:  |                  |        |------------------|
        |------------------|    A:  |       100        |
   98:  |       999        |        |------------------|
        |------------------|    B:  |        3         |
  100:  |        0         |        |------------------|
        |------------------|
  102:  |        .         |
                   .


  ------------------------------------------------------------


  After:

   96:  |                  |        |------------------|
        |------------------|    A:  |     100     98   |
   98:  |       999        |        |------------------|
        |------------------|    B:  |       999        |
  100:  |        0         |        |------------------|
        |------------------|
  102:  |        .         |
                   .
```

Decrement the A register and then move the
contents of the cell whose address is in the
updated A register to the B register.

Using a variant on the C example we just looked at, predecrement is used in C as follows:

```
static    char    x[20] ;  /*  Use memory locations 200-219 */
register char    *xp   ;  /*  Use A register.              */

xp = &x[20];     /*      MOV.W  #220,A         */
*--xp = 'c';     /*      MOV    #99,-(A)        */
```

Note that here we're initializing the pointer to the end of the array. In fact, it's initialized to point one cell past the end of the array. Since we do a predecrement before we access the cell, the A register points to (hold the address of) x[19] when the assignment is done.

You'll notice that our machine supports a *pre*decrement and a *post*increment, but there's no postdecrement or preincrement. This is the case with many real computers, mostly because predecrement and postincrement are required for stack maintenance while postdecrement and preincrement are not. We'll look at these matters in depth in a moment. A related issue in C is that two instructions, rather than one, are needed to do one of these non-supported functions. For example:

```
xp = &x[20];    /*  MOV.W  #220,A                  */
*xp-- = 'c';    /*  MOV    #99,(A)                  */
                /*  SUB    #1,A    ; decrement      */
```

3.4.7. Indexed Addressing

The notation $x(rN)$ is used to represent *indexed addressing*. In this mode, x is added to the contents of *rN* and then the contents of the cell whose address is the result of the addition is accessed. The offset, x, may be negative. The register itself isn't modified. For example, if A contains the number 100, a *MOV 10(A),B* instruction moves memory location 110 (that is, 100 + 10) into the B register. The A register itself won't be modified. This addressing mode may be used to access a single element of an array. If A holds the base address of a character array, then *MOV 12(A),B* moves the thirteenth element of the array into the B register (the first element is at offset zero from the base of the array).

In order to maintain this ability to access arrays, word moves become somewhat complex. Again, starting with 100 in the A register, *MOV.W 12(A),B* adds 24 to the contents of the A register, and then move the contents of cells 124 and 125 into the B register. That is, the index is first multiplied by two because this is a word move. This multiplied value is then added to the contents of A to give the address we want. So, this last example would access the thirteenth element of an integer (as compared to a character) array.

Another complication with word moves is alignment. As usual, we can only access word-sized objects from even addresses. Consequently, when we're doing a word move, we have to be careful that the base address is even. The automatic multiplication of the index by two guarantees that all possible target addresses will also be even.

Fig. 3-9: Indexed Addressing

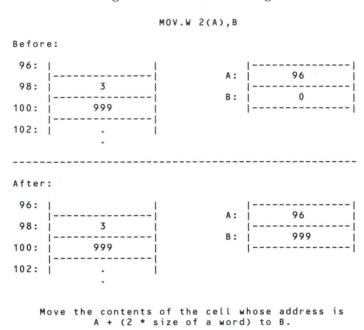

```
                            MOV.W 2(A),B

    Before:

      96: |                 |              |---------------|
          |-----------------|          A: |       96      |
      98: |        3        |              |---------------|
          |-----------------|          B: |       0       |
     100: |       999       |              |---------------|
          |-----------------|
     102: |        .        |
                   .


    ----------------------------------------------------------

    After:

      96: |                 |              |---------------|
          |-----------------|          A: |       96      |
      98: |        3        |              |---------------|
          |-----------------|          B: |      999      |
     100: |       999       |              |---------------|
          |-----------------|
     102: |        .        |
                   .
```

Move the contents of the cell whose address is
A + (2 * size of a word) to B.

In C, indexed addressing is used to access arrays. Consider this example:

```
int      array[10];       /* Use memory locations 200-220 */

array[0] = 1;             /* MOV.W  #200,A  ;  A = address of array */
                          /* MOV.W  #1,0(A) ;  A[0] = 1             */
array[6] = 2;             /* MOV.W  #2,6(A) ;  A[6] = 2             */
```

Note that we start by initializing A to point at the base address of the array. This is an important concept in C. The C language doesn't really support an array as a data type. In other words, an array is not a real object; rather, a pointer to the array is a real object. For example, when you pass an array to a subroutine, the array itself is not passed (as it can be in Pascal); instead, the address of the first element (a pointer to the first element) is passed. Consequently, an array name in C always evaluates to the address of the first element in the array. The first thing that happens when the compiler sees an array name is that it creates an implied pointer to the array in the A register. That is, it moves the base address of the array into the A register. All array accesses are then done via this pointer. In C there is no difference between

```
array[6] = 2;
```

and

```
char    *xp = array;
*(xp+6) = 2;
```

In fact, many compilers generate identical code for both statements.

In this example we're letting the machine do address arithmetic for us. Since we're accessing an integer array (where each element uses 2 bytes) and using word moves, the *MOV.W #1,0(A)* accesses memory locations 200 and 201. The *MOV.W #2,6(A)* modifies locations 212 and 213. That is, (6 * the size of an int) is actually added to the address contained in the A register before the cell is accessed (but the A register itself won't be modified). If our array was, say, an array of structures, we'd have to do the address arithmetic ourselves.

3.5. Instruction Set

3.5.1. The Move Instruction

There is only one move instruction in out demo machine. We've already seen several examples of how it's used:

MOV r1,r2   Move r1 to r2

3.5.2. Arithmetic Instructions

In addition to performing the indicated arithmetic operation, all arithmetic instructions modify one or more bits of the flag register, based on the result of the operation. In particular, the

```
Z flag is set if the result is 0.

P flag is set if the the result
      is a positive number.

N flag is set if the the result
      is a negative number.

V flag is set if the result overflows
      the register (if the result
      is larger than 16 bits).
```

These flags are used in turn by various jump instructions described in the next section. Their behavior is illustrated in figure 3-10. Again, note that all arithmetic instructions cause two registers to be modified: the target register specified in the instruction and the flag register (which reflects the result of the operation).

Fig. 3-10: Status Flags

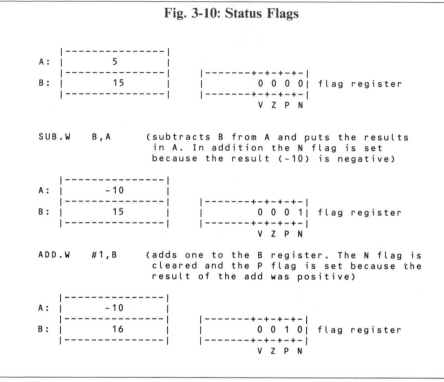

```
      |---------------|
A:    |       5       |
      |---------------|            |-------+-+-+-+-|
B:    |      15       |            |       0 0 0 0|  flag register
      |---------------|            |-------+-+-+-+-|
                                           V Z P N

  SUB.W    B,A      (subtracts B from A and puts the results
                     in A. In addition the N flag is set
                     because the result (-10) is negative)

      |---------------|
A:    |     -10       |
      |---------------|            |-------+-+-+-+-|
B:    |      15       |            |       0 0 0 1|  flag register
      |---------------|            |-------+-+-+-+-|
                                           V Z P N

  ADD.W    #1,B      (adds one to the B register. The N flag is
                      cleared and the P flag is set because the
                      result of the add was positive)

      |---------------|
A:    |     -10       |
      |---------------|            |-------+-+-+-+-|
B:    |      16       |            |       0 0 1 0|  flag register
      |---------------|            |-------+-+-+-+-|
                                           V Z P N
```

ADD r1,r2	Add r1 to r2 and store the result in r2 (r2 = r2 + r1).
SUB r1,r2	Subtract r1 from r2 and store the result in r2 (r2 = r2 - r1).
AND r1,r2	Bit-wise AND r1 and r2 and store the result in r2.
OR r1,r2	Bit-wise OR r1 and r2 and store the result in r2.
NOT rN	Bit-wise invert (one's complement) rN.
SHR x,rN	Shift rN x bits to the right ($0 < x < 16$). Duplicate the topmost bit (that is, shift in a 1 if the topmost bit was 1, 0 otherwise). This duplication preserves the sign of the shifted number.
SHL x,rN	Shift rN x bits to the left ($0 < x < 16$). Shift in a 0 to the rightmost bit.

Examples: *ADD 2000,(A)* adds the contents of the cell whose address is contained in the A register to the contents of the cell at address 2000. The result is stored at the memory location whose address is contained in the A register. *SUB #2,C* subtracts the number 2 from the current contents of the C register. *ADD C,#2* is illegal. Note that assignment operators can be implemented in one instruction. For example, $x += y$ translates directly into a *ADD.W y,x* instruction.

3.5.3. Jump Instructions

Jump instructions work by modifying the program counter (which contains the address of the instruction being executed) to point somewhere other than to the next sequential instruction. JMP is an absolute jump instruction; you just start executing instructions at the indicated address. If no instructions are located at that address, unpredictable things will happen. The other jump instructions (JP, JGE, and so on) are executed only if some condition of the flags are true.

JMP rN   PC = rN.

JP rN   PC = rN only if the P flag is set.

JGE rN   PC = rN only if the P or Z flag is set.

JZ rN   PC = rN only if the Z flag is set.

JN rN   PC = rN only if the N flag is set.

JLE rN   PC = rN only if the N or Z flags are set.

JV rN   PC = rN only if the V flag is set.

JNV rN   PC = rN only if the V flag is not set.

Other instructions can cause jumps too, as these examples demonstrate:

```
ADD  #128,PC      PC = PC + 128.
SUB  #4,PC        PC = PC - 4.
ADD  (C),PC       PC = PC + the contents of the
                       cell whose address
                       is in the C register.
```

Jump instructions are used for **goto** branches, **if/else** statements, to process **switch** statements, and for processing iterative statements like **while** and **for**. We'll look at them in greater depth in a moment. Subroutine calls are done with another mechanism that we'll look at in both the next section and the next chapter.

3.5.4. Subroutine Calls and Stacks

Two jump instructions are important enough to merit a section of their own. These are the JSR (Jump to SubRoutine) and RET (RETurn from subroutine) instructions. A subroutine is a body of code to which control may be passed from anywhere within a program. This code performs some task and then passes control back to the instruction following the original call instruction. You can't get to a subroutine with a normal jump instruction because you need to know where you jumped from (in order to be able to get back). This place to which we return is called the *return address*. The return address can't be stored in a fixed memory location because the subroutine could not itself call another subroutine. The second call would overwrite the return address set up by the first call. The solution to this problem is a data structure called a *stack*. The usual analogy is to a stack of plates in a cafeteria. The plate that is put onto the stack last is the plate that is taken off first. The data put onto the stack last is the data that is retrieved first. The process of putting data onto the stack is called *pushing*; retrieving data is accomplished by *popping*.

The SP, or *stack pointer*, register is used for stack maintenance. It always contains the address, in memory, of the object most recently pushed onto the stack. You can push something on the stack with a *MOV.W rN,-(SP)* instruction and pop an object with a *MOV.W (SP)+,rN*. Lets look in detail at how this process works (see figure 3-11).

Fig. 3-11: Push and Pop Operations

```
        | Memory  |                |-----------|      Stack before
        |---------|          SP:   |    100    |        a push
  98:   |         |                |-----------|
        |---------|          A:    |     3     |
 100:   |         |<-SP            |-----------|
        |---------|
        |         |


                                                    Do the push:
                                                       MOV.W A,-(SP)
        | Memory  |                |-----------|
        |---------|          SP:   |  100  98  |      (1) SP = SP - 2
  98:   |    3    |<-SP            |-----------|      (2) (SP) = A
        |---------|          A:    |     3     |
 100:   |         |                |-----------|
        |---------|
        |         |


                                                    Now do a pop into B:
                                                       MOV.W (SP)+,B
        | Memory  |                |-------------|
        |---------|          SP:   |  100 98 100 |    (1) B   = (SP)
  98:   |    3    |                |-------------|    (2) SP  = SP + 2
        |---------|          A:    |      3      |
 100:   |         |<-SP            |-------------|
        |---------|          B:    |      3      |
        |         |                |-------------|
```

The stack pointer holds the address of the memory cell that is the current top of stack. The push operation does two things: It first decrements the stack pointer, and then moves the object to be pushed (in this case the contents of the A register) to the memory location whose address is now in the

stack pointer (after the decrement). A push can be represented in C syntax as
$*--SP = A$.

The pop operation is just the opposite of a push operation. We now use
a *MOV.W (SP)+,B* instruction. We first move the object at the top of the
stack (the object whose address is contained in the stack pointer) into the target location (the B register), and then increment the stack pointer. The C syntax for a pop is $B = *SP++$. Note that even though the popped object isn't
actually erased when it's removed from the stack, it should never be used after
the pop. The problem here is caused by interrupt service routines and by subroutines in your compiler's run-time library, both of which use the stack.
Since you are not aware of when these routines execute, they are liable to
overwrite previous stack values at any time. Consequently, once an object is
popped, there is no way to be sure that another, invisible routine hasn't
overwritten the image of that object still on the stack.

Push and pop are such common operations that our assembler supports
special mnemonics for them:

```
PUSH   rN      is translated into      MOV.W  rN,-(SP)
POP    rN      is translated into      MOV.W  (SP)+,rN
```

A stack is a 16-bit-wide data structure. Maintenance would just be too
difficult if we had both 16-bit and 8-bit objects on the same stack. Consequently, there is no special instruction for pushing or popping byte-sized
objects, like there is for word-sized objects.

There are several things to notice about stacks:

(1)   The predecrement guarantees that the stack pointer always points at the
      last object pushed. This way, the object at the top of the stack can be
      accessed indirectly through the stack pointer, without having to do any
      arithmetic first.

(2)   Every successive push puts the object being pushed into a different
      memory location, because the SP is decremented each time. As a result,
      we won't overwrite previously pushed objects with another push.

(3)   The stack grows down in memory (towards low memory).

Rule 3 has several ramifications, especially in microcomputers. There is
no checking to see if the stack is growing over an area of memory which
already contains something else. This condition, the stack growing too large, is
called *stack overflow* and is responsible for a set of particularly nasty bugs in
C programs. Most C compilers use memory as shown in figure 3-12. The code
is put lowest in memory. The static data areas come next, and the stack exists
in high memory. The stack grows down, so the stack pointer is initialized to
the highest address in the stack area. In a machine like an IBM PC that
doesn't support protected memory, it is possible for the stack to get so large

that it starts overwriting the data areas and, in a pathological case, the code areas. When this happens, global variables start changing their values for no reason. If the code is overwritten, the CPU starts executing garbage, thinking that this garbage is legitimate instructions. We'll look at some of the causes of stack overflow in the next chapter.

Fig. 3-12: C Program Memory Usage

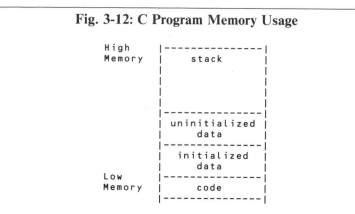

Note that most mainframes won't allow a stack-overflow condition to develop; the operating system will terminate your program first. The same goes for wild pointers, the operating system will terminate your program if the program tries to overwrite its own code area. In UNIX, this pathological behavior generates a "segmentation violation, core dumped" error message and the offending program is terminated. Stack overflow and wild pointers are a real problem on micros, however.

Now let's return to our original topic, the JSR and RET instructions. The JSR instruction does two things: it pushes the address of the instruction that follows the JSR instruction (the return address) onto the stack, and it then transfers control to the address that is its argument. The RET instruction pops the top of stack into the PC, thereby transferring control back to the instruction following the original JSR. This process is shown in figure 3-13.

JSR rN   Go to a subroutine whose address is rN:
       (1) SP = SP - 2
       (2) (SP) = PC + 2
       (3) PC = rN

RET   Return from subroutine:
       (1) PC = (SP)

Fig. 3-13: JSR and RET Instructions

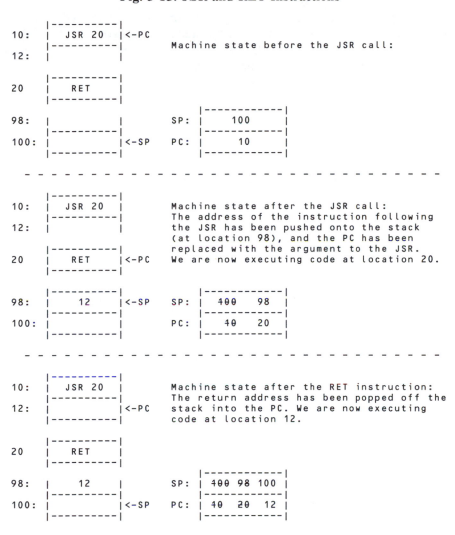

(2) SP = SP + 2

Note that rN can be an indirect address. *JSR (A)* jumps to a subroutine whose address is in the A register. In this case A is a pointer to a subroutine, a legal type in C.

3.6. Labels

Any 1-to-8-character string starting at column 1 and followed by a colon defines a *label*. (Instruction names and register names [JMP, ADD, A, B, SP, and so on] may not be used as labels.) When the label name (without the colon) is encountered by the assembler, it replaces the name with the address of the first instruction following the label. This way you don't have to keep track of the actual locations of things in memory. For example, the JSR example just given could be coded as follows:

```
          JSR        subr

   subr:   RET
```

The *subr* in the JSR instruction automatically replaces with the address of the RET instruction.

The assembler keeps track of label names by means of a *symbol table.* Every time the assembler sees a label definition, it makes a symbol table entry containing the label name and the associated memory address. Every time a label is used, the assembler looks for the name in the symbol table and replaces the label name with the associated address. Typically, an assembler goes through a program twice to take care of forward references (cases in which a label is used before it's defined, as in the example just cited). C compilers also use symbol tables, though a C symbol table is somewhat more complex.

3.7. Comments

Any text following a semicolon on a line is ignored by the assembler. This mechanism lets you explain what you're doing in the body of the code itself, rather than in a separate document.

3.8. Pseudo-ops and Static Initializers

Certain keywords serve to tell the assembler to do something other than generate code. These keywords are called pseudo-operations, or pseudo-ops, because they are not actually instructions, even though they take the same form as an instruction. The pseudo-op

```
          label:  DB      N
```

causes the assembler to reserve 1 byte of memory, initialized to N, and create a label whose value is the address of that byte (DB stands for *define byte*). That is, rather than outputting an instruction, it puts the number N into memory.

```
              label:   DW      N
```

reserves a word rather than a byte.

In C, initialization statements for static objects generate DB or DW directives like the following:

```
static int romeo;       /*   romeo:  DW 0                */
static int juliet;      /*   juliet: DW 0                */
romeo  = 5;             /*          MOV.W   #5,romeo     */
juliet = romeo;         /*          MOV.W   romeo,juliet */
```

These initialized areas of memory are saved on the disk along with the code. When a program is loaded into memory by the operating system (that is, when it is executed), the initialized data is read into its correct position in memory with its correct value. No code is generated to do these initializations; the data is just read from the disk with the correct initial value. This explains why static variables local to a subroutine have their initial value only the first time that the subroutine is executed. Once the variable is modified, it retains this new value. This behavior also explains why the static data that is not initialized explicitly is initialized to zero for you. You have to initialize the cell to something.

3.9. Exercises

3-1   Using the algorithm described in Chapter 2, write an assembly language subroutine that multiplies together two 8-bit numbers held in the A and B registers and puts the result into the C register.

3-2   Write an assembly language subroutine that moves a string. On entry, the A register contains the address of the first character in the string, the B register contains the length of the string in bytes, and the C register contains the address of the area where the string is to be moved. The source and destination string may overlap. In this case the source string is modified, but the destination string contains the original, unmodified, source string.

3-3   In the following program, list the contents of all registers (including the SP and PC, but not the FP)

(a) right before the JSR instruction is executed.

(b) right before the MOV instruction following the label *subr* is executed.

(c) right before the RET instruction is executed.

(d) right before the HALT instruction is executed

Assume that all instructions take up 2 bytes and that the first instruction is at memory location 100.

```
start:   MOV      #100,SP
         MOV      #0,A
         MOV      A,B
         ADD      #10,B
         MOV      B,C
         SHL      3,C
         MOV      C,D
         ADD      B,D
         NOT      D
         JSR      subr
         HALT                            ; stop the processor
subr:
         MOV      A,-(SP)
         MOV      B,-(SP)
         MOV      C,-(SP)
         MOV      D,-(SP)
         MOV      (SP)+,A
         MOV      (SP)+,B
         MOV      (SP)+,C
         MOV      (SP)+,D
         RET
```

CODE GENERATION

AND SUBROUTINE LINKAGE

This chapter puts to use the assembly language we learned in the last chapter. We'll look in depth at C subroutine calling and parameter passing, seeing how variables are accessed from within a subroutine. We'll also discuss simpler code generation for control flow statements.

A familiarity with argument passing conventions is useful for understanding recursion and for writing subroutines with a variable number of arguments. Most important though, an understanding of how variables are arranged internally can be an invaluable debugging aid; in fact, some bugs are almost impossible to find without this knowledge.

4.1. Subroutine Calling

This section describes the code generated when control is passed to a subroutine. The actual code produced by your compiler will be more complex, but this example serves to illustrate several important concepts.

First we'll need some background. In this chapter we will use the terms *run time* and *compile time.* A compile-time operation is performed while the compiler itself is working, generating code. The more we can do at compile time, the less we have to do when the program is actually running (at run-time). For example, constant expressions (expressions involving no variables,

77

only explicit numbers) should be evaluated at compile time since the compiler has all the information necessary to do the evaluation. This way, since we don't have to evaluate the expression with explicit code, our program will run faster at the cost of a little more time required to actually do the compilation. For example, the expression $x = (1024*3)$ should generate the single instruction *MOV.W #3072,x* rather than the considerable amount of code required to multiply together 1024 and 3.

We will also talk about the machine register we avoided in the last chapter. The frame pointer (or FP) register, like the stack pointer (SP), holds the address of a memory location on the stack. However, the FP is a fixed reference into a large area of the stack, while the stack pointer is a moving reference to a single cell (it's modified with each push or pop). The frame pointer is used for maintaining a subroutine's variables. All local variables are maintained on the stack in a contiguous block created when a subroutine is entered (at run-time). The subroutine's arguments are also kept on the stack, in the same memory block as the variables. This block of memory is a subroutine's *stack frame,* and the frame pointer is used to reference the various memory locations comprised by the stack frame.

Stack frames are created when a subroutine is entered; they are deleted when the subroutine returns (in a manner analogous to pushes and pops). Consequently the same area of memory (the stack) is constantly recycled as various subroutines execute. That is, several subroutines use the same part of the stack for their local variables.

To complicate matters, all variables don't exist on the stack. In particular, register variables are put into machine registers; global variables (those declared outside the body of a subroutine) are at fixed memory locations, as are all local variables explicitly declared with the keyword **static**. Those variables that are on the stack are called *automatic* variables.

Figure 4-1 shows a short C program and the corresponding assembly language. Don't worry if this program seems confusing at first; we're going go spend the rest of this chapter looking at it.

Before looking at the code itself in depth, let's look at the actions performed by the code, using as an example the call to *foo()* on line M of figure 4-1. Before anything else is done, a stack frame is created for *foo()* to use. Half of the stack frame is created by the calling subroutine—*main()* in this case—and the other half by *foo()* itself. *Main()* passes arguments to *foo()* by pushing them onto the stack; these pushed arguments are the first part of the new stack frame. The arguments are pushed from right to left (*p3* is pushed first). Note that in C, all argument passing (except for arrays) is done by value. That is, the value of the variable *p3* is passed to *foo()*, not *p3* itself. Another way to look at it is that *main()* makes a copy of *p3* by pushing its

Fig. 4-1: A Short C Program and Associated Assembly Language.

```
A:                      int   p1 = 1, p2 = 2, p3 = 3;
B:
C:                      foo( p1, p2, p3 )
D:                      int       p1, p2, p3;
E:                      {
F:                                int       v1, v2, v3;
G:
H:                                return 0;
I:                      }
J:
K:                      main( )
L:                      {
M:                                foo( p1, p2, p3 );
N:                      }
-----------------------------------------------------------------
1:      _p1:            DW  1           ; Reserve space for static global
2:      _p2:            DW  2           ;       variables: p1, p2 and p3.
3:      _p3:            DW  3
4:
5:      _foo:                           ; Set up stack frame:
6:                      PUSH   FP       ;       preserve the frame pointer
7:                      MOV.W   SP,FP   ;       set up new frame
8:                      SUB.W   #6,SP   ;       make room for local vars
9:
10:                     MOV.W   #0,D    ; Set up return value;
11:                                     ; Restore the old stack frame:
12:                     MOV.W   FP,SP   ;       clean up local variables
13:                     POP   FP        ;       restore old frame pointer
14:                     RET
15:
16:     _main:                          ; Set up the stack frame:
17:                     PUSH FP         ;       preserve the frame pointer
18:                     MOV.W   SP,FP   ;       set up new stack frame.
19:                     SUB.W   #0,SP   ;       There are no local variables
20:
21:                                     ; Call the subroutine "foo(p1,p2,p3):"
22:                     PUSH _p3        ;       push rightmost parameter (p3)
23:                     PUSH _p2        ;       push middle parameter (p2)
24:                     PUSH _p1        ;       push leftmost parameter (p1)
25:                     JSR     _foo    ;       call the subroutine
26:                     ADD.W   #6,SP   ;       clean arguments off the stack
27:
28:                                     ; Restore the old stack frame:
29:                     MOV.W   FP,SP   ;       clean up local variables
30:                     POP   FP        ;       restore old frame pointer
31:                     RET
```

contents onto the stack. This way if *foo()* modifies the argument corresponding to *p3*, it's actually modifying the copy of the original variable, not the variable itself. The stack, after the variables are pushed, is illustrated in figure 4-2.

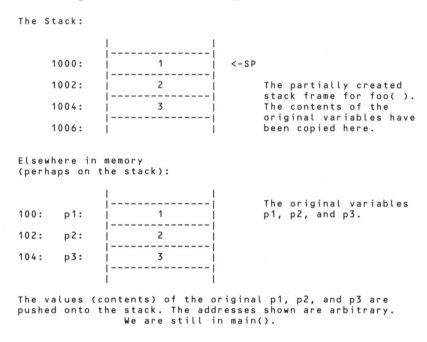

Fig. 4-2: Parameters To foo( ) Pushed on the Stack

```
The Stack:

                |               |
                |---------------|
        1000:   |       1       |       <-SP
                |---------------|
        1002:   |       2       |               The partially created
                |---------------|               stack frame for foo( ).
        1004:   |       3       |               The contents of the
                |---------------|               original variables have
        1006:   |               |               been copied here.


Elsewhere in memory
(perhaps on the stack):

                |               |
                |---------------|               The original variables
        100:  p1: |       1       |             p1, p2, and p3.
                |---------------|
        102:  p2: |       2       |
                |---------------|
        104:  p3: |       3       |
                |---------------|
                |               |
```

The values (contents) of the original p1, p2, and p3 are
pushed onto the stack. The addresses shown are arbitrary.
                We are still in main().

Next, the subroutine *foo()* is actually called. This call puts the return address onto the stack. (If this isn't clear to you review the sections on the JSR and RET instructions in the last chapter.) The new stack is shown in figure 4-3.

The first thing that *foo()* does is preserve the existing frame pointer by pushing it. Then it copies the current stack pointer into the frame pointer. Figure 4-4 shows the stack after the copy.

Next, *foo()* allocates space for its own local variables. This space is carved out of the stack by subtracting a suitably large constant from the stack pointer. Figure 4-5 shows the stack after the space is allocated.

At this juncture, the stack frame is complete. We'll look in depth at how this construct is used in a moment. For now, we'll see what happens to it when the subroutine returns. *Foo()* has to delete all the parts of the stack frame that it created. Local variables are deleted by copying the current value of the frame pointer into the stack pointer, making the stack pointer point to the same place as the frame pointer (see figure 4-6). Next, the old frame

Fig. 4-3: The Stack Immediately After foo( ) is Entered

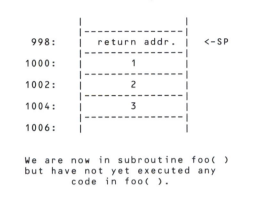

```
        |               |
        |---------------|
 998:   | return addr.  |   <-SP
        |---------------|
1000:   |       1       |
        |---------------|
1002:   |       2       |
        |---------------|
1004:   |       3       |
        |---------------|
1006:   |               |
```

```
We are now in subroutine foo( )
but have not yet executed any
      code in foo( ).
```

Fig. 4-4: The Stack After the Old Stack Frame is Saved

```
        |               |
        |---------------|
 996:   | old frame ptr |  <-SP   <-FP
        |---------------|
 998:   | return addr.  |
        |---------------|
1000:   |       1       |
        |---------------|
1002:   |       2       |
        |---------------|
1004:   |       3       |
        |---------------|
1006:   |               |
```

pointer is restored by popping its old value off the stack, as shown in figure
4-7. Then *foo()* executes a RET instruction, returning to *main()* and popping
its return address off the stack. The stack now looks just as it did before *foo()*
was called (see figure 4-8).

Now, *main()* <u>throws</u> <u>away</u> the stack variables associated with the arguments. Since the arguments to a called subroutine aren't used by *main()*, it
doesn't bother to pop them off the stack back into the original variables. Consequently, there is no way for a subroutine to directly modify the variables
used by another subroutine. (They can be modified indirectly, using pointers,

Fig. 4-5: The Remainder of the Stack Frame is Created

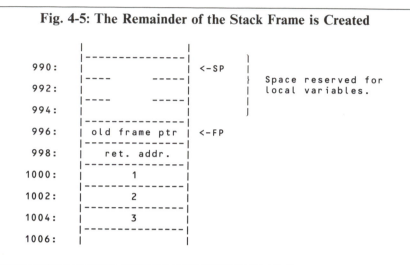

```
        |               |
        |---------------|
990:    |               | <-SP    )
        |----       ----|         }  Space reserved for
992:    |               |         |  local variables.
        |----       ----|         |
994:    |               |         )
        |---------------|
996:    | old frame ptr | <-FP
        |---------------|
998:    |   ret. addr.  |
        |---------------|
1000:   |       1       |
        |---------------|
1002:   |       2       |
        |---------------|
1004:   |       3       |
        |---------------|
1006:   |               |
```

Fig. 4-6: The Local Variables are Deleted

```
        |               |
        |---------------|
990:    |               |
        |----       ----|
992:    |               |
        |----       ----|
994:    |               |
```
Variables are deleted
by making the stack and
frame pointer point to
the same memory location.

```
        |---------------|
996:    | old frame ptr | <-FP <-SP
        |---------------|
998:    |   ret. addr.  |
        |---------------|
1000:   |       1       |
        |---------------|
1002:   |       2       |
        |---------------|
1004:   |       3       |
        |---------------|
1006:   |               |
```

Fig. 4-7: The Old Frame Pointer is Restored with a Pop

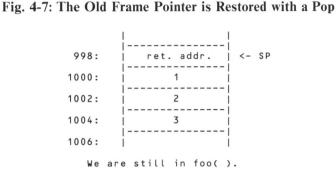

We are still in foo( ).

Fig. 4-8: The Stack After foo( ) Returns

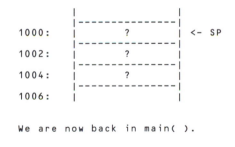

We are now back in main( ).

but not directly.) The variables are eliminated by adding a number to the stack pointer. That is, adding 6 to the stack pointer shown in figure 4-8, makes it point to address 1006, effectively deleting the arguments. (The arguments are 3 word-sized objects: 3 objects * 2 bytes = 6 bytes.)

Let's backtrack a bit and look at the code that does all this pushing and popping. Remember that the code is generated at compile time and that the compiler only goes through the code once, from top to bottom. In other words, code is generated as the input lines are encountered. The order in which subroutines are called (at run-time) has no bearing on the order that the code appears in the final object module. Just because *main()* is the first subroutine that's executed doesn't mean that the code for *main()* is generated first or put at the beginning of the object module.

Looking at the bottom part of figure 4-1, you'll note that the compiler changes the names of things (it adds a leading underscore character). The compiler often does complex operations (like finding something in a switch or doing a floating-point multiply) by calling a subroutine. These subroutines are provided for you by the compiler manufacturer as part of the run-time library. The compiler just assumes that these subroutines are available and generates calls to them. None of these predefined subroutines have leading underscores as part of their own names. Similarly, no external data used in the run-time library has a leading underscore in its name. The compiler adds the underscore to your variables to make sure that they don't accidentally conflict with objects already in the run-time library. You'll see these extra characters if you get a link map from the linker. (Note that some compilers use characters other than an underscore, and others put the extra character in a different place.) More to the point, if you write an assembly language routine that is going to be called from C, you have to add this extra underscore in the assembly language (but don't use it in the C code).

The next thing to look at is the **static** variable allocation. Lines 1 through 3 of figure 4-1 were generated by the compiler when it encountered line A of the C source code. Since these variables are global (they are declared outside the body of a subroutine), space for them is is allocated at a fixed memory location, using *DW* directives. Note that P3 is initialized to 3 as part of the *DW* directive. As was mentioned in the previous chapter, there's no explicit code for static initializations. The two basic storage classes in C, static and automatic, are treated in radically different ways. Static variables all exist at fixed memory locations, so we can reserve space for them using *DW* directives. Automatic variables must be handled differently, as we'll see in a moment.

Let's jump forward and look at a subroutine call. The call to the subroutine *foo()* on line M of figure 4-1 generates lines 22 through 26 of the assembly language listing. Remember that arguments are passed to the subroutine on the stack. It's the responsibility of the calling routine to push the arguments onto the stack and to clean up the stack after the called routine returns. (This mechanism is one of the things that makes subroutines with a variable number of arguments possible. Such subroutines don't have to know the number of arguments in advance, as long as the calling routine takes care of stack maintenance.) Parameters are pushed in reverse order (from right to left; *p3* is pushed first). The 3 arguments are the global variables we just declared; consequently, they're at fixed memory locations, and we can refer to their addresses directly in the PUSH instructions on lines 22 through 24. The subroutine is actually called on line 25. Remember that the JSR instruction also pushes the return address onto the stack.

Once *foo()* returns (we're now on line 26), the stack will be in the state it was before the call. The compiler now cleans the arguments off the stack with an *ADD.W #6,SP* instruction. The arguments are just thrown away, so instead of popping them, we just add a constant to the stack pointer. (This is the equivalent of a series of pops without actually moving anything.) The situation is analogous to the *SUB.W* on line 8 (the one used to create space for the local variables). That is, 3 *POP* instructions add 6 to the stack pointer (remember, these are word moves) and put the objects taken from the stack somewhere. Because we don't want to save the objects on the stack, we dispense with the moves and just do the add directly.

Now let's look at the subroutine itself. When we enter *foo()*, part of the stack frame will have been created by pushing the arguments. It is now the responsibility of the called subroutine to set up the rest of the frame. The subroutine *foo()* starts on line C of the source code and line 5 of the assembler code. Lines C and D affect the symbol table (more on this later) but won't actually cause any code to be generated. When the compiler encounters the open curly brace (on line E), it preserves the old frame pointer with the *PUSH FP* on line 6. After the push, a frame pointer for the current stack frame (the one we're now creating) is initialized with the MOV.W SP,FP on line 7. We are just copying the current contents of the stack pointer into the frame pointer.

The compiler then sees the local variable declarations on line F. It reserves space for *foo()*'s local variables with the *SUB.W* on line 8. It could have used 3 *PUSH #0* instructions to decrement the SP by 6 and put three zeros on the stack (again, these are word moves; 3 times the size of a word is 6). But since local automatic variables hold garbage values on entry into a subroutine, it's much more efficient to manipulate the stack pointer directly with an *SUB* instruction, rather than using three pushes. The *SUB.W* makes space on the stack for the local variables. It just moves the stack pointer to a safe place (below the local variables).

Note that each subroutine creates space on the stack for its own local variables and cleans these variables off the stack before it returns. In this way, the same area of memory (the stack) is constantly recycled by various subroutines for their own local variables.

The body of *foo()* consists of the single return statement on line H. Values are typically returned to the calling subroutine in a register. *Foo()* returns 0 to the calling routine with the *MOV.W #0,D* instruction on line 10. The calling routine expects the return value to be in the D register. There is always something in the return register, whether or not an explicit **return** statement is in the returning subroutine. If the called function doesn't return a value, the return register holds garbage. Since there's no way for the calling routine to know if the return value is valid, multiple return statements from a subroutine are dangerous. If one of them doesn't return a valid value (executes a **return** that has no argument), then garbage will sometimes be returned. Similarly, if no explicit return is present, then an implied return is generated when the close curly brace for the subroutine is executed, and this implied return statement returns garbage. Note that in C, all subroutines return a value. If the calling subroutine doesn't use that value, then the fact that it's garbage is immaterial.

The code needed to do the actual return is created on lines 12 through 14 of figure 4-1. A subroutine must return to the calling routine with the stack pointer and the frame pointer returned to their original states (as they were when the subroutine was entered); This happens on lines 12 and 13. The stack is restored by moving the current contents of the frame pointer (the FP register) into the stack pointer (SP), thereby restoring the stack pointer to the state it was in right before the global variables were created. Next, the frame pointer is returned to its original state with the *POP(FP)* statement. Finally, we return to the calling routine on line 14, popping the return address into the PC.

4.2. The Stack Frame

A machine state, as it is when line 6 of figure 4-1 is reached, is shown in figure 4-9 (the addresses shown are arbitrary).

To recapitulate, the part of the stack used by a subroutine is that subroutine's *stack frame,* and the *frame pointer* register (FP) is a fixed reference point, used to access the variables within the stack frame. The frame pointer, like the stack pointer, holds the address of a location on the stack and the arguments are always at a known offset from the frame pointer. For example, the parameter that was leftmost in the subroutine call (*p1* in this example) is at an offset of +4 from the frame pointer. (Look again at figure 4-9. The old frame pointer is at offset +0 from the current FP, the return address is at offset +2.) Parameters are accessed by means of this offset. For example, The parameter *p1* may be fetched by *foo()* with a

---

Fig. 4-9: The Stack Frame

```
        REGISTERS:                      STATIC MEMORY:

                                    Address: |--------------|
                                             |              |
        |--------------|             _p1 500: |      1       |
   SP:  |     102      |                     |--------------|
        |--------------|             _p2 502: |      2       |
   FP:  |     108      |                     |--------------|
        |--------------|             _p3 504: |      3       |
                                             |--------------|
                                    _foo 506: |  code for    |
                                             |  foo starts  |
                                             |    here       |

  STACK:

  Address: |              |   Offset from
           |              |   frame pointer
  100:     |              |   (in bytes):
           |--------------|
  102: SP->|      v3      |   -6    ⎱
           |--------------|         ⎪
  104:     |      v2      |   -4    ⎬  3 local        ⎫
           |--------------|         ⎪     variables   ⎪
  106:     |      v1      |   -2    ⎰                  ⎪
           |--------------|                            ⎪
  108: FP->|    old  FP   |    0                       ⎬ Stack frame
           |--------------|                            ⎪   for foo( )
  110:     |  return addr |   +2                       ⎪
           |--------------|                            ⎪
  112:     |      p1      |   +4    ⎱                  ⎭
           |--------------|         ⎪
  114:     |      p2      |   +6    ⎬  3 arguments
           |--------------|         ⎪
  116:     |      p3      |   +8    ⎰
           |==============|               ---------------
  118:     |    old  FP   |                               ⎫
           |--------------|        (no local variables)   ⎪
  120:     |  return addr |                               ⎬ Stack frame
           |--------------|         ⎱                     ⎪   for main( )
  122:     |     argc     |         ⎪                     ⎪
           |--------------|         ⎬  2 arguments        ⎪
  124:     |     argv     |         ⎪                     ⎭
           |==============|         ⎰
  126:     |              |
```

$$MOV.W \quad 4(FP),rN$$

P3 can be fetched with a

$$MOV.W \quad 8(FP),rN$$

instruction. Local variables are also referenced using an offset from the frame pointer, this time in the negative direction. The local variable *v3* can be referenced from within *foo()* with a

```
MOV.W    -6(FP),rN
```

Again, referring to figure 4-9, *v1* is at an offset of -2 from the FP, *v2* is at an offset of -4, and *v3* is at -6. Note that the offsets from the frame pointer of the various arguments and variables depend on the types of the objects. That is, a **long int** takes up more space on the stack than does a normal **int**. Note here that the sizes of the arguments are computed in two places: once in the calling routine and once again in the called routine. The declared type of the parameter (**int**, **long**, **float**, and so on.) in the calling routine tells the compiler how many bytes to push onto the stack. The declared type of the corresponding argument in the parameter list of the called routine tells the compiler at what offset from the frame pointer a particular variable is to be found. The compiler makes no attempt to determine whether these two declarations agree, so if a **long**-sized object is pushed onto the stack by the calling routine, and the called routine expects an **int**-sized object to be there, all the offsets are incorrect, and none of the arguments following the incorrect one will be accessed correctly. This situation is illustrated in figure 4-10. Here, the negative offsets from the frame pointer are still correct (they point at the local variables *v1*, *v2*, and *v3*, as expected), but the positive offsets are not correct. The offset +6 that's used to access the parameter *p2* is now pointing at the high word of *p1*. The offset for *p3* (+8) now accesses *p2*. *P3* can't be accessed; *foo()* thinks that the old frame pointer is at offset + 10.

An even more severe problem can be caused if an insufficient number of arguments are pushed on the stack. This situation is illustrated in figure 4-11. Again, the offsets from the frame pointer for *p1*, *p2*, and *p3* are computed when *foo()* is declared, and *foo()* expects these variables to be at these offsets. If *foo()* is called without any arguments, then *p1*, *p2* and *p3* will not be pushed onto the stack, but *foo()* will not know that they're not there. If none of these variables is used, their absence is inconsequential. If, however, the parameter *p2* is modified by *foo()*, the compiler generates code to modify the memory location that is at an offset of +6 from the frame pointer (the place where *p2* ought to be). Looking at the correct (left) stack, you'll see *p2* at the correct offset. On the incorrect stack (on the right), however, the location at offset +6 from the frame pointer holds the return address needed by the calling subroutine. If this location is modified, even though *foo()* will probably work correctly and return correctly (and the calling subroutine will probably work, too), when the calling routine itself tries to return, its return address will have been overwritten by *foo()* and the calling routine will vector into outer space, to an undefined address (whatever *foo()* put there!). This is an extremely hard bug to find because it doesn't manifest until well after the bug itself is executed. In a pathological case, anything on the stack can be randomly modified. The moral? Count the number of arguments you pass to a

Fig. 4-10: Stack Created by a Type Mismatch

```
Stack as foo( ) expects              Stack that would have been created
     to find it:                     if the global variable p1 had been
                                     declared a 4-byte, long integer:

              Offset from                            Offset from
Address:      frame pointer:         Address:        frame pointer:

                                                |--------------|
                                     100: SP->|      v3        |  -6
              |--------------|                 |--------------|
102: SP->|      v3        |  -6     102:       |      v2        |  -4
         |--------------|                       |--------------|
104:     |      v2        |  -4     104:       |      v1        |  -2
         |--------------|                       |--------------|
106:     |      v1        |  -2     106: FP->|     old FP      |   0
         |--------------|                     |--------------|
108: FP->|     old  FP     |   0     108:       |   return addr   |  +2
         |--------------|                       |--------------|
110:     |   return addr   |  +2     110:       |                |  +4
         |--------------|                       |--- p1    ---|
112:     |      p1        |  +4     112:       |                |  +6
         |--------------|                       |--------------|
114:     |      p2        |  +6     114:       |      p2        |  +8
         |--------------|                       |--------------|
116:     |      p3        |  +8     116:       |      p3        | +10
         |==============|                       |==============|
118:     |     old  FP     |         118:       |     old FP      |
         |--------------|                       |--------------|
120:     |   return addr   |         120:       |   return addr   |
         |--------------|                       |--------------|
122:     |      argc       |         122:       |      argc       |
         |--------------|                       |--------------|
124:     |      argv       |         124:       |      argv       |
```

subroutine and make sure the types match, or more to the point, use lint (it's less likely to make a mistake than you).

While we're on the subject, many newer C compilers support *function prototyping,* a mechanism for checking the types and number of arguments passed to a subroutine. Function prototyping is activated with an **extern** statement that contains a *type list.* For example,

```
extern double   foo( int, char*, long );
```

tells the compiler that *foo()* is a subroutine that returns a **double.** It takes three arguments of types **int**, pointer to **char**, and **long**. If the compiler finds a call to *foo()* with anything other than the indicated parameters, it will generate a warning message. A function with a variable number of arguments [such as *printf()*] can be specified with a trailing ellipsis in the type list:

Fig. 4-11: Stack Created when Insufficient Arguments are Listed

```
        Stack as foo( ) expects                      Stack created  when foo( ) is
              to find it:                            called incorrectly with no
                                                              arguments:


                         Offset from                                      Offset from
        Address:         frame pointer:              Address:             frame pointer:

                      |--------------|                                 |--------------|
        102: SP->|        v3        |  -6            102:          |                  |
                      |--------------|                                 |--------------|
        104:      |        v2        |  -4            104:          |                  |
                      |--------------|                                 |--------------|
        106:      |        v1        |  -2            106:          |                  |
                      |--------------|                                 |--------------|
        108: FP->|      old  FP      |   0            108: SP->|        v3        |  -6
                      |--------------|                                 |--------------|
        110:      |   return addr    |  +2            110:          |        v2        |  -4
                      |--------------|                                 |--------------|
        112:      |        p1        |  +4            112:          |        v1        |  -2
                      |--------------|                                 |--------------|
        114:      |        p2        |  +6            114: FP->|      old  FP      |   0
                      |--------------|                                 |--------------|
        116:      |        p3        |  +8            116:          |   return addr    |  +2
                      |==============|                                 |==============|
        118:      |      old  FP      |                118:          |      old  FP      |  +4
                      |--------------|                                 |--------------|
        120:      |   return addr    |                120:          |   return addr    |  +6
                      |--------------|                                 |--------------|
        122:      |       argc        |                122:          |       argc        |  +8
                      |--------------|                                 |--------------|
        124:      |       argv        |                124:          |       argv        |
                      |--------------|                                 |--------------|
```

```
            extern void      printf( char*, ... );
```

Here, *printf()* takes a pointer to **char** as its first argument, followed by any number of arguments of variable type. Function prototyping has saved me several hours of debugging time and I strongly recommend using it if your compiler supports it. Note that the **extern** statement is necessary to activate the function prototyping, even if the actual subroutine declaration is in the same file.

A final stack-related problem is stack overflow. As, we've seen, all automatic variables are kept on the stack. Space for a local array is allocated from the stack, unless the array is explicitly declared **static**. (Remember that all static variables exist at fixed memory locations rather than on the stack.) If a 10K-byte automatic array is declared in a subroutine, then that subroutine's stack frame will use a little over 10K bytes of stack. Generally, 10K bytes of stack aren't available; unfortunately, the compiler usually doesn't know this. As a consequence, the stack will now extend well into the data, and perhaps the code, areas of your program. If you modify the contents of the array, you will probably be modifying some other routine's data or, even worse, the code itself. Again, this bug won't show up until long after the offending subroutine has returned, so it's also a hard bug to find. The moral is either make all large arrays static, or use *malloc()* and *free()* to get memory for them.

By now you may be asking yourself, why have a stack frame if using it is so dangerous? There are several reasons. First, as was mentioned earlier, stack frames give us efficient RAM usage because the same memory can be recycled for different variables. The maximum required stack size corresponds to the highest level of subroutine call nesting. Second, you can't write a recursive subroutine without stack frames. We'll look in greater depth at how a recursive routine uses the stack in Chapter 8. Finally, if you can tell a subroutine how many arguments will be on the stack and the size of those arguments, you can write a routine with a variable number of arguments. In Chapter 9 we'll examine how *printf()*, which has a variable number of arguments, accomplishes this task. (It counts the number of % signs in the format string to determine the number of arguments and looks at the conversion character to determine the type.)

Another ramification of stack usage is shown in figure 4-9. In terms of code generation, *main()* is a subroutine like any other; there is nothing special about it. *Main()* generates the same code as *foo()* for setting up and restoring the stack frame, even though, strictly speaking, *main()* doesn't need a stack frame. (In fact, the only thing special about *main()* is that the linker requires it to exist.)

Part of *main()*'s stack frame are the arguments *argc* and *argv*, which are passed through from the root module. If *main()* is not going to use *argv* and *argc*, they don't have to be declared in *main()*'s formal parameter list. Since it is the responsibility of the calling routine to push and pop arguments, the presence of extraneous arguments doesn't cause any problems. In other words, when a subroutine is called (and *main()* is just a subroutine), its arguments are pushed on the stack. The compiler just sees an argument list that's part of a subroutine call and generates the necessary push instructions. The arguments are on the stack, whether or not they're used by the called routine. Nevertheless, called subroutines can't get at these arguments unless they're listed in the formal argument list that's part of the subroutine declaration. The compiler computes the offsets from the frame pointer when it processes **the formal argument list of the subroutine declaration, not the call. There's no connection at compile time between a subroutine call and a subroutine declaration. The connection isn't made until run time.**

To sum up stack frame-related issues:

(1)   There's no way for the called routine to know whether the arguments pushed on the stack are of the correct type.

(2)   The called routine cannot know whether the calling routine pushed the correct number of arguments onto the stack; it just assumes that they are there.

(3)   If a routine can be told how many and what type of arguments to expect on the stack, it can be passed a variable number of arguments.

4.3. Using Casts in Subroutine Calls

Because it is not always convenient to make a variable a particular type only to be able to pass it to a subroutine, C provides a useful operator called a *cast*. A cast tells the compiler that, for this one use of a variable or constant, it should be converted to a different type. Casts take the form of a type definition surrounded by parentheses. To figure out how to make a cast, write out a declaration for a variable of the desired type (without any trailing semicolon), surround that definition with parentheses, and then remove the variable name. Then precede the name of the variable that you want to convert with the cast. Let's look at an example:

```
foo( longvar )
long      longvar;
{
          /* ... */
}

main( )
{
          int       intvar;

          /* ... */

          foo( intvar );   <------ WRONG
}
```

Here, *main()* wants to call *foo()* and pass it intvar. Intvar is of type **int**, but *foo()* expects a variable of type **long**. If we were to execute the call to *foo()* as shown, we would create all the stack misalignment problems we just discussed. We get around this problem by *casting* intvar into a **long**. To form the cast, we start with a normal definition for a long:

```
long      x;
```

Next, we remove the semicolon and surround the definition with parentheses:

```
(long x)
```

Finally, we remove the variable name:

```
(long)
```

So, we can tell the compiler to convert intvar to a **long** (before pushing it onto the stack) by preceding the name *intvar* with the cast we just created:

```
foo( (long) intvar );
```

It's worth mentioning that in some compilers an **int** and a **long** are the same size (for example, **int**s and **long**s are both 32 bits wide on many VAX and 68000 compilers). The code just described will work correctly on these machines without the cast but when you try to move the code to another machine (or even to a different compiler on the same machine), it will stop working. Always use casts so that your code will be portable, even if they seem like unnecessary work right now. We'll discuss casts again when we discuss pointers in Chapter 6.

4.4. The Return Value

An issue related to stack frames is a subroutine's *return value*. The return value is usually passed back to the calling routine in a register. The calling routine assumes that this register contains a valid number. All subroutines return a value, but if that value is not loaded into the correct register with an explicit **return** statement, garbage is returned. (If the calling routine doesn't use the called routine's return value, then it doesn't matter that this value is garbage.) For this reason, it's a good idea not to use multiple return statements. If a subroutine does return a value, be sure that there's no path out of that subroutine that doesn't pass through an explicit return statement.

4.5. The Symbol Table

The compiler uses a *symbol table* to keep track of the locations of variables in memory. In the case of static or global variables, these locations are absolute memory addresses; in the case of local variables, they're offsets from the frame pointer. The symbol table is used at compile time. Entries are put into it as the compiler encounters declarations, and the entries are removed when the variable is no longer need. For example, a local variable is put into the symbol table when it's declared and is deleted when the compiler has finished processing the subroutine. Figure 4-12 shows the symbol table, as it would look while the compiler is processing the program shown in figure 4-1.

Only three variables are shown because the compiler has seen only three declarations so far. The *name* field holds the variable's name. *Class* holds the variable's storage class: *fixed* if the variable is at a fixed address, *auto* if the variable is on the stack, *extern* if the variable is external (declared in a different file). *Type* holds the variable's type (**char**, **int**, **long**, and so forth). The type of a subroutine refers to the subroutine's return value. *Val* is either

Fig. 4-12: Table While Line B of Figure 4-1 is being Processed

	Variable name	class	type	val
1:	p1	fixed	int	500
2:	p2	fixed	int	502
3:	p3	fixed	int	504

an absolute memory address or an offset from the frame pointer, depending on the class. Automatic variables use offsets, fixed variables use absolute addresses. A subroutine's *val* is the address of the first instruction of the subroutine. A real compiler's symbol table is more complex than the one shown, but all the essentials are in this example.

By the time the compiler gets to line E, several more variables will have been added to the table. The new situation is illustrated in figure 4-13.

Fig. 4-13: Table While Line E of Figure 4-1 is being Processed

	Variable name	class	type	val
1:	p1	fixed	int	500
2:	p2	fixed	int	502
3:	p3	fixed	int	504
4:	foo	fixed	int	506
5:	p1	auto	int	+4
6:	p2	auto	int	+6
7:	p3	auto	int	+8

Foo, being a subroutine, is at a fixed memory address; its type is the type of the return value. There are now three entries for the variables *p1*, *p2*, and *p3*. The second set of entries (on lines 5 through 7 of the table) are the three variables listed in *foo()*'s formal argument list (on lines C and D). When the compiler uses a variable, it searches the table from bottom to top, using the first entry that has the correct name. If the parameter *p2* were used inside the body of *foo()*, the compiler would look for a *p2* by going through the table backwards, and would find it on line 6 of the table. The local variable *p2* then takes precedence over the global variable having the same name (because the compiler stops searching when it finds a variable with the correct name). In C, all local variables take precedence over global variables with the same name.

Now, processing a little more code, Figure 4-14 shows the symbol after all of *foo()*'s local variables have been processed.

Fig. 4-14: Table While Line G of Figure 4-1 is being Processed.

	Variable name	class	type	val
1:	p1	fixed	int	500
2:	p2	fixed	int	502
3:	p3	fixed	int	504
4:	foo	fixed	int	506
5:	p1	auto	int	+4
6:	p2	auto	int	+6
7:	p3	auto	int	+8
8:	v1	auto	int	-2
9:	v3	auto	int	-4
0:	v3	auto	int	-6

Note here that the true local variables (as compared to the arguments) are at a negative, rather than a positive, offset from the frame pointer. When the compiler has finished processing *foo()* (that is, when it has found the close curly brace on line I), it deletes all of *foo()*'s local variable references from the table, giving us figure 4-15.

Fig. 4-15: Table While Line J of Figure 4-1 is being Processed.

	Variable name	class	type	val
1:	p1	fixed	int	500
2:	p2	fixed	int	502
3:	p3	fixed	int	504
4:	foo	fixed	int	506

Note that *foo()* itself—that is, the subroutine name—is treated as a global variable (because it is declared at the same level as global variables; it is not contained in a block of any sort). When *main()* is processed, the table looks as it does in figure 4-16. *Main()* doesn't have any local variables so the table won't get any larger.

Fig. 4-16: Table While Line L of Figure 4-1 is being Processed

	Variable name	class	type	val
1:	p1	fixed	int	500
2:	p2	fixed	int	502
3:	p3	fixed	int	504
4:	foo	fixed	int	506
5:	main	fixed	int	600

There are several important things to notice here. First, all variable references are made via the symbol table. A subroutine has no way of knowing if all its parameters were actually pushed on the stack by the calling routine; it only knows that a certain number of parameters were declared in the formal argument list.

Second, all information about a variable is determined by searching the symbol table in reverse order. The first instance of the variable encountered is the one used, even if there are other variables of the same name somewhere else in the table.

Finally, a subroutine name isn't put into the symbol table until its declaration is encountered. The only way that the compiler knows the type of a subroutine's return value is by processing this declaration. Consequently, if you use a subroutine before you declare it, the compiler doesn't have the subroutine name listed in its symbol table yet. Since it's not always convenient to arrange your code so that a subroutine's declaration always precedes any use of the subroutine, the compiler makes some assumptions. It puts the undeclared subroutine name in its symbol table as an external subroutine that returns an **int**. It's immaterial that the subroutine may be declared later in the same file; the linker will find it.

4.6. Control Flow: if/else, while, and for

Figure 4-17 shows an if/else translated into assembly language. We've made x and y static so that the code is simpler. The test $(x > y)$ requires three instructions. We put the value of x into the A register and then subtract the value of y from it $(A = x - y)$. Note that the previous contents of the A register are destroyed. If x is greater than y, then the result is positive and the P flag will be set as a result of the subtract instruction. If x equals y, then the

Fig. 4-17: If/else Statements

```
static int      x;      |   x:      DW      0
static int      y;      |   y:      DW      0
                        |
if( x > y )             |   if:     MOV.W   x,A
{                       |           SUB.W   y,A
                        |           JLE     else
                        |
    <some code>         |           <some code>
                        |
}                       |           JMP     next
else                    |   else:
{                       |
    <more code>         |           <more code>
}                       |
                        |   next:
                        |
```

result is zero and the Z flag will be set. If *x* is less than *y*, then the result is negative and the N flag will be set. The *JLE* instruction jumps only if the N or Z flags are set. We are testing for the condition opposite that specified in the test part of the *if* and jumping to the **else** clause if that opposite condition is true. That is, we are testing for $x > y$ and branching only if $x <= y$ (using a *JLE* instruction). This convoluted coding style saves us a third *JMP* instruction, which would otherwise be required. The **if** clause is terminated by an unconditional jump around the **else** clause.

Figure 4-18 illustrates a **while** loop. As in the previous example, we do the test by subtracting and then jumping outside the loop on the opposite condition. The only difference is that, instead of jumping to an **else** clause when the test fails, we jump outside of the loop. A **continue** statement would be translated into a *JMP while* instruction; a **break** would be translated into a *JMP next*.

A **for** statement is shown in figure 4-19. You'll note that the code generated to handle the loop part of the **for** is identical to that used for a **while**. The initialization and increment steps are added in the case of a for, but identical code would have been generated if we had preceded the **while** statement in the previous example with an $x = 0$ statement and put an $x++$ at the end of the loop. The moral is, use the control flow statement that makes the *source* code more readable; the object code will probably be the same.

A **continue** statement in this **for** loop would generate a *JMP endfor* instruction, while a **break** would be translated as *JMP next*.

Fig. 4-18: While Loops

```
static int      x;      |      x:      DW      0
static int      y;      |      y:      DW      0
                        |
while( x > y )          |      while:  MOV.W   x,A
{                       |              SUB.W   y,A
                        |              JLE     next
                        |
    <some code>         |              <some code>
                        |
                        |              JMP     while
}                       |
                        |      next:
```

Fig. 4-19: For Loops

```
static int      x;      |      x:      DW      0
static int      y;      |      y:      DW      0
                        |
                        |              MOV.W   #0,x
for( x = 0; x > y; x++ )|      for:    MOV.W   x,A
{                       |              SUB.W   y,A
                        |              JLE     next
                        |
    <some code>         |              <some code>
                        |      endfor:
                        |              ADD.W   #1,x
                        |              JMP     for
}                       |
                        |      next:
```

The statements *for(;;)* and *while(1)* are often used for a "do forever" situation. Most compilers generate more efficient code for the **for** loop, as in figure 4-20.

The same considerations are involved in *while(i)* as compared to *while(i != 0)*. The explicit *!=* can cause unnecessary instructions to be generated.

4.7. Switches

Switches are more complicated than an if/else. A switch is one of the few elements of the C language where you don't have a good idea of what the compiler is going to do by looking at the source code. Moreover, the compiler is

---

Fig. 4-20: Forever Loops

```
while( 1 )                  |    while:    MOV.W   #1,A
{                           |              OR.W    A,A
                            |              JZ      next
   <some code>             |              <some code>
                            |
}                           |              JMP     while
                            |    next:
                            |
                            |
for( ;; )                   |    for:
{                           |
   <some code>             |              <some code>
                            |
}                           |              JMP     for
```

---

liable to do different things in different situations. As an example, I'll quote the manual for version 2.14 of the Lattice C compiler (pp. 4–26 f.; the italics are my own comments):

> The code generator also makes a special effort to generate efficient code for the switch statement. Three different code sequences may be produced, depending on the number and range of the case values.
>
> (1) If the number of cases is three or fewer, control is routed to the case entries by a series of test and branch instructions. *(That is, the switch is treated as if it were a series of if/else statements.)*
>
> (2) If the case values are all positive and the difference between the maximum and minimum case values is less than twice the number of cases, the compiler generates a branch table which is directly indexed by the switch value. The value is adjusted, if necessary, by the minimum case value and compared against the size of the table before indexing. This construction requires minimal execution time and a table no longer than that required for the type of sequence described in Number 3.
>
> (3) Otherwise, the compiler generates a table of [case value, branch address] pairs, which is linearly searched for the switch value. *(This procedure is very inefficient, especially if the case used most often is at the end of the table.)*

Some compilers treat all switches as in case 3, with no attempt at optimization, which can render switches grossly inefficient. Other compilers make case 3 more efficient, by re-organizing the table of **case** values so that they can do a binary search. Thus, locating a case statement at the top of a switch won't guarantee that that case will be looked at first. The first **if** statement of an **if/else** is always evaluated first, however. (Don't confuse the order in which the cases are evaluated with the order in which code is executed after the machine has vectored to the correct case).

What all this means is that switches can be very inefficient, you shouldn't use them instead of **if/else**s when there are only one or two else clauses. On the other hand, switches often result in much more readable code than a long string of **if/else**s

4.8. Relocatable Code

For the sake of clarity, none of the code we've discussed so far has been relocatable. *Relocatable code* must have two attributes: it has to be able to run anywhere in memory, and it has to be linkable to other modules.

There are two ways to make code relocatable. Machines such as an 8085, which only support absolute jumps [that is, you can say *JMP 100* but you can't say *JMP 124(PC)*], use a system of dummy addresses. The compiler can't supply the target addresses for jumps at compile time (because it doesn't know where the current module will be in memory at compile time). Consequently, as the compiler creates assembly language instructions, it fills the space normally occupied by target addresses with offsets to the target address, rather than the address itself. It also keeps a table showing where all these offsets are to be found in the program. Another table contains both a list of external objects (subroutines and data not declared in this module) and a list showing where in the code these objects are used. *Where* is usually a list of offsets from the beginning of the module to every instruction that accesses the external object. A third table lists all objects in the current module that can be accessed externally. Note that the **static** keyword, when applied to a global variable, prevents that variable from being included in this third table. Consequently, **static** global objects can't be accessed from outside the file in which they are declared because the linker cannot access these objects. The linker, as it puts together the final program, uses these tables to resolve the ambiguities in the original code. It replaces references to external objects with their actual addresses and, since it now knows the base address of the current module, replaces the offsets in the jump instructions with absolute addresses as well. The intermediate modules that are input to the linker are relocatable, but the final (linked) version of the program is not. It can run only in a specific area of memory.

True relocatable code can only be made on machines that support relative addressing (such as a 68000 or a PDP–11). In this case, no absolute jumps or memory accesses are created; rather, all jumps are performed relative to the current program counter [*JMP x(PC)*]. External subroutines are usually accessed by two jumps. Code is generated to jump to a *jump table* (a long list of jump instructions) at a known location in the module, and then the linker patches that jump table to contain the correct relative addresses when it links the program together. External data is accessed relative to the base address of the data area (also supplied by the linker). Thus, this second type of code can actually be located anywhere in memory.

4.9. Exercises

4-1   Using the assembly language described in the previous chapter, write an
       assembly language program likely to be generated by a compiler when it
       sees the following source code. Assume that an **int** occupies 2 bytes; the
       return value of a called function is passed back to the calling function in
       register D.

```
test( var1, var2 )
int var1, var2 ;
{
        int     x, y;

        x = var1;
        y = var2;

        while( x < y )
                x = x + y;

        if( x >= 3 )
                return( x + y - 1 );
        else
                return 0 ;
}

main( )
{
        static int a, b;

        a = 2;
        b = 3;

        test( a, b );
}
```

4-2   Draw a picture of the stack frame for subroutine *test()* in exercise 4-1..
       Show the stack and frame pointers and all relative offsets from the frame
       pointer (as in figure 4-9).

4-3   Use the foregoing to show what the symbol table looks like just after:

       (a) the *int x,y;* statement in *test()* is processed.

       (b) the call to *test()* in the *main()* module is processed.

4-4   Write a description of how the stack frame used by your own compiler is
       organized. Explain how automatic variables and subroutine arguments
       are accessed. Include an assembly language dump of a subroutine if your
       compiler creates one.

STRUCTURED PROGRAMMING AND STEPWISE REFINEMENT

Structured programming is a generic name for a group of techniques used to write well-organized and easy-to-maintain programs. In this chapter we're going to look at how to write programs in a structured way. We will also discuss peripheral issues such as commenting, formatting, and how to organize your programs. This chapter barely touches the subject of structured programming; it talks mostly about how structured programming techniques can be used to develop small programs (say under 2,000 lines). The topic is much more involved than you might think.

Structured programming techniques are sometimes referred to as "writing goto-less code," but using or not using a **goto** statement has little to do with a program's being well structured. Not only is it possible to write good code with **goto** statements in it, but this code may be easier to read than a version without the **goto**. Structured programming is really a way to organize your thought processes and to develop your programs, so that they will come together faster and with fewer bugs.

Unfortunately, many schools use their structured programming classes to weed undergraduates out of Computer Science programs. As a consequence, the words *structured programming* have acquired a bad reputation in some circles. Many people look at structured programming as if it were an academic exercise with no practical use. They see it as just another form of busywork, meant to make an undergraduate's life more difficult. Nothing could be further from the truth. Most programs can be written in less time, and be more reliable, when they are developed in a structured way.

Structured programming techniques are indispensable when programming in C. Some languages, such as Pascal or Modula-2, build program structure into the language syntax. It's difficult (though possible if you're really determined) to write an unstructured Pascal program. C, on the other hand, has no rigid structure imposed by the language itself. The language allows a great deal of latitude in both program organization and development methods. Consequently, if you don't impose structured programming techniques on top of the C language, you can program yourself into a hole, finding yourself with a 40,000-line-long program that doesn't work and can't be fixed.

5.1. Writing a Program is Writing

It is a common misconception that programming and mathematics are somehow related. I'm differentiating here between *computer science* and *programming*, between the study of programs and the writing of them. Much of computer science has to do with mathematical analysis. On the other hand it's possible to be a good programmer without also being a mathematician. What, then, provides a foundation for programming if not math? It turns out that the techniques with which you write a program are almost identical to those that you use to write an essay. The skills you learn in an English Composition class are invaluable when applied to programming. (If more schools required English [as well as Mathematics] as a foundation for Computer Science degrees, we'd not only have better written programs but would have readable documentation for them as well.) In this chapter, we're going to use the mechanics of writing an essay as a vehicle for talking about structured programming. As we go, we'll draw parallels between the two processes.

The first, and often hardest, step in essay writing is to decide on a topic, to narrow a large field down to a subject that can be discussed adequately in the amount of space available. Once you have chosen a topic, you have to research it, learning what others have said about it and drawing your own conclusions by examining both other people's work and the original sources. To summarize: the first step in writing an essay is thinking.

Unfortunately, thinking is the step in program development that is usually omitted. Before addressing the question of how to solve a problem, you have to define that problem precisely, just as you have to narrow an essay topic down to something about which you can write. It's a mistake to try to define the problem as you're writing the code. Every loose end must be thought about in advance, every contingency must be considered. Of course, you can't really think of everything at this stage, but you can save yourself a lot of work by trying. The alternative is to spend time writing code that has to be discarded because it can't do the job and is too difficult to modify.

Once the problem has been defined, you have to research it, looking at how other programmers have solved similar problems. Again, this step is often skipped. Programmers often spend hours solving problems that have already been adequately solved—hours that would have been unnecessary if only the programmer had bothered to look for the earlier solution.

A related issue is the reluctance of many programmers to use code written by someone else. Don't be tempted to discard a piece of code that works just because you don't like the way that it looks. Admittedly, some programs are written so poorly, or have been patched so often by so many people, that it's best to put the program out of its misery and start over from scratch. But before you discard a piece of functioning code, you have to honestly assess how long it will take you to write the equivalent code and whether your code will really be better than the original.

Once you've decided what you're going to say in an essay, you have to actually write it. Similarly, once you've defined a programming problem, you have to write the code. If you just sit down and start writing your essay, though, you're going to end up with pages of unconnected thoughts, a meandering and unreadable mess rather than an essay. By the same token, you can't just sit down and start coding. You first have to think about program organization. Outlining is the first step, both in writing an essay and in writing a program. In fact, the familiar outline form is quite suitable for program design as well.

How do you write the outline? Start by defining the problem at a very high level, by summarizing what you're going to write about in a few succinct sentences that develop the idea in an orderly fashion. Write these sentences on a piece of paper, one on each line and assign each sentence a Roman numeral. The process used to design a program is identical. In a few succinct sentences, summarize how you're going to solve a program. Really do it—put them into English and write them down on paper. The importance of putting a problem into words can't be overemphasized. If you can't say it in English, you won't be able to say it in C.

Let's look at a concrete, though short, example. We've been provided (in Chapter 8) with the following subroutine:

```
int      parse( expr )
char     expr[ ];
```

This subroutine takes as input a string containing an arithmetic expression and returns the integer result of evaluating that expression. We'd like to build a small desk-calculator program around this subroutine.

Before writing any code, we must define what the program has to do. This definition is the equivalent to the topic paragraph of an essay. The description should be succinct but it should be as complete as possible. The following paragraphs are an acceptable description:

Write the program "expr" that exercises the subroutine *parse()* in Chapter 8. The program analyses arithmetic expressions and prints the results to standard output. Expressions may be composed of decimal digits, parentheses, and the operators +, -, *, and / for addition, subtraction, multiplication, and division. Space characters and tabs are not permitted in expressions. Infix notation is used.

Program invocation can take three possible forms:

```
expr
```

takes a series of expressions from standard input, one expression per line, evaluates them, and prints the result to standard output. All expressions are terminated by a newline character (\n) that is not considered to be part of the expression itself.

```
expr <exp1> ... <expN>
```

extracts the expressions from the command line, evaluates them and prints the expression and the result of the evaluation to standard output. There may be only one expression in each argv entry and each argv entry must be a complete expression.

```
expr -f <ifile>
```

works like the previous form except input is taken from the indicated file rather than from the command line. The file should have one expression per line (as in the first example).

The program should print the input expression, along with its evaluated result, to standard output. It should print an error message if the expression can't be evaluated. In interactive mode, if an expression starts with an operator, the result of the previous evaluation should be used as the leftmost term in the current expression. [Use *(-1)* if you need to use a negative number as the first term in the expression.]

The next step is to decide on how our data will be represented. The choice of data types often influences the entire structure of a program, so it's best to make these decisions early. This example requires two data types: a buffer to hold the expression and a variable to hold the result of the analysis. We can define these with two **typedef**s and a **#define** that we'll put into a file called *expr.h* (see figure 5-1).

Fig. 5-1: Expr.h

```
#define MAXBUF    128

typedef char      BUFFER[ MAXBUF ];
typedef int       ANSWER;
```

This file will be **#include**d in every file in our program (if the program extends to more than one file). All constants used by the program should be macros (like *MAXBUF* in figure 5-1). This way, if we decide to change the input buffer size we can change the *MAXBUF* macro and recompile without having to search every source file for explicit constants.

The third step is to refine our description into a series of simple operations and to put these in outline form. An outline for our program is shown in figure 5-2.

Fig. 5-2: A Simple Program Outline

```
I.   If there are no arguments on the command line
          A. Process expressions interactively.

II.  Else (there are arguments on the command line)
          A. If the first argument is -f
                    1. Process arguments from a file
          B. Else
                    1. Process arguments from the
                       command line itself
```

Of course, this outline would make both a very short essay and a very short program. There's not yet enough information in the outline to write a program. We'll refine the outline a little in figure 5-3.

You'll note that expression evaluation is done in three places (I.A.3.c, II.A.1.b.ii, and II.B.1.a.i). By observing this similarity now, we can write our code so that a single subroutine is used to do all the actual expression evaluation. Making decisions like this in advance is much easier than modifying existing code.

Now what? Returning to our essay, we'd have to start it with a topic paragraph that synopsizes the entire essay. The topic paragraph can be assembled by putting together all the major headings in the outline. In a C

Fig. 5-3: Refining the Outline

```
I.   If there are no arguments on the command line
     A. Process expressions interactively
        1. Print a sign-on message.
        2. While there is input
           a. Print a prompt.
           b. Get a line of input.
           c. Evaluate it.
              i. If the expression starts with an operator
                 (a) Modify the expression string
                     to use the result of the
                     previous expression as its
                     leftmost term.
                 (b) Parse the expression.
                 (c) If there was an error
                        (i) print an error message.
                 (d) Else
                        (i) print the result.

II.  Else (there are arguments on the command line)
     A. If the first argument is -f
        1. Process arguments from a file.
           a. Open the file and print an error message
              if we can't.
           b. While there are input lines:
                 i.  Fix up the input line so that
                     the expression analyzer can
                     handle it.
                 ii. Evaluate it.

     B. Else
        1. Process arguments from the command line itself.
           a. While there is an argument
                 i.  Evaluate it.
                 ii. Get the next argument.
```

---

program, the equivalent to a topic sentence is the *main()* subroutine and our *main()* can be assembled from the outline, just as you would develop a topic paragraph. (See figure 5-4. Don't worry if you can't follow the code itself, just look at the program structure.) Note that the nesting depth in the program corresponds exactly to the nesting depth in the outline.

A topic paragraph should be able to stand by itself, a sort of mini-essay; so should our program. The program under development should be fully functional at every stage of the development process. So the next step in writing our program is to get it working. To do this we'll have to provide a few dummy subroutines called *stubs*. A stub doesn't do anything except announce its presence. However, since *main()* calls subroutines, these routines have to exist if we are to compile and test *main()*. Figure 5-5 shows the stubs we need to get *main()* working.

Fig. 5-4: Translating the Outline into Code

```
Outline |  Code:
------- |----------------------------------------------------------------
        |
        |  main(argc, argv)
        |  int  argc;
        |  char *argv[ ];
        |  {
I.      |      if( argc <= 1 )
I.A     |          interactive_mode( );
II.     |      else
        |      {
II.A    |          if( argc==3  &&  argv[1][0]=='-' && argv[1][1]=='f')
II.A.1  |              file_mode( argv[2] );
II.B    |          else
II.B.1  |              command_mode(argc, argv);
        |      }
        |  }
```

Fig. 5-5: Stubs Used by Main

```
interactive_mode( )
{
        printf("Doing interactive input\n");
}

file_mode( filename )
char    *filename;
{
        printf("getting input from <%s>\n", filename );
}

command_mode(argc, argv)
char    **argv;
int     argc;
{
        printf("doing command mode input\n");
}
```

The stubs just print an "I'm here" message and return. If it's easy, the stub also prints its arguments. This way we can see whether a valid argument is getting through to the subroutine. Admittedly, the program doesn't do much at this point. Nonetheless, the program can be fully tested and made to work (it may not do anything useful, but it does do something). It's a mistake to write 10,000 lines of code and then try to debug them all at once; instead, you should write a few lines of code, get them working, write a few more and the get the program working again, and so on. Since you make only a few changes at a time, you always know the location of the problem when the program stops functioning.

Returning to our essay, we now have to flesh out the essay with additional paragraphs, each of which covers the material in one of the subcategories in the outline. Likewise, we can refine the program by expanding the stubs using the same procedure we used to write *main()*. This refinement is shown in figure 5-6.

We need only one stub now, for *evaluate()* (figure 5-7). Note that the *evaluate()* stub has to return a value if the rest of the program is to work correctly.

We now compile the new version *and get it working.* Then, we continue the process of refinement, proceeding through the outline one section at a time, writing a little code and some stubs, getting the existing code working, and repeating this process until the program is finished. This method for developing programs is called *stepwise refinement* and is the heart of structured program development. Its main advantage is that the program always works, so when something goes wrong, you can find the problem easily.

It's important to expand the stubs one at a time, just as you'd write an essay one paragraph at a time. It may seem tedious to make only a few changes before re-compiling, but you end up saving time in the long run (because you always know were a bug is likely to be when something goes wrong, it's in the code you just modified).

The only remaining stub is *evaluate()*. It's expanded in figure 5-8. Since there are no more stubs, we're finished.

5.2. Program Organization

As is the case with an essay, a program is both more readable and easier to revise when it is well organized. There are two good ways to organize a program.

In the first method, we use an essay as a model. An essay should start with a topic paragraph that summarizes the essay in a few sentences. It then develops a subject in an orderly way, with related ideas grouped together in paragraphs. The paragraphs themselves mirror this organization, starting with a topic sentence that describes a thought, and then developing that thought in a series of related sentences. Programs can follow the same model, beginning with a high-level routine (like *main()*) that describes a program's function by a series of well-named subroutine calls. Each subroutine corresponds to a paragraph and should develop in the same orderly manner, with the subroutine itself coming first, followed by support routines that the higher-level subroutine uses.

In this programming model, the high-level routines that do most of the work are at the top of the file, and the routines that are called by the high-level ones are below them. The subroutines become more complex and lower-level as you read down. The first subroutine in the module is *main()*.

The second method just turns the entire "essay" upside down. The lowest-level subroutines are at the top of the file, and the higher-level routines are below them. The subroutines are still developed in the same fashion, but here the development proceeds from the end to the beginning of the file. The advantage of this method is that fewer forward references (uses of subroutines that haven't been declared yet) are required in the code; neither method is inherently superior, however. Regardless of whether you're reading up or down, the file should present subroutines in an orderly way.

A third method for organizing a file is to put the subroutines in alphabetical order. Forward reference problems are resolved by **extern** statements at the top of the file. With this method, however, it's much harder to read the code (because there's no immediate connection between a subroutine and its neighbors). It is easier to find a specific subroutine in an alphabetized file, though.

Note that the program outline provides a good indication of how to break up a large program into separate modules. *Main()* is usually in a module by itself. Each of the subroutines marked with a Roman numeral is also put into a module by itself, along with the support routines represented by the subcategories in the outline. This way functionally related subroutines tend to be grouped together in a single file. Whether still more modules are required depends on the overall size of the program. These additional modules can also be organized in the same way as the outline, however.

The other organizational problem is the location of the data, external declarations, and so on. I usually organize my modules in the following order:

```
#includes
extern declarations
#defines
typedefs
global variables
code
```

Don't mix your global variable definitions, **#defines**, and so forth, in with your code, it makes the program to difficult to maintain because definitions get lost in the code.

Fig. 5-6: Expanding Stubs

```
Outline    |  Code:
---------- |-----------------------------------------------------------------
           |  #include <stdio.h>
           |  #include "expr.h"
           |
           |  /*-----------------------------------------------------------------
           |   * isopr(c) evaluates to 1 if c is one of the operators *+-/
           |   */
           |
           |  #define isopr(c) ((c)=='+' || (c)=='-' || (c)=='/' || (c)=='*')
           |
           |  /*-------------------------------------------------------------*/
           |
I.A        |  interactive_mode( )
           |  {
           |      /*  Process expressions in interactive mode. Print a
           |       *  prompt, get an expression from standard input, and
           |       *  print the result. Execution terminates at EOF or when
           |       *  a blank line is encountered.
           |       */
           |
           |      BUFFER    buf;
           |
I.A.1      |      printf("Enter expression after ? or <CR> to exit program\n");
I.A.2      |      while( 1 )
           |      {
I.A.2.a    |          printf("? ");
I.A.2.b    |          if( gets(buf) == NULL || !*buf )
           |              break;
I.A.2.c    |          evaluate( buf );
           |      }
           |  }
           |
           |  /*-------------------------------------------------------------*/
           |
II.A.1     |  file_mode( fname )
           |  char    *fname;
           |  {
           |      /*  Process expressions from a file. The file is
           |       *  opened in read mode, and is processed one line
           |       *  at a time. If the line is terminated with a
           |       *  '\n', the newline is removed. Maximum permitted
           |       *  line length is MAXBUF-1 (132) characters.
           |       */
           |
           |      int      len;
           |      BUFFER   buf;
           |      FILE     *stream;
           |
II.A.1.a   |      if( (stream = fopen(fname,"r")) == NULL )
           |          fprintf(stderr, "Can't open <%s>\n", fname );
           |      else
           |      {
II.A.1.b   |          while( fgets(buf, MAXBUF, stream) != NULL )
           |          {
           |              /* Delete the carriage return and then
           |               * evaluate the expression. Ignore blank
           |               * lines. Don't evaluate blank lines.
```

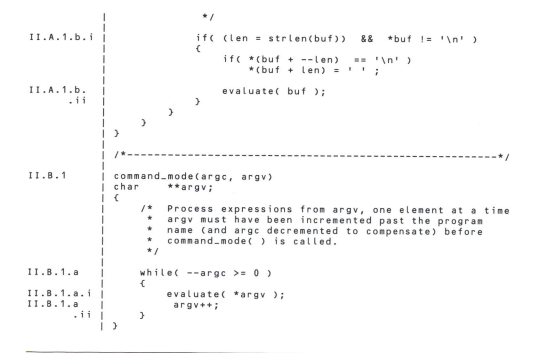

```
II.A.1.b.i |                    */
           |
           |            if( (len = strlen(buf))  &&  *buf != '\n' )
           |            {
           |                if( *(buf + --len)  == '\n' )
           |                    *(buf + len) = ' ' ;
           |
II.A.1.b.  |                evaluate( buf );
    .ii    |            }
           |        }
           |    }
           | }
           |
           | /*--------------------------------------------------------*/
           |
II.B.1     | command_mode(argc, argv)
           | char    **argv;
           | {
           |    /*  Process expressions from argv, one element at a time
           |     *  argv must have been incremented past the program
           |     *  name (and argc decremented to compensate) before
           |     *  command_mode( ) is called.
           |     */
           |
II.B.1.a   |    while( --argc >= 0 )
           |    {
II.B.1.a.i |        evaluate( *argv );
II.B.1.a   |        argv++;
    .ii    |    }
           | }
```

Fig. 5-7: A Stub for Evaluate( )

```
int     evaluate( expr )
{
        printf("Evaluating <%s>, returning 1\n", expr );
        return 1;
}
```

5.3. Commenting and Formatting

Most of this section falls into the category of "good advice." Many people preach about commenting styles and formatting conventions with an almost-religious fervor. They are misguided. Formatting conventions are intended to make your code readable, and anything you can do to further this end is acceptable. At the other extreme, some say that formatting style is unimportant as long as it's consistent. This is simply not true—your formatting can be consistently awful. You may disagree with some of the suggestions made here. Nonetheless, this section can give you a good understanding

---

Fig. 5-8: Expanding the Evaluate( ) Stub

```
Outline:           |   Code:
-------------      |-------------------------------------------------------------
I.A.2.c            |
II.A.1.b.ii        |
II.B.1.a.1         |   int     evaluate( expr )
                   |   char    *expr;
                   |   {
                   |       static int  def_val = 0;
                   |       int         err ;
                   |       BUFFER      copy;
                   |
                   |       /* Evaluate the expression contained in expr and print
                   |        * the result. If the first character in expr is an
                   |        * operator, then use def_val as the first operand in
                   |        * the expression (that is, use the result generated
                   |        * in the previous call to evaluate( )). If an error is
                   |        * encountered, print an error message instead of the
                   |        * result. In any event, return the value returned by
                   |        * parse( ) (which will be 0 on error).
                   |        */
                   |
I.A.2.c.i          |       if( isopr( *expr ) )
                   |       {
I.A.2.c.i.a        |           sprintf( copy, "%d%s", def_val, expr );
                   |           expr = copy;
                   |       }
                   |
I.A.2.c.i.b        |       def_val = parse( expr, &err );
                   |
I.A.2.c.i.c        |       if( err )
I.A.2.c.i.c.i      |           fprintf(stderr, "Error in expression: %s\n", expr);
I.A.2.c.i.d        |       else
I.A.2.c.i.d.i      |           printf("%s = %d\n", expr, def_val );
                   |
                   |       return def_val;
                   |   }
```

---

of the issues.

Comments are an essential part of every program. There's no such thing as self-documenting code (though well-written code can get by with fewer comments). Comment your code in the body of the code itself, not in a separate document (which has a way of getting lost). A reader who is unfamiliar with the code should be able to read through the comments, without looking at the code itself, and have a pretty good idea of how the program works.

Comment the code as you write it. It's a mistake to write all the code first and then go back and comment it after the program is made to work. For one thing, many large programs never do work completely, so they never get commented. In any event, it's much easier to debug code that you don't have to figure out first, and there's a limit to the amount of detail anyone can remember. Commenting the code saves you from having to remember everything about how a program works while you're debugging.

Another consideration: Code that's commented at the last minute is hardly ever commented adequately, and well-commented code is much easier to maintain. When you have to modify the program that you wrote two years ago, you'll be glad that you commented it properly.

Comments should be well-formed sentences, with subjects and verbs and objects, just as if they were part of an essay. Try to minimize the use of abbreviations and sentence fragments. Punctuate the comments correctly. In other words, the rules of English usage can't be suspended in a comment. Doing so will just make the comments as unreadable as the code.

Good programmers often write their comments first, before writing any code at all. That is, they'll write the entire program in English first, describing in depth every detail of the program's operation. They then go back and intersperse code with the comments. Describing a process in words can help clarify that process. Potential problems that hadn't occurred to you become evident. Consequently, if you write down what you're doing in English, before writing it in C, you'll often end up with a better program.

5.3.1. White Space and Indenting

Properly distributed white space is one of the most useful comments at your disposal. As in most prose documents, a space should always follow punctuation in a program (, ; and so on) and should surround operators (like +, -, and *) if at all possible. Just as a blank line should precede a paragraph, code should be arranged into short functional blocks, each preceded by a blank line. **While**, **for**, **do**, **switch**, and **if** statements should always be preceded by blank lines; **else** statements usually shouldn't because they're part of a previous **if** statement block. Generally, there should be no more than five or six lines of code without a blank.

Never place more than one statement on a line. Your code should not look like this:

```
if(isdigit(*s))for(p=s,i=0;isdigit(*p);)i+=i*10+(*p++-'0');
```

There is nothing to be gained from this practice (unless you intend your code to be unreadable and impossible to debug). The line should have been written as follows:

```
if( isdigit(*s) )
{
    i = 0;
    for( p = s; isdigit(*p); p++ )
        i += (i * 10) + (*p - '0');
}
```

Indenting is the other white-space related issue. A statement body should always be indented at least four spaces. Here are some examples:

```
while( condition )
        body( );

for( a; b>c; d++ )
{
        body_of_for( );
}

if( condition )
        action( );
else
        another_action( );
```

Some programmers begrudge even four spaces of indenting and use only one or two, but one space of indent doesn't help your code's readability at all. Use enough space so that you can see that you've done something. You're writing in C, not BASIC—extra white space will not make your code run more slowly. If your code is falling off the right side of the page because of indenting, then the lower levels of nesting should probably be a separate subroutine. Too much nesting is a sure sign of lack of design. It tends to happen when the code "just grows." That is, the real problem is that your subroutine isn't thought out well enough, not that a tab is too wide.

Note that the curly braces are at the outer indent level. This makes finding mismatched curly braces much easier; you can draw lines with a ruler. If you indent the braces, they tend to get lost in the surrounding code. Similarly, if you say

```
while( condition ){
        code( );
}
```

it's harder to find a mismatched brace (you have to draw diagonal lines and the open brace tends to get lost).

Indenting also applies to null statements. For example:

```
for( c = x;   c  ; c++ )
        ;
```

Here,the semicolon is indented and stands alone on the next line. An unwanted semicolon at the end of a **for** or **while** statement is the most common error that I make. For example:

```
while( a < b );
{
            a++;
}
```

says "while *a* is less than *b*, do nothing; then, when your done with that, increment *a*." The loop will never terminate. Similarly

```
if( condition );
       do_something( );
```

says "if the condition is true, do nothing, then call *do_something()*." By putting the semicolon on the next line, you can use grep to find this sort of error (see chapter 1). That is, the regular expression *while.*;* finds all lines with the word *while* followed by a semicolon; *for(.*);* finds incorrectly terminated **for** statements.

The one exception that can safely be made to the brace-placement rule is the **do/while** statement which can be written as follows:

```
do {
       code( );

} while( condition );
```

This construct lets you differentiate between the bug we just mentioned (the misplaced semicolon) and the one situation where a semicolon legitimately follows a **while** statement (that is, if there's a leading brace on the line, then the semicolon at the end belongs there).

One final issue is the visual separation of subroutines on a page. If the subroutines run together, it's too hard to find them. Consequently it's a good idea to put a dashed line comment such as:

```
/*-------------------------------------------------*/
```

above every subroutine declaration. Don't put this sort of comment inside the body of a subroutine or you'll defeat its purpose (separating subroutines from each other). Use a few consecutive blank lines to separate major blocks inside a subroutine.

5.3.2. How to Write Comments

Comments don't nest in C. Consider the following code:

```
the comment
starts here
|
|
|
/* This is a comment that isn't terminated
properly. It is a relatively long comment,
taking up several lines.

while( a )
        a = foo( );


/* This is another comment. It is terminated
correctly, but note that the end-of-comment
character is hard to find.*/
                    |
                    |
                    |
            and ends here
```

In this code, the **while** loop is part of the comment. This problem can be minimized by writing comments in a way that makes it easy to see the terminator. Two examples are:

```
/*   This is perhaps the best way to comment
 *   code because you can just look along the
 *   stars for the close comment. This sort of
 *   comment should always be at the same nesting
 *   level as the block in which it is found.
 */

/*   This is acceptable only if        */
/*   the open-comment and close-        */
/*   comment symbols line up in a       */
/*   neat column.                       */
```

Don't randomly place the comments on the page, or write them in columns with a ragged left or right edge. It's too easy to lose the close comment.

5.3.3. Where to Put Comments

A few comments should always be present in your code. A comment at the top of every file should give the file name, a brief description of what the program or subroutines in the file do, and a list of all externally accessible objects (subroutines and global variables). I use the format shown in figure 5-9.

At the top of every subroutine, a similar comment should describe what the subroutine does, how it does it at a high level, and what all the parameters do. The functions of all local variables should also be commented. Figure 5-10 is an example.

Don't clutter the code. If every other line is a comment, it becomes impossible to read either the comments or the code. It's as if you're trying to read two books at once by reading a line from one book, and then a line from

---

Fig. 5-9: A Header Comment

```
#include <stdio.h>                    /* All #includes go here  */

/*
 *
 *      FILE.C  -  Briefly say what the program does here, continuing
 *                 to several lines if necessary.
 *
 *      external objects:
 *
 *      foo( a, b )     - Say what foo( ) does here.
 *      int a;          - Describe what a does here.
 *      int b;          - Describe what b does here.
 *
 *      bar( d, e )     - Say what bar( ) does here.
 *      double d;       - Describe what d does here.
 *      char    *e;     - Describe what e does here.
 *
 *      int  Global_1;  - Describe what Global_1 is for here.
 */
```

Fig. 5-10: Commenting a Subroutine

```
void    foo( a, b )
int     a;                   /* Describe what a does here.  */
int     b;                   /* Describe what b does here.  */
{
        /*      Describe how foo works and what it does
         *      in this comment.
         */

        int     local1;      /* Describe what local1 does. */
        char    *local2;     /* Describe what local2 does. */

        /* Code goes here.
         */
}
```

---

the other. Comments and code should be combined into logical blocks, with a comment describing how a block of code works preceding the block that it describes. If the operation is complicated, you can put numbers in the comment that refer to the code (like footnotes). Figure 5-11 is an example. The comments ["/* 1 */," and so on.], reference the numbers [*(1)*, and so on] in the description found above the **while** statement.

Fig. 5-11: Referencing a Comment From the Code

```
/*
 *      This is a complicated comment describing what's
 *      going on in the following while loop. The loop works like
 *      this:
 *      (1)     Do something
 *      (2)     Do something else
 *      (3)     Do another thing
 */

while( condition )
{
        do_something( );                /*  1  */
        do_something( );

        do_something_else( );           /*  2  */
        do_something_else( );

        do_another( );                  /*  3  */
        do_another( );
}
```

5.3.4. Do Not Explain the Obvious

A comment should tell you something that is not immediately obvious. Comments like

```
tea += 2;               /* Add two to tea            */
elisa( )                /* Start subroutine elisa */
```

are worse than useless. They not only tell you nothing that you can't see immediately but they clutter up the page with needless verbiage. It's safe to assume that whoever's reading your code knows the language and understands how the operators work.

5.3.5. Variable Names

A variable's name is itself a comment on the variable's function. Variable names must mean something and variables should be named in a way that lets you know their scope as well as their function.

Macro names (#**defines**) should be in full capital letters. Only the first letter of global variables should be capitalized. Local variables should be all lower case. This way you can tell the scope of a variable by looking at its name, and global and local variables that have the same name can be distinguished from each other. If you capitalize letters in the middle of a variable name, you may have trouble remembering that you've done so. Use an underscore (_) to separate two-word names, and use it consistently.

A variable's name should describe its function. Moreover, whenever possible, the name should not be an abbreviation (abbreviations are harder to read). A problem here is portability. Earlier C compilers require the first 8 characters of a variable name to be unique. Additional characters, if present, are ignored. Compilers are beginning to support longer variable names, but your program might not port to another compiler if you use these longer names. Abbreviate very carefully. Abbreviations that you understand may be incomprehensible to someone else.

If your compiler supports long names but your assembler does not, you can get around this problem with macros. For example:

```
#define    this_is_a_long_variable_name    vn1

this_is_a_long_variable_name = 6;
```

You can use the long variable name in the C source code, but the assembler will see the short equivalent. Be careful with this method though. Some preprocessors look at only the first 8 characters of **#define**s, even though the compiler itself accepts longer names. Remember, the preprocessor is not part of the compiler.

5.4. Global Variables and Access Routines

Don't use global variables unless you have to. In this case, the globals should be declared **static** and modified externally via an *access routine*.

The problem here is caused by the linker. If two global variables having the same name are declared in two independently compiled modules, most linkers will assume that they are the same variable. If you wrote one of the modules five years ago and put it into a library, and then inadvertently use a global variable with the same name as the one in the library routine, you'll find the variable that you *do* know about magically changes its value from time to time (every time the library routine is called). This situation can be a frustrating one to discover and fix.

The solution to this problem is to declare all global variables **static**. Static global variables are limited in scope to the file in which they are declared. Consequently, a subroutine declared in one file can't access a **static** global declared in a second file. If two global statics have the same name, the linker will treat them as two different variables.

Sometimes, though, you need to modify a global variable from another module, and this is what an access routine is used for. An access routine is a subroutine that either fetches or modifies the value of a static global variable. The access routine is itself globally accessible. Figure 5-12 shows how such a routine is used. The routines *setvar()* and *getvar()* provide access to the variable *Global_var*. Access routines are used in the expression analyzer presented in Chapter 7, where they're discussed in greater detail.

Fig. 5-12: Access Routines

```
              file 1:
     ----------------------------------------
    |                                        |
    | static int    Global_var;              |              file 2:
    |                                        |     -----------------------------
    | setvar( x )                            |    |                             |
    | int x;                                 |    | some_function()             |
    | {                                      |    | {                           |
    |       Global_var = x;                  |    |      setvar( 123 );         |
    | }                                      |    |      do_something();         |
    |                                        |    |      x = getvar();          |
    | getvar()                               |    | }                           |
    | {                                      |    +-----------------------------|
    |       return Global_var;               |    |
    | }                                      |
    |                                        |
    | do_something()                         |
    | {                                      |
    |       /* Global_var is used here */    |
    | }                                      |
     ----------------------------------------
```

If you organize your files functionally (so that all subroutines in the same file are related in function) all subroutines that need to use a particular global variable can usually be concentrated into one file. So, in practice, access routines are not often necessary.

5.5. Portability

One of the nice things about C is that it's portable. Just about every type of microprocessor has a C compiler for it. Nevertheless, the fact that C *can* be portable, doesn't mean that it *is* portable. A well-written C program can be downloaded to another machine over a modem, recompiled, and then run, with a minimum of fuss. On the other hand, a program that isn't written with portability in mind can take days to get running on another system.

Perhaps the most important portability consideration is the compiler's I/O library. The Unix compiler's I/O library provides a de facto standard for C, and many compilers support the majority of the Unix I/O functions. If your compiler's library isn't Unix compatible, you may be better off getting another compiler (at least if you ever intend to move your code to another system). Volume I of the *Unix Programmer's Manual* (see the bibliography) describes all the Unix I/O routines and serves as a good basis for comparison with your own compiler's documentation.

Some compilers provide temptingly useful extensions to the C language. Don't use them. Similarly, don't use nonstandard (non-Unix) subroutines supplied by your compiler manufacturer unless the manufacturer also supplies the source code for these routines.

Don't assume anything about the hardware. Routines that have to manipulate the hardware should be concentrated into one file, so that they can be changed easily if necessary. Never assume that an **int** is 16 bits wide or that a pointer and an **int** are the same size. Figure 5-13 shows a subroutine that returns the width of a **int** in bytes.

Fig. 5-13: Finding the Width of an Int

```
width( )
{
          /*          Return the number of bits in an int
           */

          register int       i, j;

          for( j = ~0, i = 1;   j <<= 1 ;   i++ )
                   ;

          return i;
}
```

Integer sizes are sometimes implicit in constants. For this reason it's always better to say

```
~0x1
```

rather than

```
0xfffe
```

The latter expression won't work with a 32-bit-wide integer. Similarly you should use:

```
~(( (unsigned)~0 ) >>1)
```

instead of

```
0x8000
```

(The cast is necessary here because ~0 is an **int**, so sign extension may become active when the number is shifted, and we wouldn't end up clearing the top bit as expected.) Portability is discussed further in Chapter 10.

5.6. Things to Avoid

5.6.1. Abuse of the goto: Unstructured Programming

Don't use the **goto** statement unless you really must. There is nothing wrong with the **goto** as such. In many situations (such as having to break out of several levels of nested **while** or **for** loops), using a **goto** is the cleanest and most efficient way to solve a problem. Nevertheless, programmers who come to C from FORTRAN or BASIC tend to overuse the **goto**. Since C provides three ways to control loops (**for, while, do**) and four ways to terminate or modify the control flow in a loop [**break, continue, return** and the *exit()* subroutine] a **goto** is rarely required in any program.

Fig. 5-14: A Valid Use of a Goto

```
main( )
{
        while( ... )
        {
                while( ... )
                {
                        while( ... )
                        {
                                if( an_unrecoverable_error )
                                        goto abort;
                        }
                }
        }

abort:
        clean_up( );
}
```

Abuses of the **goto** are limited by the fact that C requires a label to be in the same subroutine as the **goto**. There are a few rules of thumb to use with the **goto**, however:

(1) Never use a **goto** if a **while, for, break, continue, return,** or *exit()* can be made to do the job. These parts of the language are there to be used, so use them.

(2) The **goto** and the label to which you're branching should be on the same page of the listing, so that you can see the control flow at a glance. Similarly, make the label easy to see by starting it in the leftmost column, rather than at the correct indent level (as shown in figure 5-14).

(3) The label for a goto should *always* be associated with a statement at the outermost block of a subroutine. You should never do something like

branch from an **if** statement to a label in an **else** clause.

(4)   Restrict yourself to using **goto** statements for panic abort situations.

(5)   There should only be one label in a subroutine. You may have several **goto** branches to that label but you should never have more than one label.

A problem related to the **goto** is the *setjmp()* and *longjmp()* subroutine calls. A *setjmp()* call preserves the current machine state in a buffer; a *longjmp()* call restores the machine to the state it was in before the *setjmp()*. These routines can create a maintenance nightmare inside your program. Stack frames are destroyed, variables are found in unknown states, and control flows through the program in ways that can't be traced by looking at the code. I've never had to use these subroutines and, if your program is structured correctly, you shouldn't have to either. All too often, a setjmp/longjmp is used to patch a bug caused by the program's not being properly structured to begin with. You're much better off taking some time to plan before you start to write code than using one of these subroutines.

5.6.2. Misuses of the #define

I've a friend that says "I can write FORTRAN in any language." Unfortunately, he really means it. Don't try to make C look like another programming language. Don't say:

```
#define begin      {
#define end        }
#define AND        &&
#define OR         ||
#define Stuff      stuff( )
```

so that you can say

```
while( condition AND condition OR condition )
begin
        Stuff;
end
```

If you want to program in Pascal, then use Pascal. Trying to make C look like another language just makes your program hard to maintain by a C programmer who doesn't know the other language. The program certainly isn't made easier to read. It's just made to look more familiar (because you happen to know Pascal). Many programmers are tempted to do this sort of thing when they're first learning the language, in an effort to make the unfamiliar look more like something they're used to. You'll find yourself getting used to C syntax very quickly, though, and will probably end up going back through much of your early C code to de-Pascal-ify it.

A related problem is:

```
#define TRUE     1
#define FALSE    0

while( something == TRUE )
            stuff( );
```

The problem here is that any non-zero value is true in C. So the test
something == TRUE can fail, even if *something* is indeed true. The expression *something != FALSE* is safe but just adds unnecessary words to your
program (*!something* works just as well). As in the previous example, you'll
get used to the proper C syntax more quickly than you think.

5.6.3. Switches

Don't let a **case** statement vector into the middle of a block. For example, the following, though legal, is not recommended:

```
switch( x )
{
case a:
        if( some_condition )
        {
                do_something( );
        }
        else
case b: {
                do_something_else( );
        }
}
```

Similarly, since a case will just fall through to the next case if no **break** is
present, all cases in a switch should end with either a **break** statement or a
comment saying that the break is deliberately missing:

```
switch( x )
{
case a:
        code( );
        /* fall through to case b */
case b:
        more_code( );
        break;
}
```

5.7. If/else

Generally, try to organize your **if/else** statements so that the block that
takes up less space is next to the **if** clause:

```
if( condition )
        short_block( );
else
{
        /*
         *
         *
         */

        long_block( );

        /*
         *
         *
         */
}
```

Here, the problem is readability. We're trying to get the statement that controls execution of the **else** to be on the same page as the **else** itself. Putting the shortest clause first usually ensures this.

5.8. A C Style Sheet

This section is a synopsis of all the formatting issues we've discussed in this chapter. It's meant not to be any sort of program, but rather to present a concise set of examples of how common constructs in C should be formatted. I strongly recommend that you format your programs in this way. If you change anything, do it because the result of the change is enhanced readability. In any event, try it for a while. Once you've used good formatting, you'll understand the reasons behind what must now seem arbitrary rules. Good formatting really does help.

```
UNACCEPTABLE:      for(i=2+16;i<=MAXCH&&i>0;i+=2)foobar=i;

BETTER:            for(i=2+16; i<=MAXCH && i>0; i+=2)
                           foobar=i;

BETTER STILL:      for(i = 2 + 16;  i <= MAXCH  &&  i > 0; i += 2)
                   {
                           foobar = i;
                   }


=========================================================================

#include <stdio.h>

/*       FILENAME.C:  Describe the routines in this module here.
 */

/*--------------------------------------------------------------*/

extern   char      *foo();     /* Name of module in which foo is declared */
extern   unsigned bar();       /* Name of module in which bar is declared */
extern   int       Globalvar;  /* Name of module in which bar is declared */

/*------------------------------------------------------
 *       #defines and typedefs should have their names in all caps.
 *       Capitalize only the first letter of global variables. Local
 *       variables should be in all lower case. When initializing
 *       structures and arrays, line everything up in neat columns.
 */

#define ARRAYSIZE          (1024 * 6)    /* Its better to say this than
                                          * 7224 because it's more readable.
                                          * The compiler should evaluate it
                                          * at compile time.
                                          */

typedef struct _foo                      /* Explain what the structure   */
{                                        /* is used for.                 */
        char            a;               /* Explain a.                   */
        int             b;               /* Explain b.                   */
        struct _foo     *ptr;            /* Explain ptr.                 */
}
FOO;

static int      Var     = 1;             /* Explain how Var is used      */
static char     *Var2   = 2;             /* Explain how Var2 is used     */


/* Explain the uses of Var3 and Var4. The comment cannot be placed to
 * the right of the definition because there's no room.
 */

static FOO      Var3    = { 'a',  "string",            &var4        };
static FOO      Var4    = { 'b',  "another string",  (FOO *)NIL   };

/*--------------------------------------------------------------*/

main( argc, argv )
int      argc;
char     **argv;
{
        /*       This comment describes the program (or subroutine)
         *       in general terms. It should explain the function of
```

```
 *          each argument, and list the possible return values
 *          and their meanings.
 */

int          local_int;              /* explain what it does */
char         array[ARRAYSIZE], *ap;  /* explain what it does */
static int   var_2;                  /* explain what it does */

while( statement )
{
        /*
         *      Explain what's happening in the while loop (if it
         *      isn't obvious).
         */

        body( );
        more_body( );
}

for( initializer = 0 ;   comparison( ) ; modify(initializer) )
{
        for_body( arg1, arg2, arg3 );
        for_body( arg4, arg5, arg6 );
}

if( a )
{
        statement( );
}
else if( b >= a   &&   d < b   )
{
        statement( );
}
else
{
        statement( );
}
}

/*--------------------------------------------------------*/

a_subroutine( a1 )
int     a1;
{
        /*      Explanatory statement goes here.
         */

        switch( a1 )
        {
        case CR:
                do_something;
                break;

        default:
                printf("a_subroutine( ): bad argument <%c> (0x%04x)\n",
                                                        a1, a1);
                break;
        }

        while(1)
        {
                if ( !do_forever)
                        break;
                else
```

```
                        do_something( );
        }

        do {
                --a;
                more_stuff( );

        } while ( a1 );
}

/*----------------------------------------------------------*/
char    *another_routine(b)
int     b;
{
        switch(b)
        {
        case 'a':           return ("a");
        case 'b':           return ("b");
        case 'c':           return ("c");
        case 'd':           return ("d");
        default :           return ("?");
        }
}
```

5.9. Exercises

5-1   Design (but don't code) a program that right-justifies text (spreads the
        words as evenly as possible on a line so that the rightmost letters all line
        up; the text in this book is right-justified). It should take input from
        standard input and write to standard output. The first line of input
        should contain the number of columns in the output text. Use *gets()* to
        get input and *printf()* or *puts()* for output. A subroutine should be
        called to do the actual justification. It should modify the contents of a
        character array in place (do not copy from one array to another).

        Submit the program outline along with a description, in English, of
        exactly what the program does and how it does it. Resolve any ambigui-
        ties in the assignment in the program description (for example, what
        should be done if an input line is longer than the specified output line
        width, what should be done with tabs, and so on).

5-2   Write the program you designed in question 5-1. Hand in all intermedi-
        ate stages of the program development process, showing all stubs.

POINTERS

This chapter explores pointers, the most misunderstood and powerful part of the C language. Pointers can dramatically improve the execution time of your programs; a tenfold improvement isn't unheard of.[1] In fact, pointers are such an integral part of C that any program that uses arrays but doesn't access them with pointers can't be considered a C program at all, but is really a FORTRAN program written in C.

Unfortunately, most textbooks either don't cover pointers at all, or cover them in inadequate depth. This chapter is meant to supplement the pointer chapters in most C textbooks, and you may want to read this chapter in parallel with another text. The first few sections describe pointers as represented in the machine; rather than resorting to analogies such as mailboxes. These sections assume that you know how to make simple declarations in C, and that you understand machine addressing. The next chapter, "Advanced Pointers," explores several complex uses of pointers. Don't move on to that chapter until you thoroughly understand the material in this chapter.

---

1. I'm talking here about a program that ran on an 8085. All direct references to a two-dimensional array of structures were changed to pointer references. The improvement isn't always this dramatic, but it's often a factor of three or four. We'll look at why in a moment.

I've used footnotes here to provide extra details that will probably be confusing the first time you read the chapter; ignore them the first time through. Pointers to structures, though mentioned towards the end of the chapter, aren't explained in depth because most texts cover this material adequately.

6.1. Simple Pointers

A *pointer* is a variable that holds the address of another variable. Memorize that definition. A pointer is a *variable* that holds the *address* of another variable. We sometimes refer to the address itself as a pointer too. Let's analyze this definition in depth. First of all, a pointer is a *variable* (as opposed to a constant). There is nothing special about it. A variable's name, when used in an expression, evaluates to the contents of that variable. A good way to see what a variable (or expression) evaluates to is with a *printf()* statement. For example,

```
printf("%d",x);
```

prints the contents of x; the variable x evaluates to its contents when used in a statement.

Declaring an object in C carves out an area of memory for that object to use.[2] The declaration

```
int     x, y;
```

allocates space for two integer-sized objects in memory. That is, the compiler reserves space somewhere for these two variables to use. Reserving space is all the compiler does. There's no way to predict what a

```
printf("%d",x);
```

executed at this point would print, because you don't know what's in x. A picture of what x and y look like in memory is shown in figure 6-1. The addresses shown are arbitrary; it helps to have specific addresses to which we can refer, though. We're also assuming here that an **int** is a 16-bit (2-byte) quantity.

Since x and y haven't been initialized, they contain garbage. We can put something into x and y by saying

---

2. The distinction between a definition and declaration is often made in books about C. Strictly speaking, a *definition* allocates space, while *declaration* just tells the compiler how to use an object. A variable definition always implies a declaration. However, you can declare an object (with an **extern** statement) without allocating space for it. The linker will find the actual object when it puts the program together. In this chapter we'll use the word *declaration* in a broader sense to mean both the declaration and the definition of the variable.

Fig. 6-1: Two int Variables

```
variable                    address of first
name:                       byte of the variable:

        |           |        50
        |-----------|
x:      |    ???    |        52
        |-----------|
y:      |    ???    |        54
        |-----------|
        |           |        56
```

```
x = 100;
y = x + 1;
```

X now contains the number 100, y contains 101. If you look at our picture in memory, you'll see the following:

```
        |           |        50
        |-----------|
x:      |    100    |        52
        |-----------|
y:      |    101    |        54
        |-----------|
        |           |        56
```

The statement $x = 100$ puts the *number* 100 into the *variable* x. (It's called a *variable* for a reason—you can "vary" its contents.) The statement $y = x + 1$ fetches the *number* contained in the variable x, adds 1 to it, and then puts it into y. That's what we mean when we say that a variable name, when *used* in an expression, evaluates to its contents. X, when used in the statement $y = x$, evaluates to the number 100, because that number is contained in x.

Now, let's apply all this to pointers. Consider this declaration:

```
int     *ptr ;
```

This statement allocates space for one *pointer-sized* (as compared to **int**-sized) object. Remember that a pointer is a variable that holds an address. Consequently, the size of a pointer is however many bytes you need to hold an address on your machine (2 bytes on an 8080, Z80, or PDP-11, 4 bytes on a VAX or 68000, and so on). Like *int x*, the statement *int *ptr* just allocates space for one pointer; the contents of the memory at this location are *undefined* because we haven't initialized the variable yet. Let's draw another picture:

```
          |              |      50
          |------------- |
     x:   |     100      |      52
          |------------- |
     y:   |     101      |      54
          |------------- |
   ptr:   |     ???      |      56
          |------------- |
          |              |      58
```

Even though we've told the compiler that *ptr* points to an integer, that integer is *not* created along with the pointer. If we declare a pointer to an array, only the pointer is created. The array is *not* created and the pointer is *not* pointing anywhere in particular. Generally speaking, all pointers are the same size, regardless of what they point to.[3] When viewed in terms of memory allocation, it doesn't matter whether a pointer variable is a pointer to an **int**, to a **long**, to an array or to a structure. Nonetheless, for reasons that will become clear later, the compiler needs to know the type of the object being pointed to.

A pointer is a *variable.* For the most part, it can be used like any other variable.[4] For example, the statement *ptr = 100;* puts the number 100 into the variable called *ptr.*[5] The statement

```
printf("%d", ptr);
```

prints out the number 100.[6] Remember, though, a pointer is a variable that

---

3.   This is not always true. For example, in the 8086 medium models, it's possible to have a 16-bit pointer to a function and a 32-bit pointer to data, or vice versa. A good deal of C code assumes that all pointers are the same size, however. Be careful when you move code to an 8086-family machine.

4.   In practice, there are limits to what you can do with a pointer. The following are legal:
     (1) Assignment. You can set a pointer to the value of another pointer or to an address derived with the & operator. (More about this in a moment.)
     (2) Adding or subtracting an integer to or from a pointer (you may not add two pointers together).
     (3) Subtracting two pointers (which yields the distance, in objects, between the two pointers). Both pointers must point to the same type of object.
     (4) Most other operations (multiplication, shifting, and so on) are illegal, though you can circumvent this problem with a cast if you must.

5.   Many compilers require you to say *ptr = (int *)100;* more on this in a moment.

6.   We're really tricking *printf()* here. We're pushing a pointer-sized object onto the stack, but telling printf that it's an **int**-sized object and should be printed as if it were a number. This is a useful thing to do during debugging, but it won't work on machines whose pointers are larger than **ints** (because the value of the pointer will be truncated). The proposed ANSI standard defines a %p argument to *printf()* that prints a pointer-sized object as if it were a number, but most compilers don't support this yet. Sometimes the problem can be circumvented by telling *printf()* that

holds the *address* of another variable. Since there's no known variable at memory location 100, the assignment of 100 to ptr, though legal, is not meaningful.

A variable's address can be found with the & operator. &*x* evaluates to the *address* of the variable *x* (not to the contents of *x*). The statement

```
ptr = &x;
```

puts the address of the variable *x* into the pointer. Since *x* is at memory location 52, *ptr* = &*x* puts 52 into *ptr*. Memory now looks like this:

```
          |             |    50
          |-------------|
     x:   |     100     |    52
          |-------------|
     y:   |     101     |    54
          |-------------|
   ptr:   |      52     |    56
          |-------------|
          |             |    58
```

Ptr = &*x* is just an assignment, like any other assignment; no magic.

To modify *x* indirectly through the pointer, a * operator is required. The * operator in C is the *object-pointed-to* operator. *ptr* means the object-pointed-to by ptr. The object-pointed-to is the object at the address contained in the pointer. *Ptr* holds the number 52, which is the address of *x*. Consequently, the object-pointed-to by ptr is the contents of memory location 52, the variable *x*.

The expression *ptr=5* puts the number 5 into *x*, the object-pointed-to by *ptr*; *x=5* does the same thing. To summarize, *ptr* (with no asterisk) evaluates to the contents of the variable *ptr*, and *ptr* (with an asterisk) evaluates to the contents of the object-pointed-to by *ptr*, the variable whose address is contained in *ptr*. The statement

```
printf("%d, %d", ptr, *ptr );
```

prints

```
52, 5
```

This declaration of *ptr*:

```
int *ptr;
```

allocates space for a pointer-sized object *but does not initialize that object*. Consequently, when the pointer is created it contains a random number rather

---

the pointer is really a **long**, as in:

```
printf("%ld",ptr)
```

than the address of an object. Moreover, the compiler is too stupid to know whether *ptr* actually contains a valid address. If we say **ptr = 5* without initializing *ptr* first (with a *ptr = &x* or its equivalent) we'll put the number 5 into memory at some random place (at the address contained in *ptr*, whatever that may be). If *ptr* contains the number 0, then the command **ptr=5* puts the number 5 into memory location 0, destroying what was previously there. Using an uninitialized pointer is a common, and dangerous, error. You can obliterate anything in memory, including your own program.[7] In MS-DOS, you can even destroy the directory on your hard disk and overwrite the operating system itself.[8] To avoid these disasters, **YOU MUST INITIALIZE A POINTER BEFORE USING IT.**

6.2. Pointers and Array Names

Even though we talk about *arrays,* there's no such thing as an array in C. Period. There *is* a method for allocating space for a block of objects that all have the same type, and we can (and do) call this block of objects an "array." Nevertheless, this "array" is not a *type* in the C language. The elements of the array can be manipulated as if they were single objects, but the entire array cannot be manipulated as a unit. That is, if an array type actually existed, you'd be able to assign one array to another with an equals sign, rather than having to copy the elements one at a time. You'd be able to pass an array to a subroutine by value. You wouldn't be permitted to index into an array with a subscript that was larger than the array size, and so forth.[9] The *concept* of an array (a block of objects, all contiguous in memory and all having the same type) exists, but the array can't be manipulated as such. It has to be manipulated one object at a time and it has to be manipulated via a pointer (more on this use of pointers in a moment).[10]

---

7.   Most large mainframes will let pointers overwrite data, but they draw the line at code. UNIX, for example, will give you a "segmentation violation: core dumped" error message if a out-of-control pointer attempts to write into the code space. Most microcomputers, on the other hand, don't do any checking of this sort. While on the subject, "core" is a file that contains an image of the computer's memory store when the program was terminated. It's a large file and not very useful. You should remove it with a *rm core* command.

8.   A part of the disk's directory structure, the FAT, is stored in memory and written out to the disk when a file is closed. A pointer in a large-model program, or a far pointer in a small-model program, can overwrite the FAT, destroying the logged-in disk's directory.

9.   You wouldn't be able to apply the brackets to a pointer, either.

10. The pointer may be an implied pointer, derived from the array name, but it's a pointer nonetheless.

The declaration

```
int       array[5];
```

allocates space for 5 integers (that contain garbage because we haven't initialized them yet). They are guaranteed to be contiguous in memory, but you should look at them as five unique objects, not as a single array. Memory, after the allocation, is shown in figure 6-2.

Fig. 6-2: Adding an Array to Memory

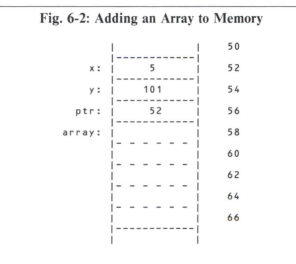

Although we've allocated five integers, these integers don't have unique names. How can we access them then? *In C, an array name always evaluates to a pointer to the first element of an array.* That is, the array name is used as if it were a pointer variable that had been initialized to point to the first object in the array. An array name is a constant, however. It can't be manipulated like a pointer.[11] More on this in a moment.

Don't confuse the array *declaration* with the way in which the array name is *used*. Even though the array name is used as if it were a pointer, arrays and pointers are very different. An array is an *aggregate type*— a collection of contiguous variables all having the same type. A pointer is a *single*

---

11. An array name, in assembly language, is the label associated with the first cell of the array. A pointer, on the other hand, is a cell in memory that contains the address of another location in memory. That is, an array name is a *label* and a pointer variable is not.

pointer-sized variable. The declaration *int array[5]* allocates space for 5 integers, which requires 10 bytes of memory. The declaration *int *ptr* allocates space for a single pointer, requiring 2 bytes in memory, but does not allocate space for the object or objects that the pointer accesses.

It's a very common error[12] to say

```
char    *p;
gets(p);                  /* WRONG   */
```

when you really mean

```
char    buf[128];
gets(buf);                /* CORRECT */
```

The subroutine *gets()* expects, as its argument, the address of a block of memory into which it puts characters taken from standard input. Since an array name evaluates to the address of the first element of the array, the call *gets(buf)* works as expected. *Buf* evaluates to the address of the first byte of a block of 128 bytes. On the other hand, *p* is a single pointer-sized variable. With no asterisk, *p* evaluates to the contents of that variable. The call *gets(p)* passes the contents of the variable *p* to *gets()*, which assumes that those contents are the address of a block of memory into which it can put characters. But *p* contains garbage. We've never initialized it to point to anything, so it still contains whatever random number happened to be there when the space was allocated. Consequently *gets()* starts putting characters into that random location in memory. If we really wanted to use *p* in the *gets()* call, we'd have to say:

```
char    buf[128];
char    *p;

p = buf;
gets(p);
```

but why bother to copy the address of the first element of *buf* into *p* when *gets(buf)* is sufficient?

A problem here is the way that *gets()* is presented in most compiler's manuals, which represent the calling syntax of *gets()* as follows:

```
gets( str )
char *str;
```

This representation means that the subroutine requires a character pointer as its argument. Programmers who are accustomed to a strongly typed language like Pascal tend to think that they have to pass to *gets()* a variable that had been declared as a character pointer. This assumption is wrong. When the

---

12. I've even found this error in an introductory-level textbook that purported to teach the C language.

manual says that *gets()* expects a pointer to **char**, it means that *gets()* expects the address of a variable of type **char**. (Remember, a pointer is a variable that holds an address, and the variable's name evaluates to its contents.) You can derive that address in several ways, the easiest of which is to use an array name (without the brackets). You can also pass *gets()* the contents of a pointer that has been initialized to point to an array of **char**s.

Gets() assumes that the character pointed to by its argument is followed in memory by several other **char**-sized objects. That is, it assumes that the pointer passed to it is a pointer to an array. Remember, however, that an array name evaluates to the address of the first element of the array. That is, instead of passing the entire array to *gets()*, you pass the address of the first element. More importantly, since *gets()* is being passed an address only, it has no way to determine whether that address is the address of an entire array or whether it's the address of a single **char**. In other words, the pointer to the array carries no information about the array size along with it. Since the subroutine can't know the array size, it just assumes that the array is big enough. *Caveat programmer.*

Fig. 6-3: Calling a Subroutine with a Pointer Argument

```
gets( str )      /* Definition of the subroutine gets: The argument str  */
char  *str;      /* is the address of first element of an array into      */
{                /* which gets() puts characters.                         */
}

main( )
{
    char array[10];
    char c, *cp ;

    gets( array );   /* Correct, passes the address of the               */
                     /* first element of "array."                        */

    cp = array;
    gets( cp );      /* Correct only because cp has been                 */
                     /* initialized. Passes the contents of cp, which */
                     /* must hold the address of a character array.    */

    gets( &c );      /* WRONG. Note that the syntax is correct and      */
                     /* no error messages are printed. Passes           */
                     /* gets() the address of a single character        */
                     /* rather than the address of the first of        */
                     /* a block of characters.                          */
}
```

Returning to array names, An array name can be used as if it were a pointer that had been initialized to point to the first cell of the array. That is, it evaluates to the address of the first element, as would a pointer that had been initialized to point to the first element. Using our example, the statement

```
printf("%d", array);
```

prints the number 58 (the address of the first element of *array*; note that we're giving *printf( )* a *%d*, not a *%s*). An array name can always be used as if it were a pointer. Given the declaration *int array[5]*, the expression **array = 20* is perfectly legal in C. The compiler uses the array name as if it were a pointer that had been initialized to point to the first cell of the array (at address 58). That is, it uses *array* as if it were a pointer containing the number 58. The expression **array = 20* puts the number 20 into memory location 58.

We can also use the pointer variable *ptr* to write into the array, *provided that we initialize ptr* to point to the array before we use it. Ptr can be initialized in either of two ways:

```
ptr = &array[0];
ptr = array;
```

The first statement is easy to understand. Remember that & is the *address-of* operator. The expression *&array[0]* translates to "the *address-of* array[0]," or the address of the first element of *array*, or the number 58. We can use the second form of assignment because the array name evaluates to the address of the first element. This second initialization also puts the address of the first element of *array* into *ptr*. Ptr now contains the number 58; it *points to* the first element of *array*. The relationship can be drawn as follows:

```
ptr:                                    array:
|------------|                          |------------|
|  58   *-----|-------->|      20       |    58
|------------|          |- - - - - -  |
                        |              |    60
                        |- - - - - -  |
                        |              |    62
                        |- - - - - -  |
                        |              |    64
                        |- - - - - -  |
                        |              |    66
                        |------------|
```

The arrow shows the relationship between the pointer and the object to which it points. Now, having initialized *ptr*, we can use it. The expression **ptr = 100;* moves the number 100 into the object whose address is contained in the pointer *ptr*. Since *ptr* contains the number 58, we'll move the number 100 into memory location 58, which is the first cell of *array*. Memory now looks like this:

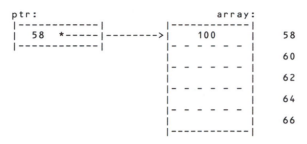

We can modify the object-pointed-to using normal pointer syntax. For example, *ptr = *ptr + 1 [or (*ptr)++] adds one to the object-pointed-to by ptr (changes it from 100 to 101).

6.3. Pointer Arithmetic

There's one major distinction between a pointer and an array name that's being used as a pointer. A pointer is a *variable.* As is the case with any variable, you can modify its contents. On the other hand, an array name, though it can be used as if it were a pointer, is *not* a variable—it's a constant. We can say *ptr++* if we like, but we *cannot* say *array++*.[13]

The statement *ptr = ptr + 1* (or *ptr++*) adds 1 to the pointer itself (just like *x++* adds 1 to *x*). The object-pointed-to isn't modified; only the pointer is. There's a catch, though, when it comes to pointers, the number 1 means *one object*. That is, we haven't actually added the number 1 to the contents of the pointer. Rather, we've added to the pointer the size of one object-pointed-to. Since *ptr* is a pointer to **int** (defined as such by the declaration: *int *ptr*),[14] we'll add 2 to it (because the size of an **int** is 2 bytes). The statement *ptr++* changes the contents of *ptr* from 58 to 60, and *it now points to the second element of the array.* If we now say **ptr = 10*, we'll put the number

---

13. An earlier footnote mentioned that an array name is a label. There's another way to look at it. Array names are constants because the address of the first element is stored in the symbol table. That is, there's no variable created that holds the address of the first element. Rather, the compiler remembers that address in the symbol table and generates an immediate instruction (or a reference to the frame pointer for automatic arrays) every time the array name is used. Since the symbol table doesn't exist at run time, you can't modify an address that is actually part of the symbol table.

14. It's important to note that it is the pointer's *declaration* that tells the compiler how much to add to a pointer when you increment it. The compiler doesn't care whether a variable declared as a pointer to **int** is actually pointing at an **int**, when you increment the pointer, you'll add sizeof(**int**) to it, regardless of to what it actually points. Printf (which we'll look at in Chapter 9) has a good example of a pointer, pointing to something other than its declared object type.

10 into the cell at address 60. Memory now looks like this:

```
ptr:                                    array:
|------------|                    |------------|
|  60    *-----|---+              |    100     |      58
|------------|    |              |- - - - - - |
                   |              |    10      |      60
                   +---->|       |- - - - - - |
                                  |            |      62
                                  |- - - - - - |
                                  |            |      64
                                  |- - - - - - |
                                  |            |      66
                                  |------------|
```

Pointer arithmetic differs from normal arithmetic only in that all integers are multiplied by the size of one object-pointed-to before they're used in an expression.[15] The expression

                              ptr += 3;

adds *[3 * sizeof(int)]* to the previous contents of *ptr* (making it point to address 66). The expression

                              ptr -= 3;

puts it back where it was. Both of these expressions evaluate to a pointer, so we could say

                         *(ptr -= 3) = 'x';

to decrement *ptr* and modify the object-pointed-to at the same time. (More on this in a moment.)

Subtracting two pointers from each other is also legal. Subtraction yields the distance between the two pointers *in objects* (not in bytes). For example, subtracting a pointer to the first element of an array (array[0]) from a pointer to the fourth element (array[3]) yields the integer 3. A subtraction yields an integer rather than a pointer. Both pointers must point to the same type of object. All other arithmetic operations on pointers are illegal.

Pointer arithmetic and accessing the object-pointed-to may be combined into one expression. For example, you can combine the * and ++ or -- operators into a single expression. When you do this, though, you have to be careful about operator precedence. Let's look at some examples.

                              x = *ptr++;

does two things at once: Something is being put into *x* at the same time that

_____

15. Actually, any integral quantity will do. You can use an expression or a **long int**, though not all compilers will accept the latter. For example, *p+(x*4)* is legal, provided that p is a pointer and *(x*4)* evaluates to an *int*.

something is being incremented. But what's being incremented, the pointer itself or the object-pointed-to? This question can be answered by fully parenthesizing the expression. A glance at the precedence chart in Appendix A tells you that the * and ++ operators are at the same precedence level, but they *associate* from right to left. Consequently, our expression parenthesizes to

```
x = *( ptr++ );
```

The * applies to the entire expression *p++* (in other words the ++ *binds tighter* to the name than does the *). The pointer itself is incremented. Next, note that the ++ *follows* the variable name, therefore this is a postincrement. We'll increment the pointer *after* we've used it. The next thing to ask is "to what does the expression evaluate?" Here the asterisk comes into play: the expression evaluates to the contents of the object-pointed-to by *ptr* (before the increment). So, we'll copy the object-pointed-to by *ptr* into *x*, and then we'll increment *ptr*.

Now, consider this:

```
x = *++ptr;
```

This expression behaves as we just described, except that now, since the ++ precedes the variable name, *ptr* is incremented *before* the object-pointed-to is fetched. The implied parentheses are

```
x = *( ++ptr );
```

How about

```
x = ++*ptr;
```

The ++ and the * have exchanged positions. The behavior here is very different than it was before. The expression parenthesizes to

```
x = ++( *ptr );
```

The ++ applies to the object-pointed-to. The object-pointed-to is incremented, and the incremented value of the object-pointed-to is copied into *x*. The pointer itself is not modified. The equivalent operation with a postincrement is

```
x = ( *ptr )++ ;
```

The parentheses are required here.

All the expressions we just described *evaluate* to the object-pointed-to. In other words, we're telling the compiler to fetch the object and put it into *x*. The *x* = is required. We can't tell the compiler to fetch an object and not put it anywhere. The statement

```
*p;
```

alone on a line makes no more sense than the statement

$$x;$$

alone on a line. This sort of omission can generate an "lvalue required" error message. (More on this in chapter 10.)

6.4. The Square Bracket Notation

You don't have to actually modify the pointer to use pointer arithmetic. For example, if *ptr* points into an array, we can modify the cell that is at offset 3 from the cell being pointed to with this expression:

$$*(ptr + 3) = 5;$$

The expression is interpreted by the compiler as "move the number 5 into the memory cell whose address is found by taking the contents of *ptr* and adding *(3 * sizeof(int))* to it."[16] In other words, the object-pointed-to is at the following address:

$$contents-of-ptr + (3 * sizeof(one-object)).$$

Ptr itself isn't modified.

Let's look at a concrete example, given the situation shown in figure 6-4. we can modify the third element of the array with this expression:

$$*(ptr + 2) = 6;$$

(The third element is at offset 2 from the base of the array.)

The compiler fetches the contents of *ptr* (the number 58) and then adds 4 (2 * sizeof(**int**)) to it, yielding the number 62. It then moves the number 6 into the object-pointed-to, to the object at address 62. *Ptr* itself won't be modified (the addition is done in a scratch variable).

Since an array name can be used exactly as if it were a pointer initialized to point to the first element of the array, and since *ptr* is indeed pointing at the first element of the array, we could perform the same operation with

---

16. That is, 3 times the size of 1 object-pointed-to. You can't say

$$ptr + 1 \ = y;$$

or

$$*ptr + 1 = y;$$

any more than you can say

$$x + 1 = y;$$

Fig. 6-4: A Pointer to an Array.

```
                              *(ptr + 2) = 6;

 ptr:                     array:           index    address:   Offset
 |------------|           |------------|                       in objects:
 |  58   *----|--------->|             |    array[0]    58       0
 |------------|           |- - - - - - |
                          |             |    array[1]    60       1
                          |- - - - - - |
                          |     6       |    array[2]    62       2
                          |- - - - - - |
                          |             |    array[3]    64       3
                          |- - - - - - |
                          |             |    array[4]    68       4
                          |------------|
```

```
                              *(array + 2) = 6;
```

The name *array* is treated just like *ptr* was treated in the previous example.

All this is beginning to look suspiciously familiar. In fact, the identity

```
             *(array + 2)       ==        array[2]
```

holds for all arrays. The square bracket notation is just a shorthand representation of the pointer operation. We can generalize this identity to

```
             *(array + i)       ==        array[i]
```

Remember that arrays don't exist as such. The compiler knows only about pointers. An array name, whether or not it's followed by square brackets, always evaluates to a pointer to the first element of the array. The square bracket notation tells the compiler to do the following:

(1)   Multiply the number in the brackets by the size of one array element (one object-pointed-to).

(2)   Add this as an offset to the contents of the pointer implicit in the array name (that is, the array name evaluates to a pointer to the first element of the array).

(3)   Fetch the object at the computed address.

Since C is very regular in the way that it handles operators, it turns out that *the square bracket notation can be applied to any pointer.* That is, the following holds when *ptr* is any pointer:

```
             *(ptr + i)       ==        ptr[i]
```

It happens to work with arrays because an array name evaluates to a pointer.

The $i==0$ case of this identity is interesting.

```
*(ptr + 0)   ==   *ptr   ==   ptr[0]
```

Or, to put it into words, any time we see a *[0]* at the right of a pointer name, we can replace that *[0]* with an * to the left of the pointer name.[17]

The name to the left of the square brackets doesn't have to be an array name, any pointer will do. Since an array name is a pointer, given

```
int     array[5], *ptr;
ptr = array;
```

all of the following do the same thing:

```
*(array + 3) = 5;
*(ptr    + 3) = 5;
array[3]      = 5;
ptr[3]        = 5;
```

Since *ptr* is a variable, you can also say

```
ptr = array;
ptr += 3;
*ptr = 5;
```

here, however, *ptr* itself is modified. Since *array* is a constant, not a variable, you can't say *array += 3.*

If all these statements are equivalent, why use pointers instead of the square bracket notation? The answer lies in efficiency considerations. Think about what you are actually instructing the compiler to do when $x = p[i++]$ is executed.

(1)   Fetch the contents of i.

(2)   Multiply it by the size of one object-pointed-to. Store the result in an anonymous scratch variable.

(3)   Then, increment i and put it back.

(4)   Fetch the contents of p.

(5)   Then add the results of the multiply to it.

(6)   Finally, fetch the contents of the cell whose address we just computed, and put it into x.

That's three fetches and one multiply. Now consider the expression $x = *p++$, which performs the same operation.[18] This second expression causes

---

17. Strictly speaking, this isn't true for multi-dimensional arrays (which we'll discuss in the next chapter). The real identity is as follows:

$$(ptr [x] [y] ... [z]) [0] == *(ptr [x] [y] ... [z])$$

18. This is true as long as p has been initialized to point to the correct array element. Of course, the initialization itself may be no more efficient than the process

the compiler to generate code to do the following:

(1)   Fetch the contents of p.

(2)   Fetch the object at that address and put it into x.

(3)   Add to p the size of an object-pointed-to.

(4)   Store the result of the addition in p.

Here there are only 2 fetches and there's no multiply. That multiply is the major inefficiency. As we saw in Chapter 2, a multiply is an expensive operation and we should do anything we can to avoid it. This is especially true for machines like the 8085 that don't support a hardware multiply; even so, a hardware multiply in most machines is still going to take more time than a hardware addition. Another factor is the actual size of the object. Multiplication by a power of 2 is just a shift. A multiply by 6 (which you'll get with a pointer to a structure or array) is not. On the other hand, many compilers don't have the sense to shift rather than call a multiplication subroutine, even for a power of 2.

You should note that, in terms of overhead, there's no difference between p[i] and *(p+i). There is a run-time multiply in either case. However, if i is a constant—p[1] or *(p+1)—then the compiler can do the multiply at *compile* time rather than at run time. Array accesses that use constants are much faster than those that use variables. Accessing an array using brackets and constants is a reasonable action. If the array is declared **static**, the actual address of the desired cell can be determined at compile time.

By the same token, if you need to access an array randomly, then use the brackets; they're easier to read. An array hardly ever has to be accessed randomly, however. Most often you're going through it in some orderly fashion: row by row, column by column, diagonally, and so forth. In these cases, pointers will be faster.

6.5. Implicit Character Arrays; Initialization

Most variables can be initialized when they are declared by following the declaration with an equal sign and the initial value. For example,

```
int     x = 5;
```

allocates space for x and simultaneously initializes x to 5. Arrays at fixed addresses (global or explicitly declared with the **static** keyword) can be initialized as well:

---

described above but it only has to be done once.

18.   More correctly, the multiply is still there but it's done at compile time rather than run time.

```
static int       array[5] = { 5, 4, 3, 2, 1 };
```

Here, array[0] is initialized to 5, array[1] to 4, and so on. In fact, the array size need not be specified if you explicitly initialize the array. For example:

```
static int       array[ ] = { 4, 5, 6 };
```

creates a three-element-long array of **ints**. The first element is initialized to 4, the second to 5, and the third to 6. You can determine the number of elements in the array with

```
sizeof(array) / sizeof(array[0])
```

This is the size of the entire array, in bytes, divided by the size of one element, in bytes.[19]

In C, there is one kind of array that is implicitly declared: a literal character string. Any collection of ASCII characters surrounded by double quotes (") forms such a string. The characters are put into sequential bytes in memory, and an ASCII NULL ('\0', the number zero) is appended to the end. The whole expression *evaluates* to a pointer to the place in memory where the first character is stored. For example, when you say:

```
printf("Hello");
```

the compiler puts the 5 characters ('H', 'e', 'l', 'l', and 'o') into five sequential memory locations that are invisible to the programmer (there's no easy way to find their address). It then puts the number zero (not the ASCII character '0,' which has the numeric value 0x30) into a sixth location and passes the *address* of the first character to *printf()* (see figure 6-5).[20]

---

19. This is often made into a macro:

    #define array_size(x) (sizeof(x)/sizeof(*x))

20. The string " " evaluates to a pointer to a **char**-sized memory cell containing a '\0';

Fig. 6-5: A Literal String

```
                    printf("Hello");
        causes the following implicit array to be created:
                         |----------|
                 50:  |     'H'    |
                         |----------|
                 51:  |     'e'    |
                         |----------|
                 52:  |     'l'    |
                         |----------|
                 53:  |     'l'    |
                         |----------|
                 54:  |     'o'    |
                         |----------|
                 55:  |    '\0'    |
                         |----------|

        and the number 50 is passed to printf( ).
```

Because a double-quoted string evaluates to a character pointer, you can
use it to initialize a character pointer. For example,

```
        char    *msg = "Hello" ;
```

does two things. First it allocates 6 bytes for the string "Hello" and initializes
them. Then it allocates a pointer-sized object called *msg* and initializes it to
point to (hold the address of) the 'H'. The situation is illustrated in figure 6-6.

Fig. 6-6: An Implicit String

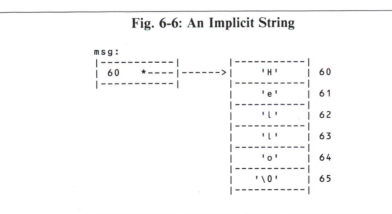

There are a few things to note here. First, the array is not an array in the usual sense. That is, the array is nameless, so it can't be accessed directly. The only way to get at it is through the pointer. Next, *msg* is indeed a variable, not an array. It has been initialized to point to an array, but it is a single, pointer-sized object. Since msg is a pointer, it can be used to access the array, just like any other pointer to an array. For example,

```
x = msg[2];
```

will move an ASCII 'l' (the number 108) into x. Similarly, *msg* evaluates to the character 'H'. Since *msg* is a variable, we can modify it. That is, we can say *msg++* if we like. This modification wouldn't be permitted if *msg* were an array name. Of course, if you modify *msg* to point somewhere else in memory, there's no way to get back to the original string because that string, even though it is stored as an array, doesn't have a name.[21]

To confuse matters, it's also legal to initialize a character array as follows:

```
char      a[128] = "foo";
```

This declaration creates a 128-byte array, however, not a pointer. The first four elements of the array are initialized to the characters 'f', 'o', 'o' and '\0'. You could also say

```
char      a[128] = {'f', 'o', 'o', '\0'};
```

---

21. It is possible to modify the literal string with something like the following:

```
msg[2] = 'C' ;
```

Nevertheless, it's considered bad programming style to modify the contents of a literal string constant. Another interesting point. Two string literals with the same contents are stored in separate areas of memory, even though the contents are the same. For example

```
char   *msg1 = "Hello" ;
char   *msg2 = "Hello" ;
```

creates two pointer-sized objects (*msg1* and *msg2*) and also creates two, 6-byte character arrays, each of which will be initialized to the string "Hello." Note that a few compilers (Lattice ver. 2.x, for example) don't guarantee that all literal strings will be unique, however.

—less confusing but more inconvenient. Because some compilers put a limit of 128 characters on implicit strings, you may have to use this second form of initialization with very long strings.[22]

There is an interesting application of quoted strings in one of *printf()*'s support routines. Consider the following statement:

```
putchar(   "0123456789abcdef"[ x & 0xf ]   );
```

All quoted strings evaluate to a pointer to the first character in the string. Also, the square bracket notation can be applied to *any* pointer, even to an implicit one. Consequently, if x is a number in the range 0 to 15 (and the *& 0xf* guarantees that it is), x vectors into the string as if it were an array and picks out a single character. If the value of x is 0, the ASCII character '0' is printed; if the value of x is 10 (0xa) then the ASCII character 'a' is printed, and so forth. In other words, x is used to compute an offset from the array base address, and the character at that offset is sent to *putchar()*. The base address of the array is implicit in the double-quote notation. So this rather odd-looking expression does a hex to ASCII conversion. The conciseness of this expression is appealing, but the code is pretty abstruse and therefore not very maintainable. For the sake of readability, it's probably better to say

```
char     a[ ] = {  '0',  '1',  '2',  '3',  '4',  '5',  '6',  '7',
                   '8',  '9',  'a',  'b',  'c',  'd',  'e',  'f' };

putchar(   a[ x & 0xf ]   );
```

The effect of explicit initialization of a variable depends on the storage class. Automatic variables (those that are local to a subroutine and have not be explicitly declared **static**) are initialized every time the subroutine is entered. Moreover, automatic aggregate types (arrays and structures) may not be explicitly initialized. Variables at fixed addresses (all global variables and any local variables whose declarations include the keyword **static**) are treated differently. Aggregates at a fixed address can be initialized, even if they're local to a subroutine. Local **static** variables retain their values between successive subroutine calls. The first time a subroutine is called, a static local variable has the value to which it was explicitly initialized. The second time the same subroutine is called, the variable has the value it had when the subroutine returned the first time.

---

22. You could also declare a 4-byte character array by saying

$$char \quad a[\,] = \text{"foo"};$$

but this is even more confusing. The one advantage to this method (as compared to *char *p="foo"*) is that *a* is a constant and is stored in the symbol table. That is, there's no pointer-sized object created to hold the address of the first element of the array.

No code is generated to initialize variables at fixed addresses. The initial value is read in from the disk. That is, the code and the initialized data for a program are stored together on the disk. When the program boots, the data is just read in along with the code. Because you have to have something up on the disk to hold the place of a fixed variable, all such variables that aren't explicitly initialized, are initialized to zero (rather than to garbage) by the compiler. This practice adds a few milliseconds to your compile time, but it is a real convenience, especially with large arrays. Code is generated to initialize automatic variables, however.

6.6. Exercises

In the following exercises do not use the notation p[i], except in array declarations. Do not use the notation *(p+i) anywhere. (Increment the pointer, not the index.)

6-1   If you used explicit array indexes in your solution to exercise 5-2, rewrite your code using pointers.

6-2   Write a subroutine that reverses a character string in place (without copying from one string to another).

6-3   Write the subroutine

```
subst( str, pattern, replacement )
char    *str, *pattern, *replacement;
```

that scans through *str* searching for the *pattern* and replacing all occurrences of it with *replacement*. For example, the call

```
char    array[128] = "this foo is a foofooo string";

subst( array, "foo", "<->" );
```

would return with "array" modified to

```
"this <-> is a <-><->o string"
```

ADVANCED POINTERS

7.1. Complex Declarations

One of the assets of the C language is its regularity. The same syntax is used for both the declaration and the application of a pointer, and the same operator precedence and associativity rules apply in both situations. We've seen how important these can be with combinations of the ++ and * operators, and the same is true for complex pointer declarations. We've already discussed the simplest sorts of declarations:

```
int     *ip;    /* pointer to int */

int     ia[3];  /* array of ints  */
```

In the latter, the name *ia* can be used as if it were a pointer initialized to point to the first element of the array (except that it's a constant, so it can't be modified). What if we combine the two notations? What is

```
int     *api[3];
```

declaring? Is it a pointer to an array or an array of pointers? The key to answering this question is, again, the order-of-precedence chart (Appendix A). Which operator is higher in precedence, the * or the [ ]? Consulting the chart we see that the [ ] is on the line above the *; therefore, the [ ]s are of higher precedence. That is, they *bind tighter* to the name *api* than does the *. Using this fact, we can parenthesize our declaration:

```
int        (  *( api[3] ) );
```

To find out what *api* is, we start with the innermost set of parentheses and work outward. The innermost expression, were it by itself on the line, would be declaring an array, so *api* is an array, three elements long. An array of what? Going out one level of parentheses, we encounter the *. Were the * by itself on the line, we'd be declaring a pointer. So *api* is an array of pointers. Pointers to what? Go out one more level to find the keyword **int**. Putting this all together:

```
int        *api[3];
```

```
is : an array, three elements long, of...    [3]
        pointers to...                          *
        int.                                   int
```

Remember, even though we've just declared an array of pointers to **int**s, *we have not* declared the **int**s themselves. Our array, properly initialized, is shown in figure 7-1.[1] In this figure (and in most of the figures in this chapter) the addresses of all the cells are shown as a number followed by a colon. These addresses are arbitrary, but they serve to illustrate what's going on in the diagrams.

In this figure, the three elements of *api* are initialized to point at the integer variables *x*, *y*, and *z*. Note that these variables must be explicitly declared. *X* and *y* are then accessed using the same operator precedence with which *api* was declared. Since the [ ]s are of higher precedence than the * ([ ] binds tighter than *), we can initialize *x* with the following:

---

1.   If the array were either global or declared **static**, we could have initialized it as we declared it:

```
int    x, y, z;
int    *api[3] = { &x, &y, &z };
```

Fig. 7-1: An Initialized Array of Pointers to Ints

```
int       *api[3];   /* Declare the array ... */
int       x, y, z;   /* and the objects at    */
                     /* which the elements of */
                     /* the array point.      */

api[0] = &x;      /* Initialize the array */
api[1] = &y;
api[2] = &z;

*api[0] = 1;      /* Put 1 into x */
*( api[1] ) = 2;  /* Put 2 into y */
```

```
Will look like:
                                x:
                         100:|-------|
             api:         +-->|   1   |
             |-------|    |   |-------|
     400:  | 100 *-|---+       y:
             |-------|       200:|-------|
     402:  | 200 *-|---------->|   2   |
             |-------|           |-------|
     404:  | 300 *-|---+       z:
             |-------|   | 300: |-------|
                         +----->|   ?   |
                                |-------|
```

```
 api  ==               the address of the first element of the array == 400
*api  ==  api[0] == the contents of the cell at address 400        == 100
**api == *api[0] == the contents of the cell at address 100        == 1
**api == *api[0] == api[0][0]

     api[1] == the contents of the cell at offset 1 from
               api (the cell at memory location 402)        == 200

    *api[1] == the contents of the cell at address 200      == 2
```

```
       *api[0] = 1;       /* Put 1 into x */
```

We can also parenthesize the expression for clarity:

```
       *( api[1] ) = 2;  /* Put 2 into y */
```

The * operates on the entire expression *api[1]*; the object-pointed-to by *api[1]* is modified.

Surprisingly (at least to me), *x* can also be referenced using **api*. Here, the array name evaluates to a pointer to the first element, so **api* is the contents of the first element, and ***api* is the object-pointed-to by the first element: *x*. To put it another way, since **api == api[0]* and *(api[0]) == x*, it follows that ***api == x*.

The procedure we just used to interpret *api*'s declaration can be generalized:

(1)   Fully parenthesize the declaration, using the order of precedence chart. The name of the object must be at the innermost level.

(2)   Start with the name by writing the phrase

```
                    name is...
```

(3)   Working from the innermost set of parentheses outward,

```
When you see:    Substitute the following phrase:

    *            (a)  pointer(s) to...
   [n]           (an) array(s),  n elements long, of...
   ( )           function returning...
```

Continue in this manner until the actual type keyword (**int**, **long**, and so forth) has been reached.

Let's try a few more examples.

```
            int      aai[3][2]
```

is not a "two-dimensional array," though it can be used as such. To find out what it really is, apply the rules we just defined. The two sets of brackets are clearly at the same precedence level. They associate from left to right, however. We can parenthesize our declaration as

```
            int     ( aai[3] )[2]
```

Now, applying our rules, and working from the inside out, we get

```
        aai is...
        an array, 3 elements long, of...
        arrays,   2 elements long, of...
        int.
```

That is, *aai* is an array of arrays. The layout in memory is shown in figure 7-2.

There are a few subtle things going on in this figure. First is the assignment *ip = (int *) aai*. An array name evaluates to a pointer to the first element. Since *aai* is an array of arrays, the first element of *aai* is an *entire,* two-element, array. Ip, on the other hand, is declared as a pointer to a single **int**, not as a pointer to a two-element array. We get around this problem with a cast. A *cast* tells the compiler to perform a type conversion on a variable before it is used. We want to convert *aai* (which is a pointer to a two-element array of *int*) to a simple pointer-to-**int**. We form the cast by making a declaration of a variable of the required type, removing the variable name and the semicolon, and then surrounding the result with parentheses. Since an integer pointer can be declared

Fig. 7-2: An array of arrays

```
#define ROWSIZE 3
#define COLSIZE 2

int        aai[ ROWSIZE ][ COLSIZE ];
int        *ip ;

ip = (int *) aai;
*(ip + 2) = 6;

       ip:
       |--------|
100:   | 200 *  |
       |- - -|-|
             |
             |
       aai:  V
       |=======|
200:   |       |    aai[0][0] == *ip
       |- - - -|
202:   |       |    aai[0][1] == *(ip + 1)
       |=======|
204:   |   6   |    aai[1][0] == *(ip + 2) == *(ip + (COLSIZE * 1) + 0)
       |- - - -|
206:   |       |    aai[1][1] == *(ip + 3) == *(ip + (COLSIZE * 1) + 1)
       |=======|
208:   |       |    aai[2][0] == *(ip + 4) == *(ip + (COLSIZE * 2) + 0)
       |- - - -|
210:   |       |    aai[2][1] == *(ip + 5) == *(ip + (COLSIZE * 2) + 0)
       |=======|
       |       |


       ip == the contents of the cell at location 100        == 200

  ip + 2  == since ip points at an int, ip + 2 adds 4
            (2 * sizeof(int)) to the contents of ip. 200 + 4 == 204

 *(ip + 2) == the contents of the cell at location 204       == 6
```

```
int        *ip;
```

we can create a cast, using the foregoing procedure:

```
(int    *)
```

Preceding *aai* with this cast temporarily changes the type of *aai* to pointer to **int**. The contents of aai are not changed, just the way that the compiler handles *aai*.

Having initialized *ip* to point to the beginning of the array, we can now use it in interesting ways. First note that whenever an integer is accessed indirectly through a pointer, the compiler doesn't know what the object-pointed-to actually is. If all it has to go on is a pointer to one element, it can't differentiate between a two-by-three integer array and a six-element integer array. When *aai* is accessed directly, the compiler does know what it's looking at (because this information was specified in the declaration). The expressions *aai[1][1]* and *(ip + 3)* both reference the same cell. This can be useful if we want to initialize the array quickly. We can go through it as if it were a simple array. Since a compound array index (using the [ ]) requires three multiplies,[2] and incrementing a pointer requires none, we've gained considerable efficiency. *Aai* can be initialized using the loop in figure 7-3.

Fig. 7-3: Initializing a Multi-dimensional Array with a Simple Pointer

```
#define ROWSIZE 2
#define COLSIZE 3

int             aai[ ROWSIZE ][ COLSIZE ];
register int    *ip , i ;

for( i = ROWSIZE * COLSIZE, ip = (int *)aai;  --i >= 0;  *ip++ = 0)
     ;
```

Now look at how we actually access one element of *aai.* Remember that it's an array of two-element-long arrays. Consequently, *aai[x]* selects one of these two-element-long arrays. It selects an entire array. To get a single element, we need another set of brackets.

$$(\ aai[x] \ )[y]$$

selects a single integer in *aai* (the y'th element of the array referenced by *aai[x]*). Since brackets associate left to right anyway, we can dispense with the parentheses and just say *aai[x][y].*[3]

---

2.   To find the address of *aai[i][j]* the compiler has to do the following:

$$addr = aai + (i * COLSIZE * sizeof(int)) + (j * sizeof(int))$$

where *aai* is the base address of the array. Three multiplies and two additions are required.

3.   As was mentioned earlier, true random access into an array, using brackets, is a very inefficient operation. Moreover, most applications of large arrays don't actually require random access, you're usually going through the array in an orderly way: row by row, or column by column, or whatever. Consequently, you can usually come up with a way to access the array using pointers and constants that will be much more efficient than the double brackets.

We'll come back to arrays of arrays in a moment. Let's move on to another example:

```
int     **ppi;
```

Again, parenthesizing the declaration yields

```
int     *( *ppi );
```

Reading from inside outwards we get

```
ppi is...
a   pointer to...
a   pointer to...
an int.
```

Don't be confused by the two asterisks. In particular, don't think of *ppi* as an "**int** pointer pointer" which makes no sense in English, much less in C. *Ppi* is one, pointer-sized, object. In terms of space allocation, it's immaterial that it points at another pointer. *Ppi*, and the data structures needed to initialize it, are shown in figure 7-4.

Fig. 7-4: A Pointer to an Integer Pointer

```
int     i;
int     *pi;
int     **ppi;

ppi   = &pi; /* ppi gets the address of a  pointer-to-int */
pi    = &i;  /* pi  gets the address of an int            */
**ppi = 2;   /* put 2 into i                              */


            ppi:            pi:            i:
    100: |-------|    200: |-------|   300: |-------|
         | 200 *-|-------->| 300 *-|------->|   2   |
         |-------|         |-------|        |-------|


    &pi == the address of pi == 200
     &i == the address of  i == 300

    ppi == the contents of ppi                      == 200
   *ppi == the contents of the cell at location 200 == 300
  **ppi == the contents of the cell at location 300 == 2
```

As we've seen, the compiler can't distinguish between a pointer to a single object and a pointer to the first element of an array of these objects. In other words, when we're dealing with a pointer, there's no telling what the object-pointed-to really looks like. For example, *ppi* could also be a pointer to a pointer to an array. This situation is illustrated in figure 7-5.

Fig. 7-5: A Second Way to use ppi

```
int   iarray[3], **ppi, *pi ;

ppi = &pi;
pi  = iarray;
*( *ppi + 2 ) = 6;
```

```
ppi:                    pi:                 iarray:
|-------|       200: |-------|     300: |-------|
| 200 *-|------->| 300 *-|------>|       |
|-------|            |-------|          | - - - |
                               302: |       |
                                    | - - - |
                               304: |   6   |
                                    |-------|
```

```
    &pi          == the address of pi                        == 200
  iarray         == the address of the first element of iarray == 300

    ppi          == the contents of ppi                       == 200
   *ppi          == the contents of the cell at address 200   == 300
   *ppi + 2      == 300 + (2 * sizeof(int))                   == 304
 *( *ppi + 2 )   == the contents of the cell at address 304   == 6
```

There's another possibility. Again, since a pointer to one object can also point at an array of those objects, the middle pointer in the previous examples (*pi*) could also be an array (see figure 7-6). The moral? The compiler doesn't keep track of anything for you. It's your responsibility to remember whether a pointer points to an array or not.

Let's consider another use for pointers to pointers. Figure 7-7 shows the composition of *argv* and *argc*, the two default arguments to *main()*.[4] The *vectors* array is usually created by the root module when the program boots. It is assembled from the command line arguments and then passed to main via *argv*. The declaration for *vectors* parenthesizes to

---

4.   Whether or not you use them, *main()* always has two default arguments on the stack, *argv* and *argc*. We'll look at how these are used in a moment. In newer compilers there's often a third argument as well: *envp*. This last is a pointer to an array of string pointers, each of which holds an environment string. The last element in the array is NULL (so there's no *envc*). They are declared:

```
                    main( argc, argv, envp )
                    int     argc;
                    char    **argv;
                    char    **envp;
```

Fig. 7-6: Yet Another Way to use ppi

```
int    array_of_ints[3]
int    *array_of_ptr[3]
int    int0, int1;
int    **ppi;

ppi = array_of_ptr;
array_of_ptr[0] = &int0;
array_of_ptr[1] = &int1;
array_of_ptr[2] = array_of_ints;

**(ppi + 1) = 6;
*( *(ppi + 2) + 2) = 7;
```

```
                                         int0:
                               200: |-------|    |
ppi:          array_of_ptr:    +---->|       |    |
|-------|      100: |-------|    |    |-------|
| 100 *-|------->| 200 *-|---+      int1:
|-------|         |-------|    300: |-------|
              102: | 300 *-|---------->|   6   |
                  |-------|         |-------|
              104: | 400 *-|---+
                  |-------|    |  array_of_ints:
                               +-->|-------|
                          400: |       |
                               | - - - |
                          402: |       |
                               | - - - |
                          404: |   7   |
                               |-------|
```

```
      ppi        == the contents of ppi                        == 100
      ppi + 1    == 100 + sizeof(int)                           == 102
   *(ppi + 1)    == the contents of the cell at address 102     == 300
  **(ppi + 1)    == the contents of the cell at address 300     == 6

   ppi           == the contents of ppi                         == 100
   ppi + 2       == 100 + (2 * sizeof(int))                     == 104
  *(ppi + 2)     == the contents of the cell at address 104     == 400
  *(ppi + 2) + 2 == 400 * (2 * sizeof(int))                     == 404
*( *(ppi + 2) + 2) == the contents of the cell at address 404   == 7
```

```
      char      *(vectors[ ])...
```

Reading from the inside out,

```
      vectors is...
      an array (of indeterminate length)...
      of pointers to...
      char
```

The array length is defined by the initialization. Since there are three objects in the initializer list, *vectors* is three elements long. Each of these objects evalu-

---

Fig. 7-7: Argv

```
char      *vectors[ ] = { "first", "second", "third" };
char      **argv = vectors;
int       argc   = sizeof(vectors)/sizeof(*vectors) ;
                                       |-------------------------|
argv:                  vectors:     +-->|'f'|'i'|'r'|'s'|'t'|'\0'|
|-------|              |-------|     |   |-------------------------|
|   *---|------------->|   *---|---+
|-------|              |-------|        |---------------------------|
                       |   *---|------->|'s'|'e'|'c'|'o'|'n'|'d'|'\0'|
argc:                  |-------|        |---------------------------|
|-------|              |   *---|---+
|   3   |              |-------|    |   |-------------------------|
|-------|                          +-->|'t'|'h'|'i'|'r'|'d'|'\0'|
                                       |-------------------------|
```

Since argv points to the first element of vectors, the names *vectors*
and *argv* are interchangeable in the following five examples:

```
    *argv         ==  vectors[0]    ==  a pointer to the string "first"
   **argv         == *vectors[0]    ==  argv[0][0] == the character 'f'
   *(argv + 1)    ==  vectors[1]    ==  a pointer to the string "second"
  **(argv + 1)    == *vectors[1]    ==  argv[1][0] == the character 's'
*(*(argv + 1) +2) == *(vectors+1)[2] ==  argv[1][2] == the character 'c'
```

---

ates to a pointer to the first character in the string. The *vectors* variable is initialized with three *pointers,* not with three character arrays. Since vectors is an array of pointers, its name evaluates to a pointer to a pointer, so we can make the assignment to *argv* with no difficulty (since *argv* is also a pointer to a pointer). Finally, *argc* holds the number of elements in *argv*. The formula

```
        sizeof(vectors) / sizeof(*vectors)
```

evaluates to the size of the array, in bytes, divided by the size of the first element of the array, in bytes—to the number of elements.

Several examples of how to use *argv* are at the bottom of figure 7-7, and there are several more in subsequent figures. Since *argv* is a pointer to the first element of *vectors*, and an array name evaluates to a pointer to the first element of the array, *vectors* and *argv* can be used interchangeably in these examples.

Note that **argv* is the object-pointed-to by *argv*, the contents of vectors[0]. Since *argv* and *vectors* can be interchanged, we can also say *argv[0]*. Remember, the square bracket notation is just telling the compiler to add an offset to a pointer and fetch the object at the computed address. Since **argv* is a string pointer, we can print the string *first* with a *puts(*argv)* call.

The next expression accesses the second element of vectors by adding an offset of 1 to *argv*. **(argv + 1)*, **(vectors + 1)*, *argv[1]*, and *vectors[1]* all do this. The expression *puts(*(argv+1))* prints the string *second*. Argv isn't modified; the addition is done in a temporary scratch variable.

Since **argv* evaluates to the contents of the first element of *vectors,* **(*argv)* (the parentheses are not required) evaluates to the object-pointed-to by the first element of *vectors,* to the character 'f' in "first." Similarly, since **(argv+1)* is the second element of the *vectors* array, ***(argv+1)* is the object-pointed-to by the second element of *vectors,* to the character 's' in "second."

Finally we come to **(*(argv+1)+2)*. Working from the inside out, **(argv+1)* is the object-pointed-to by *argv*, after an offset of one object has been added to it. It evaluates to the second element of *vectors* (*vectors[1]*). *Vectors[1]* is a pointer to the first character in "second" (to the 's'). Adding 2 to this pointer creates a pointer to the third character in "second" (to the 'c'). But so far, we just have a pointer to the 'c'. Adding the the leftmost * yields the 'c' itself. So *putchar(*(*(argv+1)+2))* prints a 'c'. This example is detailed in figure 7-8. Figure 7-9 shows the same example, but with actual addresses inserted.

Fig. 7-8: *(*(argv+1) +2)

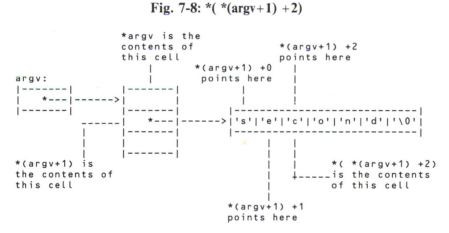

Fig. 7-9: *(*(argv+1) +2) Shown With Addresses

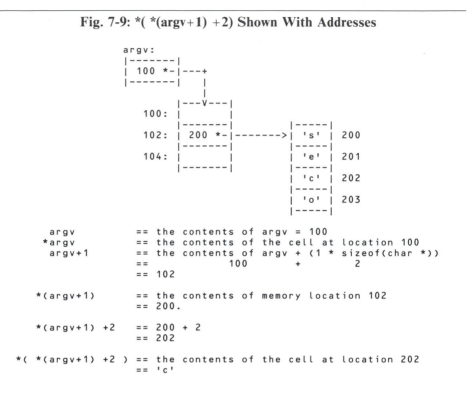

```
          argv                == the contents of argv = 100
         *argv                == the contents of the cell at location 100
          argv+1              == the contents of argv + (1 * sizeof(char *))
                              ==             100      +         2
                              == 102

        *(argv+1)             == the contents of memory location 102
                              == 200.

        *(argv+1) +2          == 200 + 2
                              == 202

    *( *(argv+1) +2 )         == the contents of the cell at location 202
                              == 'c'
```

Since *(ptr + i) can be represented as ptr[i], we can simplify this statement considerably. Applying the rule once, we get this:

```
        *(      ptr    +i) ==      ptr    [i];
        *( *(argv+1)   +2) ==  *(argv+1) [2]
```

Applying it once more yields the following:

```
        *(      ptr    +i)      ==      ptr    [i];
        *(      argv   +1) [2]  ==      argv   [1]  [2]
```

Curiously, we're using the same notation to access a string via two pointers
that we'd use to access a two-dimensional array. And argv is nothing like a
two-dimensional array. All the more proof that arrays don't really exist as
such. The square-bracket notation is really just shorthand for complex expressions involving pointers and offsets; argv[1][2] is certainly easier to read than
((argv+1)+2).

Since *argv* is a variable, it can be modified, as can the various contents of *vectors.* Figure 7-10 shows the effect of

```
++ * ++argv;
```

This one expression, parenthesized to *++(*(++argv)), does two things. The innermost ++ is attached to *argv* itself. Consequently, *argv* is incremented to point to *vectors[1]*. Because it's a preincrement (the ++ precedes the name), all subsequent operations use this new value of *argv*. The * is evaluated next, so the outer ++ is applied to *argv* (after the increment). Again, it's a pre-increment, so the object-pointed-to by the incremented *argv* is itself incre-mented. (It now points at the character 'e' in "second.") A second * would be required to access the 'e' through the pointer. The operation is illustrated in figure 7-10.

Of the examples at the bottom of figure 7-10, the only ones we haven't seen yet are the last two. The expression ***(argv-1)* subtracts an offset of one from the current value of *argv*, creating a pointer to *vectors[0]*; **(argv-1)* is the object-pointed-to by *(argv-1),* the object whose address is derived by subtract-ing the size of one object from argv. The expression ***(argv-1)* is the object-pointed-to by *vectors[0],* the character 'f' in "first." Note that the -1 can also be used in the brackets to represent a negative offset (as in **argv[-1]* or *argv[-1][0]).*

The last example in figure 7-10 uses -1 differently. Here the -1 is applied to **argv* (the object-pointed-to by *argv*) not to *argv* itself. Since **argv* is a pointer to the 'e' in "second," *(*argv)-1* is a pointer to the character that pre-cedes the 'e' (the 's'). Finally, **((*argv)-1)* is the object at that address, the 's' itself.

Fig. 7-10: Incrementing Argv

After performing the following instruction:

```
++ * ++argv          ==        ++( *( ++argv ) )
```

Argv and vectors have the following relationship:

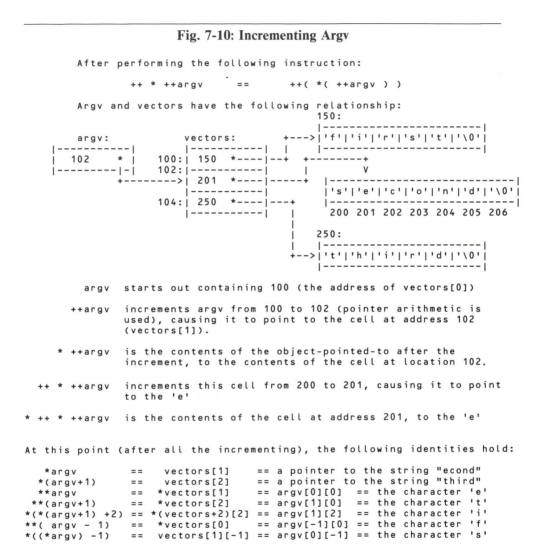

```
argv    starts out containing 100 (the address of vectors[0])

++argv  increments argv from 100 to 102 (pointer arithmetic is
        used), causing it to point to the cell at address 102
        (vectors[1]).

* ++argv  is the contents of the object-pointed-to after the
          increment, to the contents of the cell at location 102.

++ * ++argv  increments this cell from 200 to 201, causing it to point
             to the 'e'

* ++ * ++argv  is the contents of the cell at address 201, to the 'e'
```

At this point (after all the incrementing), the following identities hold:

```
   *argv           ==     vectors[1]     == a pointer to the string "econd"
  *(argv+1)        ==     vectors[2]     == a pointer to the string "third"
  **argv           ==    *vectors[1]     == argv[0][0]   == the character 'e'
 **(argv+1)        ==    *vectors[2]     == argv[1][0]   == the character 't'
*(*(argv+1) +2)    == *(vectors+2)[2]    == argv[1][2]   == the character 'i'
 **( argv - 1)     ==    *vectors[0]     == argv[-1][0]  == the character 'f'
*((*argv) -1)      ==    vectors[1][-1]  == argv[0][-1]  == the character 's'
```

Let's move on to another example:

```
int     (* pai)[3] ;
```

Here we've supplied the parentheses as part of the declaration. Looking at the innermost set of parentheses first, we see that

```
pai is...
a pointer to...
an array, three elements long, of...
ints.
```

Again, remember that we've only declared a single pointer. (It will eventually point to an array, but it doesn't as of yet.) *Pai*, is initialized in figure 7-11.[5]

Fig. 7-11: Initializing a Pointer to an Array of Ints

```
int       (* pai)[3];      /* Declare the pointer. */
int       ai[3];           /* Declare the array.   */

pai       = ai;            /* Initialize it.       */
**pai     = 0;             /* And use it.          */
(*pai)[1] = 1;
*(*pai + 2) = 2;
```

```
Which looks like:
              +
    pai:      |       ai:
|-------|     |  100: |-------|
| 100 *-|-->|       |   0   |   ai[0] == (*pai)[0] == **pai;
|-------|     |       |- - - -|
              |  102: |   1   |   ai[1] == (*pai)[1] == *( pai + 1 )
              |       |- - - -|
              |  104: |   2   |   ai[2] == (*pai)[2] == *( pai + 2 )
              +       |-------|
```

Since *pai* is a pointer to an *array*, the object-pointed-to (**pai*) is the entire array, not any single element of the array.[6] To access a single element of the array, we must "index off of" (apply the square bracket notation to)

---

5.   We could also have initialized *ai* and *pai* with

```
int   ai[3] = {0, 1, 2};
int   (* pai)[3] = ai;
```

6.   For this reason, many compilers (the Microsoft compiler, for instance) will complain about the following assignment:

```
pai = ai;
```

The problem here is that ai, being an array name, evaluates to a pointer to the first element of the array, that is a pointer to an **int**. Since *pai* is a pointer to an array, rather than to a single **int**, the compiler thinks there's a type mismatch. You can get around the problem with a cast—in other words casting *ai* into a pointer to a three-element-long array:

```
pai = (int (*)[3]) ai;
```

pai, not *pai*. Since the brackets are of higher precedence than the asterisk, the parentheses are required. We can access ai[1] with (*pai)[1].

Let's take this a step further. The first element of the array (ai[0]) can be accessed with *(*pai)[0]*; you'll remember, though, that any time we see a *[0]* to the right of a pointer, we can replace it with a * to the left of the pointer. Consequently, *(*pai)[0]* can also be accessed by ****pai*! Since the rule we just applied is a degraded case of

```
p[i] == *(p + i)
```

we can substitute **pai* for *p* in this equation to get:

```
(*pai)[i] == *( (*pai) + i )
```

Let's look at this example again, attacking it from a different angle. All expressions in C evaluate to something, and that something is of a definite type. *Pai* evaluates to its contents, to the number 100. *Pai* is of type pointer-to-array-of-**int**, so **pai* is the object-pointed-to by a pointer-to-array-of-**int**, the array itself. **pai* is then of type "array-of-**int**." An array is usually referenced by its name, and this name evaluates to a pointer to one element of the array. In this example, **pai* references an entire array. Consequently, **pai* evaluates as if it were an array name, to a pointer to the first element of the array, to the address of the first element of the array, to 100. *Pai* (by itself) and **pai* (with the *) both evaluate to the same number: 100. However, *pai* (by itself) is of type pointer-to-array-of-**int**, while **pai* (with the *) is of type array-of-**int**. Since **pai* is of type array-of-**int**, ***pai* is of type **int**, and it evaluates to the contents of the first element of the array.

There is another interesting property of *pai*. Since the object-pointed-to is the entire array, the size of that object is the size of the entire array in bytes. Pointer arithmetic is used when we increment *pai,* so the size of the object-pointed-to (of the entire array) is added to the contents of *pai*. Assuming a 2-byte **int**, the size of a three-element-long integer array is 6. Incrementing *pai* causes it to skip past the entire array, as shown in figure 7-12. This behavior starts making sense when applied to arrays of arrays (see figure 7-13). Here, *pai* is incremented to point past the first subarray to the second subarray.

Let's apply what we just learned about *pai* to the two-dimensional array itself. *Aai[x]* (with only one set of brackets) references an entire three-element array. Consequently, it can be used as if it were a *pointer* to a three-element array. *Pai* can be initialized to point to the second element of the array by saying

---

Fig. 7-12: Incrementing a Pointer to an Array of Ints

```
int       (* pai)[3];       /* Declare the pointer. */
int       ai[3];            /* Declare the array.   */
pai = ai;                   /* Initialize pai       */
++pai;                      /* Does the following:  */

        pai:                        ai:
        |-------|                   |-------|
        |   *---|--+                |   0   |
        |-------|  |                |- - - -|
                   |                |   1   |
                   |                |- - - -|
                   |                |   2   |
                   |                |-------|
                +--->|                   |
```

Fig. 7-13: Pointer to an Array of Ints used in Arrays of Arrays

```
int       (* pai)[3];       /* Declare the pointer  */
int       aai[2][3];        /* Declare the array    */
++pai;                      /* Does the following:  */

pai:                aai:
|-------|           |-------|
|   *---|--+        |       |    aai[0][0]
|-------|  |        |- - - -|
           |        |       |    aai[0][1]
           |        |- - - -|
           |        |       |    aai[0][2]
           |        |=-=-=-=|
        +--->|       |    aai[1][0] == (*pai)[0] == **pai
           |        |- - - -|
           |        |       |    aai[1][1] == (*pai)[1]
           |        |- - - -|
           |        |       |    aai[1][2] == (*pai)[2]
           |        |-------|
```

```
        pai = aai[1] ;
```

In other words, since *aai* is a compound array, the array name with one set of brackets evaluates to a pointer to an entire subarray. Since a reference to an entire array evaluates to a pointer to the first element of that array, *aai[i]* also evaluates to the type pointer-to-pointer-to-**int**. Moreover, this partial reference can itself be used as a pointer. In other words, we can extend our identity

```
                              *(p + i)  ==  p[i]
```

to

```
    p[ ]...[ ][i] ==  (p[ ]...[ ]) [i]  ==  *( (p[ ]...[ ]) + i )
```

Let's look at it another way. The identity can be applied continuously until we run out of square brackets:

```
        aai[i][j]  ==  *( (aai[i]) + j)  ==  *( *(aai + i) + j )
```

The various relationships are shown in figure 7-14. Any pointer to a three-element array can be used in place of *aai* in these examples.

Fig. 7-14: An Array of Arrays

```
#define ROWSIZE 2
#define COLSIZE 3

int       aai[ ROWSIZE ][ COLSIZE ];

aai[i][j]  ==  *( (aai[i]) + j)  ==  *( *(aai + i) + j )

aai:
|-------|
|       |   aai[0][0] == *(  aai[0] )       == **aai ;
|- - - -|
|       |   aai[0][1] == *( (aai[0]) + 1 ) == *( *aai        + 1 )
|- - - -|
|       |   aai[0][2] == *( (aai[0]) + 2 ) == *( *aai        + 2 )
|=-=-=-=|
|       |   aai[1][0] == *(  aai[1] )       == *( *(aai + 1) + 0 )
|- - - -|
|       |   aai[1][1] == *( (aai[1]) + 1 ) == *( *(aai + 1) + 1 )
|- - - -|
|       |   aai[1][2] == *( (aai[1]) + 2 ) == *( *(aai + 1) + 2 )
|-------|
```

Again, all these parentheses and asterisks drive home the utility of the square bracket notation. To my mind *aai[1][2]* is much more readable than *(*(aai+1)+2)*. On the other hand, the second expression is closer to what the compiler is actually doing.

7.2. Function Pointers

C supports another kind of pointer—a pointer to a function. Just as

```
        int     (* array)[ ];
```

declares a pointer to an array of **int**,

```
int        (* pfi)( ) ;
```

declares a pointer to a function that returns an **int**. The parentheses are required in both declarations; without them, *array* would be an array of pointers, and *pfi* would be a function returning a pointer to an **int**. As we've seen, an array name always evaluates to the address of the first element of the array. Similarly, a function name always evaluates to the address of the first line of code in a function. This address can be put into a function pointer, which can then be used to call the function indirectly. Figure 7-15 shows how this is done.

Fig. 7-15: A Pointer to a Function

```
int        foo( a, b )
{
        /* ... */
}

main( )
{
        int        (* pfi)( );
        int        x, y;

        /* ... */

        pfi = foo;                  /* Initialize pfi to point to foo */
        (* pfi)( x, y );            /* Same as: foo(x, y);            */
}
```

Note that there are no parentheses following *foo()* in the assignment *pfi = foo.* If parentheses were present, foo would be called and *pfi* would be initialized to hold whatever value *foo()* returned. Without the parentheses, the subroutine name evaluates to its address (just like an array name without the square brackets evaluates to its address), and the subroutine is not called.[7] A function is called indirectly through a pointer with:

```
(* pfi)( args );
```

"Call the function whose address is contained in *pfi.*" The parentheses are required here too. It's easiest to show why with an example:

---

7.   A bug in early releases of Lattice C forces you to say *pfi* = &*foo.* The & shouldn't be required.

```
extern   int       *funct( );

x = *funct( );
```

Here, the declaration can be parenthesized as follows:

```
extern   int       *( funct( ) );
```

So *funct* is a function...that returns a pointer...to an **int**. The statement
$x = $ *funct()* puts into x the contents of the object-pointed-to by the pointer
that *funct()* returns. That is, *funct()* returns the address of an **int** and *funct()*
evaluates to that **int**.

Function pointers are different than other pointers in that you can't have
an array of functions. (You can have an array of function pointers, but not of
the functions themselves.) Consequently, it's illegal to increment a function
pointer. (In fact all pointer arithmetic is illegal on function pointers.)

Note that a function pointer is implied every time the parentheses are
not appended to a function name. For example, if the subroutines *laurel()*
and *hardy()* take the same arguments, you can say:

```
extern int       laurel( ), hardy( );

( *(condition ? laurel : hardy)  )( arg1, arg2, arg3 );
```

Here, either *laurel()* or *hardy()* will be called, depending on whether the condition is true. In either case, the same arguments will be passed to the called
function. The conditional itself evaluates to a function pointer because its
arguments are subroutine names without the parentheses. The * then causes
the function to be called indirectly through its pointer. The line could be restated as follows:

```
extern int       laurel( ), hardy( );
int              (* ptr)( );

ptr = condition ? laurel : hardy ;

( *ptr  )( arg1, arg2, arg3 );
```

Note here that the parentheses in a subroutine call are an operator.
They are not part of the subroutine name. That is, the parentheses operator
can be applied to any function pointer in order to generate a subroutine call.
A subroutine name evaluates to a pointer to a function, just as an array name
evaluates to a pointer to the first element of the array. The parentheses operator can be applied to any pointer to a function, just as the square brackets can
be applied to any pointer to an array element.

Function pointers have several uses. Among these are jump tables, look-
up tables (an array of structures in which one field is a key and another field is
a pointer to a function to call when that key is encountered), and object-
oriented programming (a function can hold specific knowledge about a

particular object, and that knowledge can be passed to a subroutine via a pointer to the function).

A good example of this last use is *ssort()*, a general-purpose Shell sort subroutine, modeled after the UNIX qsort( ). Before looking at the general-purpose version, we'll look at one tailored to sorting *argv: argv_sort()* (see figure 7-16).

If you're not familiar with how Shell Sort works, review the description in Appendix B before continuing.

Fig. 7-16: A Nongeneral-purpose Shell Sort

```
 1 void      argv_sort( argc, argv )
 2 int       argc;
 3 char      **argv;
 4 {
 5            /* Sort argv using a Shell sort */
 6
 7            register int     i, j;
 8            int              gap, k;
 9            char             **p1, **p2, *tmp ;
10
11            for( gap = argc >>1 ;  gap > 0  ; gap >>=1 )
12                    for( i = gap; i < argc; i++ )
13                            for( j = i-gap; j >= 0 ; j -= gap )
14                            {
15                                    p1 = argv +   j;
16                                    p2 = argv + ( j+gap );
17
18                                    if( strcmp( *p1, *p2 ) <= 0 )
19                                            break;
20
21                                    tmp = *p1;     /* Swap two elements */
22                                    *p1 = *p2;
23                                    *p2 = tmp;
24                            }
25 }
```

Argv_sort is a Shell sort tailored to sort *argv*. *P1* and *p2* are pointers to the two elements being considered during a single pass. These two pointers are initialized on lines 15 and 16 of figure 7-16. Remember that pointer arithmetic is used so *argv+j* evaluates to the address of *argv[j]*. Similarly, *argv+(j+gap)* evaluates to the address of *argv[j+gap]*. The two elements are compared using *strcmp()*, which returns a negative value if **p1 < *p2*, a zero if **p1 == *p2*, and a positive value if **p1 > *p2*. Note that *p1* and *p2* are pointers into the *argv* array; consequently, they're pointers to character pointers. *Strcmp()* requires simple character pointers as arguments, so one level of indirection must be removed in the *strcmp()* call. The two elements are swapped on lines 21 through 23.

The basic Shell sort can be made truly general purpose (so that we can sort arrays of anything: arrays of pointers, arrays of structures, and so on). Two changes are needed to give *argv_sort()* this capability. First, we need to tell it the size of one cell of the array in bytes. In *argv_sort()*, this information is implicit in the array declaration. That is, since *base* is defined as an array of character pointers, the compiler knows that every element of the array is character-pointer-sized and can perform the pointer arithmetic correctly. The general-purpose routine can't do this because it doesn't know the size of one element at compile time, it won't have this information until run time. Thus, we have to pass the size of one element into the sort routine as a parameter and do the pointer arithmetic ourselves.

The second piece of information needed by the general-purpose routine is a pointer to a comparison routine. Since *argv_sort()* knew that it was sorting *argv*, it could call *strcmp()* directly. *Ssort()* can't do this because it knows nothing about the object being sorted except its size.

We need a comparison routine to replace *strcmp()*, one that knows what an element of the array looks like and can compare two such elements. Since this comparison function will change with every kind of array being sorted, we'll pass a pointer to it to the sort routine. We'll have to write a different comparison function for every kind of array that we want to sort. The comparison function will be passed pointers to two array elements but should otherwise act like *strcmp()*.

When sorting *argv* with *ssort()*, the comparison function will be passed two pointers to elements of *argv*. It removes one level of indirection and calls *strcmp()* to do the comparison. When sorting an array of **ints**, the comparison function is passed two pointers to **ints** and compares the **ints** themselves (indirectly via the pointer). When sorting an array of structures, the comparison function is passed two pointers to structures and compares the key fields of the structures. These three situations are illustrated in figures 7-17, 7-18, and 7-19. *Ssort()* itself is shown in figure 7-20.

The changes we just discussed are all incorporated here. *Base* is declared as a character pointer on line 2. Since a **char** is 1 byte wide, pointer arithmetic on a character pointer is normal arithmetic. The size of an object-pointed-to by a pointer to **char** is 1. So, when we initialize *p1* and *p2* (on lines 29 and 30), we can do the pointer arithmetic ourselves, using the *width* parameter as the size of 1 element of the array. In *argv_sort()*, the compiler did this multiply for us, using normal pointer arithmetic. Instead of using *strcmp()*, *ssort()* uses the comparison function that we supplied, calling it indirectly on line 32. Finally, the two objects must be swapped 1 byte at a time (because we don't know the size of one element until run time). This

---

Fig. 7-17: Using ssort( ) to Sort an Array of Ints

```
Given:
        int         array[ 10 ];

        cmp( ip1, ip2 )
        int         *ip1, *ip2;
        {
                return *ip1 - *ip2 ;
        }

The array can be sorted with:

        ssort( array, 10, sizeof(int), cmp );
```

Fig. 7-18: Using ssort( ) to Sort argv

```
cmp( cpp1, cpp2 )
char        **cpp1, **cpp2;
{
        return strcmp( *cpp1, *cpp2 );
}

main( argc, argv )
int         argc;
char        **argv;
{
        ssort( ++argv, --argc, sizeof(*argv), cmp );

        while( --argc >= 0 )
                printf("%s\n", *argv++ );
}
```

---

swapping is accomplished with the **for** loop on lines 35 through 40.

7.3. Going in the Other Direction

So far we've only looked at how to interpret complex declarations. This section has a few examples of how to go in the other direction and declare variables. The process is identical to the one we've been using, except that all the steps are reversed. To declare a variable

---

Fig. 7-19: Using ssort( ) to Sort an Array of Structures

```
Given:

            typedef struct
            {
                    int       key, element1, element2, etc;
            }
            ELEMENT;


            ELEMENT array[10];


            compare( e1, e2 )
            ELEMENT *e1, *e2;
            {
                    return( e1->key - e2->key );
            }

The array can be sorted with:

            ssort( array, 10, sizeof(ELEMENT), compare );
```

---

(1) Write a description of what you're declaring. If the data structure is complex enough, draw a picture; it's always helpful to see what you're doing. In the picture, circle the name of the object that you're actually declaring.

(2) Write down the name of the object. If that object is a pointer, put an asterisk to the left of the name; if it's an array, put brackets to the right and put a number in the brackets. Finally, parenthesize what you've just written.

(3) Continue this process, working away from the name. If you've drawn a picture you'll also be working in the direction of the pointer-reference arrows.

A few examples: A variable named *papa* that is a pointer to an array of pointers to arrays of **int**s is declared as follows:

Fig. 7-20: Ssort( ): A General-purpose Sort Routine

```
1 void      ssort( base, nel, width, cmp )
2 char      *base;
3 int       nel, width;
4 int       (*cmp)( );
5 {
6           /*        A general purpose Shell sort:
7            *
8            *        Base .. is the base address of the array to be sorted.
9            *        nel ... is the number of elements in the array,
10           *        width . is the width of one element in bytes, and
11           *        cmp ... is a pointer to a comparison function which,
12           *                when called with
13           *                        x = (*cmp)( a, b )
14           *                where a and b are pointers to two elements in
15           *                the array, should return:
16           *                        x <  0     if    a <  b
17           *                        x == 0     if    a == b
18           *                        x >  0     if    a >  b
19           */
20
21          register int    i, j;
22          int             gap, k, tmp ;
23          char            *p1, *p2;
24
25          for( gap = nel >>1 ;  gap > 0  ; gap >>=1 )
26                  for( i = gap; i < nel; i++ )
27                      for( j = i-gap; j >= 0 ; j -= gap )
28                      {
29                              p1 = base + ( j       * width);
30                              p2 = base + ((j+gap) * width);
31
32                              if( (*cmp)( p1, p2 ) <= 0 )
33                                      break;
34
35                              for( k = width; --k >= 0 ;)
36                              {
37                                      tmp   = *p1;
38                                      *p1++ = *p2;
39                                      *p2++ = tmp;
40                              }
41                      }
42 }
```

	Write the name.
papa	
	It's a pointer, so add an asterisk and parenthesize.
(*papa)	
	Papa is a pointer to what? An array, so add the brackets and parenthesize.
((*papa)[ ])	
	Arrays of what? Pointers, so add another asterisk and parenthesize.

```
(*((*papa)[ ]))
                              Pointers to what? Arrays, so a
                              second set of brackets is needed.
(*((*papa)[ ]))[ ]
                              Arrays of what? Ints, so write
                              the word int and we're done.
int (*((*papa)[ ])[ ]
```

In this example, all of the parentheses are actually required because the asterisk is of lower precedence than the brackets.

Another example: To declare a variable called *too_complex* that is a pointer to an array of pointers to functions returning pointers to **long**s, do the following:

```
                              Write the name.
too_complex
                              It's a pointer, so add an asterisk.
(*too_complex)
                              A pointer to an array, so add
                              brackets.
((*too_complex)[])
                              An array of pointers, so add
                              another asterisk.
(*((*too_complex)[]))
                              Pointers to functions, so add
                              a set of parentheses to signify
                              function.
(*((*too_complex)[]))()
                              Functions returning pointers, so
                              add another asterisk. Since the ()
                              needed for function are of higher
                              precedence than *, we don't
                              need another set of parentheses
                              here.
*(*((*too_complex)[]))()
                              Pointers to longs, so add the
                              word long
long   *(*((*too_complex)[]))()
```

One final example: Because of our inside-out declaration syntax, a function that returns a pointer to a function must be declared in an odd way. To declare a function that returns a pointer to a function, that in turn returns a **double** (that is, the function-pointed-to returns a **double**), do the following:

```
                              Write the name.
funct
                              Funct is a function, with two
                              arguments, a and b.
funct(a, b)
                              It is a function that returns a
                              pointer, so add an asterisk.
                              Parentheses aren't required because
                              ( ) is of higher precedence than *.
*funct(a, b)
                              But the return value is a pointer to a
                              function. Parentheses are required here.
(*funct(a,b))( )
                              Finally, the function-pointed-to by
                              the return value of funct returns
                              a double.
double (*funct(a,b))( )
                              Now, declare the types of the function
                              arguments as usual.
double (*funct(a,b))( )
int a,b;
{
}
```

7.4. Typedefs

Very complex declarations are generally not a good idea. They're too hard to interpret (and to declare). It's preferable to use a system of **typedef**s to create intermediate types that are in turn used to declare the complex type. A **typedef** is used to define a new type in terms of previously defined types. For example, a type for "array of 10 **int**s" can be created with

```
typedef int      INTARRAY[10];
```

The syntax is identical to the normal variable-declaration syntax except that the declaration is preceded by the word **typedef**. *INTARRAY* is now a real type and it can be used to declare variables as in:

```
INTARRAY      array;
```

and

```
struct
{
        int       key;
        INTARRAY array;
}foo;
```

The expression **sizeof**(*INTARRAY*) evaluates to 20 (the size of 10 **int**s).

We can also use the INTARRAY type to create other types. If we want to create an array of twenty, 10-element arrays, we can say

```
typedef INTARRAY      2D[ 20 ];
```

2D's are 20-element-long arrays of *INTARRAY*s and each of these *INTARRAY*s are 10-element-long arrays. We can use this same procedure to redeclare the *papa* array that we declared earlier. (It's a pointer to an array of pointers to arrays of **int**s.)

```
typedef int        AI [10];     /* Array of 10 ints.                  */
typedef AI        *( API [20] ); /* Array of 20 pointers to arrays    */
                                 /* of 10 ints.                       */
API               *papa;         /* Pointer to above.                 */
```

Another good use of **typedef**s is for objects like pointers to functions that have a confusing declaration syntax. For example

```
typedef int      (* PFI)( );
```

creates a type for "pointer to function returning **int**." An array of pointers to functions can now be declared with

```
PFI       functions[ 20 ];
```

rather than the more confusing

```
int       (*functions[20])( );
```

A pointer to an array of function pointers can be declared with

```
PFI       (*pfunct)[ ];
```

rather than

```
int       ( *(*pfunct)[ ] )( );
```

A **typedef** is particularly useful in a cast

```
(PFI) xp
```

is much more readable than

```
(int (*)( )) xp
```

A **typedef** is also useful for structure definitions, as in

```
typedef struct  _tnode
{
        char     *key;
        struct  _tnode  *right ;
        struct  _tnode  *left  ;
} LEAF;
```

LEAF can be used to do things like

```
LEAF      *root;
LEAF      heap[10];

root      = (LEAF *) malloc( sizeof(LEAF) );
```

7.5. Using Pointers to Talk to Hardware

7.5.1. Absolute Memory Addressing

Absolute memory addresses can also be accessed through pointers. For example, the number 10 could be put into absolute memory location 0x80 with

```
char    *p;
p   = (char *) 0x80;
*p  = 10 ;
```

P is a simple character pointer, initialized with the number 0x80. Since a pointer holds an address, *p* is now pointing to address 0x80. The cast [*(char *)0x80*] is required by many compilers. This cast tells the compiler to treat the number 0x80 (which is an **int**) as if it were the contents of a character pointer. **p=10* puts the number 10 into address 0x80. Since *p* is a pointer to **char**, only a **char**-sized area of memory (1 byte) is modified. Had *p* been declared an **int** pointer, 2 bytes would have been modified.

This example is more complicated than it need be. Since *p* is initialized and then used immediately, we can actually dispense with it entirely, substituting *(char *)0x80* for the *p* in **p = 10* to yield

```
*( (char *)0x80 ) = 10;
```

Again, it's the cast that makes this possible. We're telling the compiler to treat 0x80 as if it were the contents of a character pointer.

More complicated data structures, such as memory-mapped video displays, can be accessed in this way. For example, on a 68000, a memory mapped 80-column by 25-line display can be seen as a two-dimensional array. Assuming a base address for the display of 0x10000, the character in the upper left corner of the screen is at 0x10000, the next character is at location 0x10001, and so on. You can compute the location of any character with

```
#define addr(row,col) ((char *)0x10000 + (row * 80) + col)
```

where the top left corner is at (0,0). The whole expression evaluates to a character pointer. Alternately, you could say the following:

```
#define NUMROWS 25
#define NUMCOLS 80

typedef char    DISPLAY[ NUMROWS ][ NUMCOLS ]
#define SCREEN  ( *((DISPLAY  *)0x10000) )

SCREEN[ 2 ][ 3 ] = 'a';
```

Here, we make a typedef for a 80x25 character array. Then the number 0x10000 is cast into a pointer to an array of this type. So, *(DISPLAY *)0x10000* is a pointer to an array, adding another asterisk gives us the array itself (the object-pointed-to by the array pointer) and we can apply brackets to reference one element of the array. Note that some compilers get very confused when pointer operations become this complex. Code like this, though useful, is not necessarily portable.

7.5.2. Directly Accessing the IBM PC Video Memory from C

Direct memory addressing is not as easy on the 8086 family CPUs. In most compilers, if you try to use *((char*)0x80) in the 8086 small model, you'll access the cell at offset 0x80 from the current Data Segment, not the cell at absolute address 0000:0080. Accessing a cell outside the current Data Segment can be complex. Moreover, this process is very compiler-dependent.

Nevertheless, casting a number into a pointer is possible. Let's do the above example again, this time writing directly to the screen on an IBM PC, equipped with a monochrome adapter. This code is for the Microsoft C Compiler (Version 3 or higher). The program shown in figure 7-21 writes the characters '1', '2', '3', and '4' in the four corners of the screen. The 1, 2, 3, and 4 are displayed in normal, underlined, boldface (high intensity), and blinking modes, respectively.

There are several problems to solve in this program. First, every character on the IBM display requires 2 bytes. The low byte is the character and the high byte is the attribute. We'd like to be able to modify either character or attribute without affecting the other, so we create the typedef for *CHARACTER,* a structure with two byte-sized fields, one for the character itself and the second for the attributes. Since the 8086 stores the low-order byte of a 16-bit word at the lower address, the character field must be declared first within the structure. Next, we create a second typedef called *DISPLAY*, a 25x80 array of *CHARACTER*s. Finally, we create a #**define** for *SCREEN*, casting the base address of the video memory into a pointer to a *DISPLAY*, and then adding another asterisk to reference the *DISPLAY* through that pointer. This last syntax is identical to that used in the previous example; the object-pointed-to by a pointer-to-array is the array itself, and the square bracket notation can be applied to the cast constant as if it were an array name.

A few idiosyncrasies of the Microsoft Compiler come into play here. The keyword *far* is unique to this compiler. It's used to create a 32-bit *far pointer* in a small-model program. A far pointer can reference any location in memory, unlike a 16-bit *near pointer* which can only access data within the current Data Segment. Microsoft stores its far pointers with the segment address in the high-order (16-bit) word and the offset in the low-order word. Video memory in an IBM is at absolute address 0xb0000. Since the segment address is a paragraph address (that is, it has to be multiplied by 16 to derive the absolute address), 0xb0000 can be represented to the 8086 in

Fig. 7-21: Writing to the IBM PC's Memory-mapped Display

```
#define NORMAL          0x07     /* Basic attributes. Only one  */
#define UNDERLINED      0x01     /* of these may be present.    */
#define REVERSE         0x70

#define BLINKING        0x80     /* May be ORed with the above  */
#define BOLD            0x08     /* and with each other         */

typedef struct
{
        char    letter;
        char    attribute;
}
CHARACTER;

typedef CHARACTER       DISPLAY[25][80];

#define SCREEN  ( *( (DISPLAY far *)0xb0000000 ))

main( )
{
        SCREEN[ 0  ][ 0  ].letter = '1' ;
        SCREEN[ 24 ][ 0  ].letter = '2' ;
        SCREEN[ 0  ][ 79 ].letter = '3' ;
        SCREEN[ 24 ][ 79 ].letter = '4' ;

        SCREEN[ 0  ][ 0  ].attribute = NORMAL               ;
        SCREEN[ 24 ][ 0  ].attribute = UNDERLINED           ;
        SCREEN[ 0  ][ 79 ].attribute = REVERSE | BOLD       ;
        SCREEN[ 24 ][ 79 ].attribute = NORMAL  | BLINKING ;
}
```

segment:offset form as B000:0000. All 8 digits are required to initialize the far pointer, so we have to say

```
( *( (DISPLAY far *)0xb0000000 ) )
```

The outermost set of parentheses are required here (they weren't needed in the previous example) because we're using the expression to reference a structure. Since * is of lower precedence than the dot (.), the expression wouldn't evaluate properly without these extra parentheses.

Given all this preparation, we can use *SCREEN* to access the screen. *SCREEN[0][0]* is the upper left corner, *SCREEN[24][0]* is the lower left corner, *SCREEN[0][79]* is the upper right, and *SCREEN[24][79]* is the lower right. The character is referenced by

```
SCREEN[row][col].character
```

The attribute is referenced as follows:

```
                    SCREEN[row][col].attribute
```

The various attributes supported by the monochrome adapter are **#define**d as *NORMAL*, *UNDERLINED*, and *REVERSE*. In addition, any of these may be bitwise ORed with *BLINKING* or *BOLD* as needed (to get a blinking, bold faced, underlined character for example). Unfortunately, you can't have an underlined, reverse-video character.[8]

7.5.3. Using Structures to Model Hardware

In a memory-mapped I/O system, any piece of hardware controlled by a contiguous block of registers can also be modeled as a structure. A memory map for a SCSI disk controller host adapter is shown in figure 7-22. This controller can be represented as the structure defined in figure 7-23.

Fig. 7-22: A SCSI Host Adapter

```
offset from
base address of
device:
        |---------------|
    0:  |  cmd register |
        |---------------|
    1:  |  unused       |
        |---------------|---------------|
    2:  |  unused                       |
        |-------------------------------|-------------------|
    4:  |  pointer to data to transfer                      |
        |---------------------------------------------------|
    8:  |  pointer to SCSI command block                    |
        |---------------------------------------------------|

        |    1st byte   |   2d byte    | 3rd byte | 4th byte |
```

---

8. More information about the IBM display can be found in Peter Norton, *The Peter Norton Programmer's Guide to the IBM PC* (Bellevue, Wash.: Microsoft Press, 1985) pp. 67–97.

Fig. 7-23: The Host Adapter Defined as a Structure

```
typedef char    BYTE;           /*  8 bits     */
typedef short   WORD;           /* 16 bits     */
typedef char    *ADDRESS;       /* 32 bits     */

typedef struct
{
        BYTE    cmdreg;         /* Command register            */
        BYTE    unused0;
        WORD    unused1;
        ADDRESS data_block;     /* Address of data block       */
        ADDRESS cmd_block;      /* Address of SCSI command block */
}
HOST_ADAPTER;

#define DISK    ((HOST_ADAPTER *)0x10000) /* Address of host adapter */
                                         /* in system memory        */
```

The **#define** for *DISK* performs the same function as the *(char *)0x80* in our first example. Here, however, the constant 0x10000 is treated as if it were the contents of a pointer to a *HOST_ADAPTER* structure. Using these definitions, we can put a 0xa7 into the host adapter's command register with a

```
DISK->cmdreg = 0xa7;
```

Since we're using the -> operator, which expects a pointer to a structure on its left, we don't need the second *, which was required in previous examples. The data pointer is initialized with

```
char    buffer[1024];

DISK->data_block = buffer;
```

7.5.4. Hardware Interfacing and Portability

Portability is a problem with all routines that interface to hardware. First, the width of a given type is undefined. There's no telling how big an **int** is or whether an **int** and a pointer are the same width. The **#define**s for *BYTE*, *WORD*, and *ADDRESS* in figure 7-23 try to minimize this problem. These **#define**s are used in all hardware definitions, rather than the less portable **char**, **long**, and so on. If we change compilers, we can redefine them, and all other definitions will modify themselves accordingly.

Alignment may also cause problems. This host adapter was used with a 68000 CPU, which requires alignment on word boundaries for 16-bit or 32-bit memory accesses. 8-bit objects can be accessed at either even or odd address. The hardware was designed with alignment in mind; all multibyte objects are aligned on even addresses. We force alignment by including the *unused0* field in the structure. This field doesn't have to be explicitly defined because the compiler guarantees alignment in structures. (This means that an occasional byte is inserted into a structure if a byte-wide field in a structure is followed by a word-width field. In other words, contiguity of fields within a structure is not guaranteed. The size of a structure may be larger than the sum of the sizes of the fields.) Explicitly defining *unused0* gives us portability. We can move the code to a machine that doesn't have the 68000's alignment restrictions (such as the 8088).

A final problem: Large numbers are stored differently in different machines. For example, a 68000 stores a 2-byte **int** with the MSB at the lower address, whereas an 8086 stores the same **int** with the LSB at the lower address. Consequently, software that drives hardware that has word-width registers may have problems when the hardware and software are ported to a different CPU; the bytes within a word may need swapping. The byte-swap operation can be done with

```
#define swapb(x) (((x) >> 8) & 0xff) | ((x) << 8)
```

7.6. Exercises

7-1   What does the following program print? Explain.

```
#include <stdio.h>

main( )
{
        static int array[6][2] =
        {
                {' ', 's'}, {'d', 'r'}, {'a', 'w'},
                {'k', 'c'}, {'a', 'b'}, {'c', 'd'}
        };

        int     *p = (int *)(array + 4);

        for( ++p; p >= (int *)array; putchar( *p-- ) )
                ;
}
```

7-2   What does the following program print? What is *array* (in words). Draw a picture of it. Explain what's happening in all five arguments to *printf()* and why they evaluate to what they do.

```
main( )
{
        static char     *array[2][3] =
        {
                { "   c", "ng ", " no" },
                { "usi", "fun", "onf" }
        };

        printf("%s%s%s%s\n", **array,   *(*(array+1)+2),
                                *array[1], array[0][1]    );
}
```

7-3   What does the following program print? Explain what's happening on each line; draw pictures when necessary.

```
main( )
{
        static char     *p[ ] = { "moldy\n", "jello" };
        static char     **pp  = p ;

        ** ++ pp -= 2 ;
        printf("%s ", *pp );

        *(p[0] + 4) = *(*p+3);
        pp[-1][3]   = *(*(pp-1)+2);
        ++*--pp ;
        *++*p       = 'r';
        *(*pp - 2)  = **p + 5;

        printf( pp[0] - 2 );
}
```

7-4   Write declarations for the following:

(a) A pointer to an array of pointers to arrays of **int**s.

(b) An array of pointers to functions that return pointers to functions that in turn return pointers to an **int**s.

(c) A function returning an array of pointers to arrays of **float**s.

(d) A function returning a pointer to an array of pointers to functions each of which returns a pointer to a **char**.

(e) A function returning a pointer to an array of pointers to functions that return (pointers to) 10-element arrays of **double**s.

7-5   Write the general-purpose binary search routine:

```
                bsearch( key, array, nel, width, cmp )
```

where *key* is a pointer to the key for which you are searching, *array* is a pointer to the first element of the array, *nel* is the number of elements in the array, *width* is the size of one element in bytes, and *cmp* is a pointer to a comparison function. The function should return a pointer to the found object, or *NULL* if the object corresponding to *key* isn't in the array.

7-6   A matrix is a rectangular array of numbers often used as a shorthand to represent systems of equations in engineering and graphics applications. They can be represented in a computer as two-dimensional arrays. Two matrixes can be multiplied together if the number of columns in one is equal to the number of rows in the other. The result of the matrix multiply is also a matrix. It will have the same number of rows as the first matrix and the same number of columns as the second. The process is illustrated in the following examples:

$$[1 \ \ 2 \ \ 3] \ \times \ \begin{bmatrix} 4 \\ 5 \\ 6 \end{bmatrix}$$

evaluates to

$$[(1\times4)+(2\times5)+(3\times6)] = [4+10+18] = [32]$$

That is, the product is a 1×1 matrix. The product of

$$\begin{bmatrix} 1 & 3 \\ 2 & 4 \end{bmatrix} \ \times \ \begin{bmatrix} 5 & 7 & 9 \\ 6 & 8 & 10 \end{bmatrix}$$

has three columns and two rows. It is found by:

$$\begin{bmatrix} ((1\times5)+(3\times6)) & ((1\times7)+(3\times8)) & ((1\times9)+(3\times10)) \\ ((2\times5)+(4\times6)) & ((2\times7)+(4\times8)) & ((2\times9)+(4\times10)) \end{bmatrix}$$

Write the following subroutine:

```
matrix_mult( prod, a, b, a_row, a_col, b_row, b_col )
char *prod, *a, *b;
int   a_row, a_col, b_row, b_col;
```

A and *b* are pointers to the first cells of two matrixes represented as two-dimensional arrays of **int**. *Prod* is a pointer to an area of memory in which the product of *a* and *b* is to be placed. *A_row* and *a_col* are the number of rows and columns in matrix *a*. *B_row* and *b_col* are the number of rows and columns in matrix *b*. Remember, you may not use the square bracket notation except in array declarations, nor may you use the notation *(p+i)*. Access all array elements using pointers and advance the pointers by manipulating them directly.

RECURSION
AND COMPILER DESIGN

A *recursive* subroutine is a subroutine that calls itself. Though most books on programming talk about recursion, they usually give such simple examples of recursive subroutines that it's hard to see why anyone would use the technique. Recursion just seems to be a way to make a simple operation more difficult to understand. In the case of computing a factorial, for instance, you'd be right—using recursion for finding a factorial is not only silly, but is needlessly wasteful of memory. However, some applications of recursion, notably compilers and tree manipulation, are truly useful. A recursive solution to this type of problem uses considerably less code and is often easier to understand than an iterative equivalent.

In this chapter, we'll take an in-depth look at a reasonable use of recursion: compiler design. In the interest of clarity, we'll reduce the problem from the recognition of a real computer language to a small arithmetic expression analyzer. The techniques used for one are applicable to the other. Our expression analyzer takes as input an ASCII string representing an arithmetic expression. Only numbers, parentheses, and the operators +, −, /, and * are legal. The analyzer returns the result of the evaluation. For example, if you give it the string "(3+1)*2", the analyzer returns the number 8. The routine is pretty stupid, but the point of this exercise is to understand compilers, not to analyze complicated expressions.

189

As we look at compilers, we'll also look at a standard notation for describing programming languages: the Backus-Naur Form (or BNF). Since this notation is used regularly to explain the syntax used by C compilers, understanding BNF can help considerably in deciphering some of the better C language reference books.

8.1. How Recursion Works

Before we leap into compiler design itself, an explanation of how recursion actually works is in order. To do this, we'll use the factorial example that I just maligned (because it's so short). The factorial function computes this series:

$$N * (N-1) * (N-2) * (N-3) \ldots * 3 * 2 * 1$$

For example, 5 factorial (usually abbreviated *5!*) is:

$$5 * 4 * 3 * 2 * 1 = 120$$

This series has an interesting property. N factorial is identical to N * (N-1 factorial). To look at a concrete example, the expression

$$5!$$

can be restated as

$$5! == 5 * 4!$$

or

$$5! == 5 * (4 * 3 * 2 * 1)$$

Factorial, then, can be defined in terms of itself (that is, our definition of factorial can include the expansion of a factorial). It's this sort of self-referential definition that points at a recursive solution to a problem. We're missing something, though—a way to stop the process. We do this by defining 0! as a special case:

```
(1) 0! (zero factorial) and 1! are both equal to 1.
(2) For all other numbers, N! = N * (N-1)!
```

Using these rules, we can create the following C subroutine, which returns N!.

```
factorial( N )
int        N;
{
        if( N <= 1 )                    /* 0! == 1! == 1 */
                return 1;
        else
                return( N * factorial(N-1) );
}
```

To see how this routine works, we need to watch what happens on the stack when a subroutine is called. (Reread Chapter 4 if you're not clear about what a stack frame is and how it's created.) When the subroutine *factorial()* is called with the argument *3*, the stack frame shown in figure 8-1 is created.

Fig. 8-1: Stack Frame Created When factorial(3) is Executed

```
              |----------------|    ----------
 FP-->        |     Old FP     |
              |----------------|
 FP+2         |  Return Addr.  |    factorial's stack frame
              |----------------|
 FP+4    N:   |       3        |
              |----------------|    ----------
              |                |
              |                |    calling subroutine's stack frame
              |                |
```

There aren't any local variables, so the stack frame has only three things in it: the parameter passed to *factorial()* (*N*), the return address, and the old frame pointer. The variable *N* is always accessed by *factorial()* by using an offset from the frame pointer. That is, *N* is at offset +4 from the frame pointer [that is, 4(FP)]. Remember, this *N* is <u>not</u> at a fixed memory address; rather, it's on the stack and is *always accessed via an offset from the current value of the frame pointer.*

Now, what happens inside *factorial()* itself? It first tests *N <= 1*, fetching the contents of the memory cell at offset 4 from the frame pointer to get **the value of *N*.** The test fails, so the **else** clause is executed. Before the computation can be made, however, the subroutine *factorial()* is called (recursively). The fact that *factorial()* is calling itself is immaterial from the compiler's point of view. It just treats the recursive call as it would any other subroutine call, pushing the value of *N* onto the stack and then transferring control to the first line of *factorial()*. Note here that *N-1*, not *N*, is passed through to the recursive invocation of *factorial()*. The first thing that *factorial()* does is set up another stack frame, as shown in figure 8-2.

Note that there are now two *N*'s on the stack, one in the stack frame of the original call and a second in the recursive call's stack frame. However, since the value used as *N* inside *factorial()* is whatever the machine finds at offset 4 from the frame pointer, the *N* in the second stack frame is used by the second invocation of *factorial()*. Short of a serious error, there is no way for a subroutine to directly access a variable in another subroutine's stack frame, so the recursive invocation of *factorial()* can't modify the *N* in the original *factorial()*'s stack frame.

The recursive process continues in the same way for one more iteration. There are now three stack frames in existence. The stack at this point is

Fig. 8-2: Stack After Recursive Call

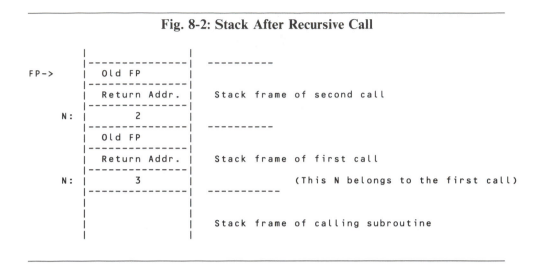

```
        |                |
        |----------------|     ----------
FP->    |    Old FP      |
        |----------------|
        |  Return Addr.  |     Stack frame of second call
        |----------------|
   N:   |       2        |
        |----------------|     ----------
        |    Old FP      |
        |----------------|
        |  Return Addr.  |     Stack frame of first call
        |----------------|
   N:   |       3        |               (This N belongs to the first call)
        |----------------|     -----------
        |                |
        |                |
        |                |     Stack frame of calling subroutine
        |                |
```

shown in figure 8-3. The value of N being used is that in the most recently created stack frame.

At this point, all the elements of the factorial series (3, 2, and 1) are on the stack, in the N's associated with the various stack frames, so all we have to do is multiply these N's together. We accomplish this multiply with the **return** statements. The subroutine performs the test $N<=1$. N is fetched from the cell at offset 4 from frame pointer. The cell at this address holds a 1, so the test now succeeds and 1 is returned to the calling subroutine. The most recently created stack frame is deleted, restoring the stack to the condition shown in figure 8-2. Before the stack frame is deleted, though, the return value (the 1) is copied into a register.

Now we're in the previous *factorial( )* call, executing the line:

Fig. 8-3: Final State of the Stack

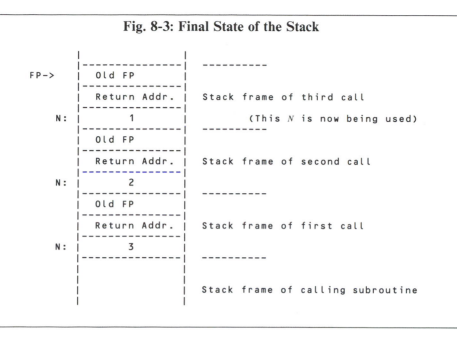

```
              |               |
              |---------------|      ----------
     FP->     |   Old FP      |
              |---------------|
              | Return Addr.  |   Stack frame of third call
              |---------------|
         N:   |      1        |         (This N is now being used)
              |---------------|      ----------
              |   Old FP      |
              |---------------|
              | Return Addr.  |   Stack frame of second call
              |---------------|
         N:   |      2        |
              |---------------|      ----------
              |   Old FP      |
              |---------------|
              | Return Addr.  |   Stack frame of first call
              |---------------|
         N:   |      3        |
              |---------------|      ----------
              |               |
              |               |
              |               |   Stack frame of calling subroutine
              |               |
```

```
          return( N * factorial(N-1) );
```

We've just returned from the call to *factorial()*, and that call has returned the value 1 to us. We now multiply that 1 (in a register) by *N* (on the stack). This copy of *N* holds the number 2 so we'll return *2*1* or 2 to the calling subroutine, deleting the current stack frame and copying the return value (the 2) into the same register used to pass the 1 to us from the previous *factorial()* call.

At this juncture we're in the original call to *factorial()*, having just returned from the *factorial(N-1)* call. The register used for return values will contain the number 2. The stack has been restored to the state shown in figure 8-1. We multiply the 2 returned from the previous call by *N* (at offset 4 from the frame pointer), yielding *3*2* or 6. The 6 is returned back up to the original calling routine. The whole process is shown graphically in figure 8-4.

Factorial() can use a lot of stack. In fact, with our 6-byte stack frame, *factorial(170)* creates a stack overflow on a 1K stack (it needs more stack than is available). This is a general problem with recursive subroutines. We have to think constantly about what the stack is likely to be doing and abort a program gracefully if the stack is getting too large. A version of our *factorial()* routine that monitors stack depth is shown in figure 8-5. The modified subroutine returns 0 if the number of recursion levels exceeds *TOO_DEEP* (since

Fig. 8-4: Subroutine Trace of a factorial(3) Call

```
              Calling routine
                   |    ^
         n = 3  |    |  returns 6
                   v    |
            inside factorial(3)
                   |    ^
         n = 2  |    |  returns 2
                   v    |
            inside factorial(2)
                   |    ^
         n = 1  |    |  returns 1
                   v    |
            inside factorial(1)
```

0! == 1, 0 is not normally returned). Note that *recursion_level* is declared
static so that it will retain its value for the next recursion level to use. Static
variables are at fixed addresses, not on the stack.

There's another problem here that makes the stack-overflow problem
moot. The factorial series grows quite quickly. In fact, 12 is the largest value
of N that can be represented in a signed 32-bit **long int** (12! == 479,001,600,
13! == 6,227,020,800 and 0x7ffffff == 2,147,483,647). Consequently, we
should really test for $N>12$ at the top of *factorial()* and return 0 if it is.
Twelve recursion levels use only 96 bytes of stack, so we don't have to worry
about stack overflow if we limit N. (I'm assuming the stack frame consists of
a 4-byte **long** for N, a 2-byte return address, and a 2-byte old frame pointer
[*recursion_level* doesn't use any stack because it **static**]; the actual size might
vary depending on how your compiler does things.)

8.2. The Anatomy of a Compiler

Now, let's apply all this to something real—a very small compiler. Every
compiler has three functionally distinct parts. These parts are often combined, but it's best to look at them as separate functions. The first part of the
compiler is a *token* recognizer. A token is some collection of ASCII characters from the input stream that are meaningful to the compiler when taken as
a group. That is, a program can be seen as a collection of tokens, each of
which is made up of one or more sequential ASCII characters. For example,
in C the ASCII character *;* is a token, similarly the keyword **while** is a token.
The matter is complicated by operators like + , ++ , and += , all of which are
single tokens. A token is then a sort of programming atom, an indivisible part
of the language (you can't say *wh ile*). Tokens are usually represented internally as an enumerated type or as a set of integer values corresponding to

Fig. 8-5: A Safer Factorial Routine

```
#include <stdio.h>

#define TOO_DEEP   18

long      factorial( N )
long      N;
{
          static   int recursion_level = 0;

          /* A safer factorial routine. Returns N! or 0 if routine
           * exceeds TOO_DEEP recursion levels.
           */

          if( N <= 1 )                    /* 0! == 1! == 1 */
                  N = 1 ;
          else
          {
                  if( ++recursion_level >= TOO_DEEP )
                          N = 0 ;
                  else
                          N = N * factorial(N-1) ;

                  --recursion_level;
          }

          return N;
}
```

#defines in a header file somewhere. A token recognizer is a subroutine that returns an integer corresponding to the next token from the input stream. We're not going to use a token recognizer in our example; rather, tokens are recognized by actually looking at the input characters as we interpret the input.

The second part of the compiler, and the part that does most of the work, is the *parser*. The verb *to parse* is borrowed from linguistics and it has the same meaning in both linguistics and computer science: "to resolve (a sentence, etc.) into its component parts of speech and describe them grammatically."[1] Just replace the word *sentence* with *program*. Computer languages may be described by means of a formal grammar (we'll look at these in a moment) and the parser breaks up a program into its component parts and interprets the parts in a larger, grammatical context. That is, a parser organizes the tokens returned from the token recognizer in such a way that the

---

1. *The Compact Edition of the Oxford English Dictionary,* (Oxford: Oxford University Press, 1971), p. 2083.

compiler can conveniently generate code.

The process can be viewed as the creation of a *parse tree*. For example, the expression *(a+b)*(c+d)* can be organized into the tree shown in figure 8-6.

Fig. 8-6: A Simplified Parse Tree for (A+B)*(C+D)

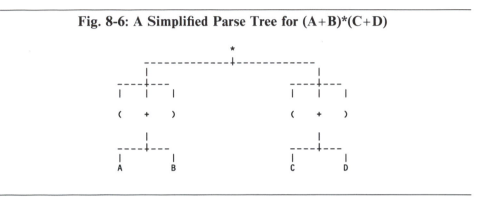

The third part of the compiler, the code generator, traverses the parse tree in an orderly way, generating code according to certain rules. For example, if we do a *postorder* traversal of the tree shown in figure 8-6. (visit the left node, middle node, the right node, and then the root recursively) the tokens are read in the following order:

$$(\quad a \quad b \quad + \quad) \quad (\quad c \quad d \quad + \quad) \quad *$$

Now, the expression may be evaluated by applying the following rules to each token in the tree as it is visited:

(1)   If the token is a parenthesis, do nothing.

(2)   if the token is a variable (a, b, c, or d), push the variable onto a stack.

(3)   if the token is a plus sign pop two items off the stack, add them, and push the result.

4)   if the token is an asterisk pop two items off the stack, multiply them, and push the result.

When you've finished parsing (traversing the tree), the answer is on the top of the stack. Owners of Hewlett-Packard calculators will be familiar with the process.

In a real compiler, the actual rule applied is some function of the type of token found and the position of that token in the parse tree. Also, most compilers (including the expression analyzer we're going to develop) don't generate an actual tree made up of structures, pointers, and so on. Rather, the structure of the parse tree is implied either by the parser's subroutine-calling sequence or by the internal state of the program at any given moment in the parse process.

There are several flavors of parsers. Many compilers use table-driven parsers that can be created automatically with a compiler-compiler program. The Unix utility YACC (Yet Another Compiler Compiler) is an example of such a program. When given a formal description of a programming language, YACC creates a set of tables that can be used by a generic, table-driven parser.

Most public domain compilers (such as Small C) don't use the more sophisticated methods. These compilers use a parsing method known as *recursive descent.* Recursive descent parsers are easier to understand than their table-driven cousins. They can also execute faster and usually give better error messages. On the other hand, they have to be built by hand. To change the way a recursive descent compiler works, you have to change the compiler itself. To change a table-driven compiler, you need only to change the table. Maintenance can thus be a problem with recursive descent compilers.

8.3. Grammars: Representing Computer Languages

The best way to start writing any program is to reduce the problem to some sort of symbolic form. Outlines, flow charts, and Warnier-Orr diagrams are examples of this kind of symbolic reduction. Compilers are no exception to this process. When writing a compiler, start by representing the programming language to be compiled in a formal, symbolic format called a *grammar.* Any one programming language can be described by several grammars. The type of parser you're going to use determines which of these is correct for your application. The most useful notation used for grammars is the Backus-Naur Form (abbreviated BNF) which we'll see in a moment.

In order to create our expression analyzer, we must start with a grammar. The first question to ask is what exactly is an expression? You'll remember from high school that an expression is composed of factors. A factor by itself (a single number) is an expression, as are two factors separated by an operator. The following are BNF representations of these two rules:

```
<expression> ::= <factor>
<expression> ::= <factor> <operator> <factor>
```

The ::= symbol means "is defined as." The word to the left of the ::= is the name of the definition, everything to the right of the ::= is the definition itself. The first line can be interpreted as "an <expression> is defined as a <factor>." The whole line is called a *production.* We can save some typing by using the vertical bar (|) to represent a logical OR in our productions:

```
<expression> ::=    <factor>
                 | <factor> <operator> <factor>
```

You'll note that no element of the BNF definition of the <expression> is a real symbol, one that can actually be found in the input stream. That is, <factor> and <operator> both must be defined further before they can be related to a real program. Symbols, such as <factor>, that need further definition, are called *nonterminal* symbols. Symbols that *can* be found in the input are called *terminal* symbols. In this chapter, nonterminals will be surrounded by angle brackets and terminal symbols will not. The four terminal symbols that can be operators are +, −, /, and *. A BNF rule for <operator> is:

```
<operator> ::=  +  |  -  |  *  |  /
```

Defining a factor is a little harder. A factor can be a number but it can also be another expression (in: a+b−d, *a* is one factor and *b-d* is a second factor). A BNF definition of factor is:

```
<factor> ::=    <number> | <expression>
```

The only symbol yet to be defined is <number>. Since a number is an easy thing for the token recognizer to find, we'll cheat a little and just define <number> in English. Our entire grammar is shown in figure 8-7.

Fig. 8-7: A Simple Expression-Recognition Grammar

```
1) <expression> ::=    <factor>
                    | <factor> <operator> <factor>

2) <operator>   ::=  + | - | * | /

3) <factor>     ::=    <number> | <expression>

4) <number>     ::=  A string of ASCII characters in the set
                     {0 1 2 3 4 5 6 7 8 9}
```

Note that every nonterminal used to the right of a ::= is also defined to the left, and that no terminal symbols are found at the left of a ::=. Let's test the grammar by plugging in an example: 1+2. *1* and *2* are both <number>s, so we can replace them with the equivalent nonterminal symbols by using rule four:

```
          1  +  2
       <number> + <number>
```

According to rule three, a single number is also a factor, so we can do another replacement:

```
<number> + <number>
<factor> + <factor>
```

The + can be evaluated using rule two:

```
<factor>      +      <factor>
<factor> <operator> <factor>
```

Finally, by using rule one, we can replace the above with a single <expression>:

```
<factor> <operator> <factor>
         <expression>
```

We can reduce the input tokens *1 + 2* to an <expression> using the rules of the grammar. Therefore, we conclude that *1 + 2* is a legal expression in our grammar.

What if there is an error in the expression? Let's try to parse *1+**. We can apply rules two and four to yield

```
<number> <operator> <operator>
```

and then apply rule three to get:

```
<factor> <operator> <operator>
```

But there's no rule we can apply to reduce this any further, however, so we conclude that *1+** isn't an expression as defined by our grammar.

8.4. Parsing with a Grammar

A parser can be viewed as a program that reduces a collection of input tokens to a single nonterminal. We have just *parsed* the expression 1 + 2. To turn a parser into a real compiler, we need to make it do something active, too, to generate code. So, we associate an action rule with each grammatical rule. Our grammar, slightly shuffled around and with action rules added, is shown in figure 8-8.

Every time we apply a grammatical rule, we'll also perform the action specified in the equivalent action rule. 1+2, parsed with the grammar in figure 8-8. is shown in figure 8-9. A somewhat more involved example is given in figure 8-10.

You're probably beginning to see how the process works. If the action rules had generated the code necessary to perform the operation, rather than actually doing the operation itself, we'd have a compiler.

Unfortunately, the grammar we just defined isn't very useful. At the very least, we'd like to have parentheses and negative numbers. We'd also like to be able to make an entire expression negative, [for example, *-(17*11)*). You'll also note in figures 8-9 and 8-10 that the expression is just parsed left to right, making all possible substitutions as we parse. A more realistic

Fig. 8-8: Adding Actions to the Grammar

```
Grammar:

    (1) <expression> ::= <factor>
    (2) <expression> ::= <factor> <operator> <factor>
    (3) <operator>   ::= + | - | * | /
    (4) <factor>     ::= <number>
    (5) <factor>     ::= <expression>
    (6) <number>     ::= Any string of ASCII characters
                         in the range '0' to '9'

Action rules:

    (1) Do nothing.
    (2) Pop two objects off the stack, apply the
        operator from in rule three), and then
        push the result.
    (3) Remember the operator for rule two.
    (4) Push the number onto the stack.
    (5) Do nothing.
    (6) Translate the ASCII string into a
        number.
```

Fig. 8-9: Parsing 1+2 Using Grammar in Figure 8-8

```
                                     rule:  action:
        1              +      2         -   Original input string
    <number>           +      2         6   Translate ASCII "1" to int.
    <factor>           +      2         4   Push 1 (result of previous step)
    <factor> <operator> 2               3   Remember the +
    <factor> <operator> <number>        6   Translate ASCII "2" to int.
    <factor> <operator> <factor>        4   Push the 2.
    <expression>                        2   Pop the 1 & 2, apply +,
                                            and push the result.
```

grammar does its substitutions in a somewhat more complex way, and the grammar has to reflect this complexity. Moreover, a grammar has to be organized so that the parser can always tell what rule to apply based on the current input symbol and the rule being processed. A better expression recognizing grammar is given in figure 8-11. We'll use this grammar in our actual program.

Fig. 8-10: Parsing 1 + 2 − 3

```
                                    Apply    Action:
                                    rule:

1 + 2 - 3                             -       Start here.
<number> + 2 - 3                      6       Translate "1" to int.
<factor> + 2 - 3                      4       Push 1.
<factor> <operator> 2 - 3             3       Remember +.
<factor> <operator> <number> - 3      6       Translate "2" to int.
<factor> <operator> <factor> - 3      4       Push 2.
<expression> - 3                      2       Pop two numbers, apply +,
                                                and push result.

<factor> - 3                          1       Do nothing.
<factor> <operator> 3                 3       Remember -.
<factor> <operator> <number>          6       Translate "3" to int.
<factor> <operator> <factor>          4       Push 3.
<expression>                          2       Pop two numbers off the.
                                                stack, subtract, and
                                                push the result.
```

Fig. 8-11: A More Realistic Expression Recognizing Grammar

```
<expr>      ::=   <factor>                      (1)
              |   <factor> * <expr>             (2)
              |   <factor> / <expr>             (3)
              |   <factor> + <expr>             (4)
              |   <factor> - <expr>             (5)

<factor>    ::=    ( <expr> )                   (6)
              |   -( <expr> )                   (7)
              |    <constant>                   (8)
              |   -<constant>                   (9)

<constant> ::=  A string of ASCII characters
                in the range '0'-'9'            (10)
```

8.5. A Recursive Descent Parser

The best way to see how a parser works is to look at one. A complete parser for the grammar in figure 8-11 is shown in figure 8-12.

Before discussing the parser proper, we'll talk about how the program is organized. The actual subroutines in the parser are highly recursive. As such, they'll use up a lot of stack space as they work. (This is a problem with recursive routines in general: They use a good deal of stack space.) Because of this stack usage, we want to pass as few parameters as possible to the subroutines (because all these parameters take up stack space). By making global those variables that would normally be passed to the subroutines as arguments, the amount of stack that we use can be reduced. However, this practice introduces new problems. In C, all nonstatic global variables are shared between all modules in a program. But the expression parser is probably going to be a library routine, and we don't want it to interfere with the normal workings of the rest of a program. Moreover, we don't want the programmer to have to remember that certain globals are used by a particular library routine and can't be used anywhere else. This problem is solved by declaring the global variables **static**. We'll also make **static** those subroutines that are used only internally. Now, however, we need some way to initialize the static globals from outside the parser module. We do this initialization with the *access routine* starting on line 84 of the listing (the only externally accessible subroutine in the module). This access routine, called *parse()*, does nothing but initialize our globals and then call *expr()* to do the work.

Another organizational concern is the *main()* routine on lines 34 through 79. The primary purpose of *main()* is to test *parse()*— thus the **#ifdef/#endif** on lines 32 and 81. DEBUG isn't #defined when we compile for inclusion in a library. The *main()* routine given is moderately useful in its own right. You can enter the expression from the command line [*expr 17/(2*12)*] or you can just type *expr* and then enter expressions as the program prompts you—sort of a rudimentary desk calculator.

Moving back to parsers, there are a few things to observe in the grammar in figure 8-11. First, the leftmost symbol following the ::= is always either a terminal or the same nonterminal for all rules. That is, all rules associated with <expr> have <factor> as their leftmost symbol. The leftmost symbol of all <factor> rules is either a terminal [(or -] or the nonterminal <constant>. The leftmost symbol of a constant has to be an ASCII digit. This property of the grammar is required if the parser is to know which rule to apply in a given situation. For example, when evaluating an <expr>, the parser always applies a rule associated with <factor> first.

A second property of the grammar is that the definitions for <expr> and <factor> are recursive. An <expr> is defined in terms of other <expr>s. The recursion in <factor> is two levels deep. A <factor> is defined in terms of an <expr>, which is in turn defined in terms of a <factor>. The recursion in the grammar suggests that we can also use recursion in a parser that implements the grammar.

Given an appropriate grammar, we can translate that grammar directly into a parser. In the program given here, all nonterminal symbols in the grammar have an equivalent subroutine with the same name. The routine for <expr> starts on line 104, <factor> on line 124, and <constant> on line 155.

Fig. 8-12: A Parser for Simple Expressions

```
 1: #include <stdio.h>
 2:
 3: /* EXPR.C:  A small arithmetic expression analyzer.
 4:  *
 5:  * Evaluate an expression pointed to by str. Expressions evaluate
 6:  * right to left unless parentheses are present. Valid operators are
 7:  * + * - / for multiply, add, subtract, and divide. The expression
 8:  * must be formed from the character set {  0123456789+-*( )/  }.
 9:  * White space is not allowed.
10:  *
11:  *     <expr>      ::=     <factor>
12:  *                   | <factor> * <expr>
13:  *                   | <factor> / <expr>
14:  *                   | <factor> + <expr>
15:  *                   | <factor> - <expr>
16:  *
17:  *     <factor>   ::=      ( <expr> )
18:  *                   | -( <expr> )
19:  *                   |  <constant>
20:  *                   | -<constant>
21:  *
22:  *     <constant> ::=   A string of ASCII chars in the range '0'-'9'.
23:  *
24:  *-------------------------------------------------------------------
25:  *   Global variables:
26:  */
27:
28: static  char    *Str ;  /* Current posn. in string being parsed */
29: static  int     Error; /* # of errors found so far              */
30:
31: /*----------------------------------------------------------------*/
32: #ifdef DEBUG
33:
34: main(argc, argv)
35: char    **argv;
36: {
37:         /*  Routine to exercise the expression parser: If an
38:          *  expression is given on the command line, it is
39:          *  evaluated and the result is printed, otherwise,
40:          *  expressions are fetched from stdin (one per line)
41:          *  and evaluated. The program will return -1 to the
42:          *  shell on a syntax error, 0 if it's in interactive
43:          *  mode; otherwise it returns the result of the
44:          *  evaluation.
45:          */
46:
47:         char buf[133], *bp = buf ;
48:         int err, rval;
49:
50:         if( argc > 2 )
51:         {
52:                 fprintf(stderr, "Usage:  expr [<expression>]");
53:                 exit( -1 );
54:         }
55:
56:         if( argc > 1 )
57:         {
58:                 rval = parse( argv[1], &err );
```

```
59:                        printf(err ? "*** ERROR ***" : "%d", rval );
60:                        exit( rval );
61:          }
62:
63:          printf("Enter expression or <CR> to exit program\n");
64:
65:          while( 1 )
66:          {
67:                  printf("? ");
68:
69:                  if( gets(buf) == NULL  ||  !*buf )
70:                          exit(0);
71:
72:                  rval = parse(buf, &err);
73:
74:                  if( err )
75:                          printf("*** ERROR ***\n");
76:                  else
77:                          printf("%s = %d\n", buf, rval);
78:          }
79: }
80:
81: #endif
82: /*-------------------------------------------------------------------*/
83:
84: int      parse( expression, err )
85: char     *expression;
86: int      *err;
87: {
88:          /* Return the value of "expression" or 0 if any errors were
89:           * found in the string. "*Err" is set to the number of errors.
90:           * "Parse" is the "access routine" for expr( ). By using it, you
91:           * need not know about any of the global vars used by expr( ).
92:           */
93:
94:          register int    rval;
95:
96:          Error = 0;
97:          Str   = expression;
98:          rval  = expr( );
99:          return( (*err = Error) ?  0  :  rval );
100: }
101:
102: /*-------------------------------------------------------------*/
103:
104: static int expr( )
105: {
106:          int      lval;
107:
108:          lval = factor( );
109:
110:          switch (*Str)
111:          {
112:          case '+': Str++;   lval += expr( );      break;
113:          case '-': Str++;   lval -= expr( );      break;
114:          case '*': Str++;   lval *= expr( );      break;
115:          case '/': Str++;   lval /= expr( );      break;
116:          default :                                break;
117:          }
118:
119:          return( lval );
120: }
121:
122: /*-------------------------------------------------------------*/
```

```
123:
124: static int factor( )
125: {
126:          int      rval = 0 , sign = 1 ;
127:
128:          if ( *Str == '-' )
129:          {
130:                  sign = -1 ;
131:                  Str++;
132:          }
133:
134:          if ( *Str != '(' )
135:                  rval = constant( );
136:          else
137:          {
138:                  Str++;
139:                  rval = expr( );
140:
141:                  if ( *Str == ')' )
142:                          Str++;
143:                  else
144:                  {
145:                          printf("Missing close parenthesis\n");
146:                          Error++  ;
147:                  }
148:          }
149:
150:          return (rval * sign);
151: }
152:
153: /*-----------------------------------------------------------*/
154:
155: static int constant( )
156: {
157:          int      rval = 0 ;
158:
159:          if( !isdigit( *Str ))
160:                  Error++;
161:
162:          while ( *Str && isdigit(*Str) )
163:          {
164:                  rval = (rval * 10) + (*Str - '0') ;
165:                  Str++;
166:          }
167:
168:          return( rval );
169: }
```

Looking again at the grammar in figure 8-11, we see that the leftmost element of all the <expr> rules (1-5) is <factor>. Similarly, the first thing the subroutine *expr()* does is call the subroutine *factor()* (on line 108). Looking back at the grammar, the next thing <expr> does is look for a terminal symbol (either *, /, +, −, or a null string). The equivalent code is the switch on lines 110 through 117. The default case takes care of the null terminal (rule one). The recursive evaluation of <expr> in rules 2 through 5 is also done in the switch. On line 119, *expr()* returns the evaluated expression.

The subroutine *factor()* is somewhat more complex. It first checks (on lines 128-132) for the leading minus sign required by rules seven and nine. After stripping off the minus, rules six and seven become identical; similarly, rules eight and nine are identical once the minus is gone. Now *factor()* decides which rule to process by looking for a leading '(' (on line 134). If it doesn't find the parenthesis, rule eight is processed (line 135) by calling the subroutine *constant()*; otherwise rule six is processed by skipping past the parenthesis and then calling *expr()* (lines 138-139). We can also do some error checking here by looking for a closed parenthesis when *expr()* returns (lines 143-147).

The final part of the parser is the routine *constant()* on lines 155 through 169. This routine is essentially *atoi()*, however it advances the string pointer past the end of a number and flags an error if a number isn't found.

You'll note that in this program, the three functional parts of the compiler are merged. There is no explicit token recognizer; rather, each routine is responsible for advancing the global string pointer, *Str,* past the token being processed. Similarly, the code-generation part of the compiler is integrated into the parser itself. (The code generation is actually simulated by the various return statements.)

A subroutine trace for a call to *parse()* is shown in figure 8-13. Interestingly, this trace is also the parse tree for the expression *2+3.* Thus a parse tree, in kind, is created by the parsing process, but that tree is implied by the subroutine calling sequence.

8.6. Improving the Parser

Our expression parser is a good example of recursion, but it still has problems. Though it parses the expression from left to right, the expression is actually evaluated from right to left (because we do the evaluation as we come up from the previous recursion level). In addition, all the operators are at the same precedence level (we'd like + and – to be of lower precedence than / and *). Both of these problems can be eliminated by changing the grammar, however.[2]

Operator precedence is the easy problem to fix. All we need to do is translate the grammatical rules in figure 8-11 to the form shown in figure 8-14, introducing a new nonterminal called a <term>. (The rules for <factor> and <constant> are the same as before so they aren't reproduced here).

---

2.   I'm presenting the grammatical transformations here without any explanation of why these particular transformations work. Just take it on faith that they do. The subject of formal grammars and their manipulation is more properly that of a compiler design book, several of which are listed in the bibliography.

Fig. 8-13: Subroutine Trace for parse("2+3",&err)

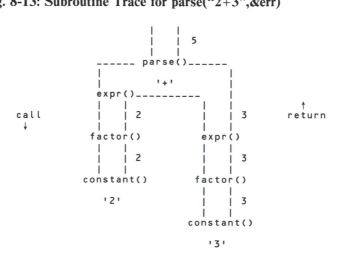

Fig. 8-14: Expression Grammar with Operator Precedence

```
<expr>   ::= <term>   + <expr> | <term>   - <expr> | <term>
<term>   ::= <factor> * <term> | <factor> / <term> | <factor>
```

Operator associativity can be changed by shuffling the grammar around a little more. The grammar in figure 8-14 is *right recursive* (the recursive call is at the far right of the production). All right recursive productions associate from right to left. To change the associativity, we make the grammar *left recursive* as is shown in figure 8-15.

Fig. 8-15: Expression Grammar with Left to Right Associativity

```
<expr>   ::=   <expr> + <term>  | <expr> - <term>  | <term>
<term>   ::=   <term> * <factor> | <term> / <factor> | <factor>
```

This last transformation causes problems for recursive descent parsers, though. Were we to code it in the simplest possible way, we'd end up with something like this:

```
expr( )
{
          expr( );
          ...
}
```

That is, *expr()* calls itself recursively—forever—there's no way to stop the process, and the stack will eventually overflow. This problem can be fixed by modifying the grammar still more to the condition shown in figure 8-16.

Fig. 8-16: The Final Version of the Expression Grammar

```
<expr>   ::=    <term>  <expr'>
<expr'>  ::= + <term>  <expr'> | - <term>  <expr'> | ε
<term>   ::=    <factor><term'>
<term'>  ::= * <factor><term'> | / <factor><term'> | ε
```

In these productions, ε means "if the expression doesn't start with any of the previous operators, do nothing." Our final grammar can now be translated directly into the subroutines in figure 8-17. (As in the grammar, the subroutines *factor()* and *constant()* are the same ones we used earlier so they aren't reproduced here.)

Fig. 8-17: A better expression parser

```
 1 #include <stdio.h>
 2 #include <ctype.h>
 3
 4 expr( )
 5 {
 6         return  expr_prime( term( ) );
 7 }
 8
 9 /*- - - - - - - - - - - - - - - - - - - - - - - - - - - - - - */
10
11 expr_prime( left )
12 {
13         if( *Str == '+' )
14         {
15                 Str++;
16                 return expr_prime(  left + term( ) );
17         }
18         else if( *Str == '-' )
19         {
20                 Str++;
21                 return expr_prime(  left - term( ) );
22         }
23         else
24                 return left;
25 }
26
27 /*------------------------------------------------------------*/
28
29 term( )
30 {
31         return  term_prime( factor( ) );
32 }
33
34 /*- - - - - - - - - - - - - - - - - - - - - - - - - - - - - - */
35
36 term_prime( left )
37 {
38         if( *Str == '*' )
39         {
40                 Str++;
41                 return term_prime(  left * factor( ) );
42         }
43         else if( *Str == '/' )
44         {
45                 Str++;
46                 return term_prime(  left / factor( ) );
47         }
48         else
49                 return left;
50 }
```

There's still plenty of room for improvement in these subroutines. Both *expr_prime()* and *term_prime()* are *right recursive*. That is, calling themselves recursively is the last thing they do. (There's no code between the recursive call and the return.) Consequently, the recursion can be replaced with a **while** loop. We can also replace the **if/else** statements with conditionals. These changes are made in figure 8-18.

Fig. 8-18: The Parser Modified to Eliminate Right Recursion

```
 1 expr( )
 2 {
 3        return  expr_prime( term( ) );
 4 }
 5
 6 /*- - - - - - - - - - - - - - - - - - - - - - - - - - - - - */
 7
 8 expr_prime( left )
 9 {
10        register int    c;
11
12        while( (c = *Str) == '+' || *Str == '-' )
13        {
14            Str++;
15            left = (c == '+') ? left + term( ) : left - term( );
16        }
17
18        return left;
19 }
20 /*----------------------------------------------------------*/
21
22 term( )
23 {
24        return  term_prime( factor( ) );
25 }
26
27 /*- - - - - - - - - - - - - - - - - - - - - - - - - - - - - */
28
29 term_prime( left )
30 {
31        register int    c;
32
33        while( (c = *Str) == '*' || *Str == '/' )
34        {
35            Str++;
36            left = (c == '*') ? left * factor( ) : left / factor( );
37        }
38
39        return left;
40 }
```

There's another easy change to make now that we've eliminated all the direct recursion from *expr_prime()* (it doesn't call itself any more, though subroutines that *expr_prime()* calls will call *expr_prime()* indirectly)]. Since all *expr()* does is call *expr_prime()*, the subroutine call to *expr_prime()* on line 3 can be replaced with *expr_prime()* itself. The same goes for *term()* and *term_prime()*. Final versions of *expr()* and *term()*, with these changes made, are shown in figure 8-19.

Fig. 8-19: The Final Versions of expr( ) and term( )

```
 1 expr( )
 2 {
 3          register int     c;
 4          register int     left;
 5
 6          left = term( );
 7
 8          while( (c = *Str) == '+' || *Str == '-' )
 9          {
10              Str++;
11              left = (c == '+') ? left + term( ) : left - term( );
12          }
13
14          return left;
15 }
16
17 /*-------------------------------------------------------------*/
18
19 term( )
20 {
21          register int     c;
22          register int     left;
23
24          left = factor( );
25
26          while( (c = *Str) == '*' || *Str == '/' )
27          {
28              Str++;
29              left = (c == '*') ? left * factor( ) : left / factor( );
30          }
31
32          return left;
33 }
```

8.7. Exercises

8-1 Write the recursive subroutine:

```
                search( array,  key,  array_size )
                int     *array,  key,  array_size;
```

that does a binary search for the indicated key in the indicated integer array. Array_size is the size of the array in elements, not in bytes. The routine should return a pointer to the cell in which the key is found (or -1 if the key isn't in the array).

8-2   Write a C subroutine that prints the size, in bytes, of its own stack frame. It should compute this size at run-time. (If your subroutine is longer than 10 to 15 lines of code you're doing something seriously wrong.)

8-3   Using the principles in Exercise 8-2, modify the expression parser so that parse( ) prints the maximum amount of stack used for an entire expression evaluation (that is, the sum of the sizes of all stack frames that are active at the deepest level of recursion). The size of the stack frame used by parse( ) itself should be included in this number. How much stack will be used to evaluate "((1*2)+(3*4))" ?

8-4   Using the parser described in this chapter, parse the expression "1+(2*3)," showing the stack and the subroutine trace diagram after every subroutine call. Assuming that all variables and addresses require 2 bytes, how much stack space is required to parse this expression? How could the amount of required stack space be reduced? How could you modify the parser to restrict the number of recursion levels?

8-5   Write a desk calculator program that gets statements interactively from standard input and evaluates them. The calculator must support an arbitrary number of variables having arbitrary, alphabetic, names. The statement "<name> = <expr>;" creates a variable (if it doesn't already exist) and assigns the value of <expr> to it. Thereafter, the variable can be used in place of a number in any expression. A *print* statement ("print <expr>;") prints the result of the expression evaluation to standard output. Use the following grammar:

```
<stmt>    ::= print <expr> ; <stmt> | <name> = <expr> ; <stmt> | ε
<expr>    ::=   <term> <expr'>
<expr'>   ::= + <term> <expr'> | - <term> <expr'> | ε
<term>    ::=   <fact> <term'>
<term'>   ::= * <fact> <term'> | / <fact> <term'> | ε
<fact>    ::= ( <expr> )        | -( <expr> )        | <const> | -<const>
<const>   ::= <num> | <name>
<num>     ::= A string of ASCII characters in the range '0' - '9'
<name>    ::= A string of ASCII characters in the range 'a' - 'z'
```

Note that all statements are terminated by semicolons. Take intelligent action when an error (such as a missing semicolon or equal sign) is encountered.

THE ANATOMY

OF PRINTF( )

In this chapter, we're going to apply several of the points we've covered in previous chapters by writing an implementation of *printf()*, a subroutine that makes a thorough use of the C language. It must use pointers in sophisticated ways; it has a variable number of arguments; and it requires a sophisticated understanding of casts, type conversion, and so forth. *Printf()* is also an example of realistic programming. Many compromises were made when it was written, and many of the same compromises are made in any piece of real code (as compared to textbook code).

9.1. Stacks Revisited

Before leaping into *printf()* proper, we'll reduce the scope of the problem a little. The following subroutine prints its own return address:

```
typedef int      (*PFI)( ) ;

printaddr( arg )
{
        PFI             *argp = &arg ;

        printf( "printaddr: called from 0x%04x\n", argp[-1] );
}
```

To see how *printaddr()* works, let's look at its stack frame:

```
                    |                | address  <-SP
                    |----------------|
          argp:  |       106      |   100
                    |----------------|
                    | old frame ptr  |   102        <-FP
                    |----------------|
                    |  return addr.  |   104
                    |----------------|
          arg:  |   parameters   |   106
                    |----------------|
                    |                |
```

The expression *&arg* evaluates to the address of *arg,* the number 106.
Consequently, *argp = &arg* puts the number 106 into *argp*. Since *argp* is a
pointer, *argp[0]* is the contents of the cell at address 106. Since *argp* is a
pointer to a pointer-sized object, *argp[-1]* accesses the cell whose address is
derived by subtracting the size of a pointer from the contents of *argp*. In our
machine, a pointer requires 2 bytes and *argp* contains the number 106, so
argp[-1] references the cell at address 106-2 (at location 104). Cell 104 holds
the subroutine's return address.

This routine isn't portable, but it works with most compilers. It assumes
that the stack frame is organized in a certain way and, in practice, the stack
frame's organization varies somewhat from compiler to compiler. Nevertheless, the relative positions of the return address and the arguments are usually
the same. *Printaddr()* also assumes that both a pointer to a subroutine and a
subroutine's return address are the same size. This is a pretty good bet but
may not necessarily be true. The routine does serve to illustrate how a C program can directly access the stack, however, and you need to understand this
process to see how *printf()* works.

9.2. printf( )

The source code for *printf()* and *fprintf()* is shown in figure 9-1. The
syntax of the **extern** statements may be unfamiliar. It's the syntax specified in
the proposed ANSI standard that allows strong type checking of subroutine
arguments. The statement is called a *function prototype* in the standard. (It's
supported by the Microsoft & Lattice compilers at this writing, and other
compiler manufacturers are beginning to follow suit.) The declaration

```
      extern   void     doprnt ( int (*)( ), int, char*, char** );
```

says that *doprnt()* is a subroutine that doesn't return a value (that's the **void**).
It takes four arguments; The first is a pointer to a subroutine that returns an
int, the second   of type **int**, the third is a pointer to **char**, and the fourth is a
pointer to a **char** pointer. The syntax in the type list is just like the syntax for
a cast (except that the outer parentheses aren't there). If the compiler sees a
type mismatch in the argument list, the wrong number of arguments, or the
return value being used improperly, it will print an error message (usually a

Fig. 9-1: printf( ) and fprintf( )

```
1    #include <stdio.h>
2
3    extern  void      doprnt ( int (*)( ), int, char*, char** );
4    extern  void      fputc  ( int, FILE * );
5
6    printf( format, args )
7    char     *format, *args;
8    {
9            doprnt( fputc, stdout, format, &args );
10   }
11
12   fprintf( stream, format, args )
13   FILE      *stream;
14   char      *format, *args;
15   {
16           doprnt( fputc, stream, format, &args );
17   }
```

warning, not a hard error). If possible, the compiler will also make whatever type conversions are necessary for the subroutine to be called successfully. Subroutines with a variable number of arguments can also be specified. For example:

```
extern void      printf(char *, ... );
```

The ellipsis in the type list says that the first **char** pointer argument can be followed by any number of arguments of any type.[1]

As you can see, *printf()* is only 5 lines long. It calls a workhorse function, *doprnt()*, to do most of the work. *Fprintf()* calls the same workhorse function, so *doprnt()* is a good example of reducing the code size of a program by writing a single general-purpose workhorse function rather than several specialized functions.

Before moving on to *doprnt()*, let's look at the arguments passed to it. The first argument to *doprnt()* is a pointer to an output function. The function is indirectly called with

```
(* out)( c, o_param );
```

where c is the character to go out, and *o_param* is the second argument to doprnt( ). That is, *o_param* provides a mechanism for passing the *stream* argument through to *fputc( )*. It isn't used by *doprnt( )* itself. The third argument

---

1. Earlier drafts of the standard didn't use the ellipsis, just the trailing comma.

to *doprnt()* is the same pointer to the format string that was passed to
printf(), and the fourth is a pointer to the other arguments. In other words,
the fourth argument is the address, on the stack, of the argument to *printf()*
that immediately follows the format string pointer. The situation is illustrated
in figure 9-2.

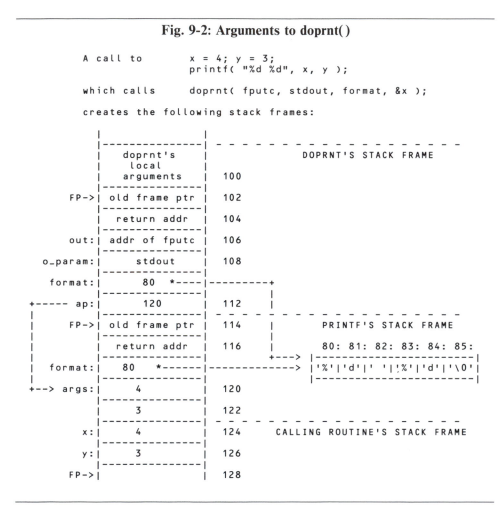

Fig. 9-2: Arguments to doprnt( )

```
A call to          x = 4; y = 3;
                   printf( "%d %d", x, y );

which calls        doprnt( fputc, stdout, format, &x );

creates the following stack frames:
```

When *printf()* is called, the three arguments to it are pushed onto the
stack in reverse order, so the contents of the variable *y* are pushed into location 122, the contents of *x* are pushed into location 120, and a pointer to the
format string is pushed into memory location 118. The return address is

pushed as part of the subroutine call and then *printf( )* itself pushes the old frame pointer. Since *printf( )* has no local variables, its stack frame is now complete.

Printf( ) calls *doprnt( )*, and the arguments to *doprnt( )* are pushed onto the stack in reverse order as part of the calling process. The address of *args* is pushed first. Then the contents of the *format* argument to *printf( )* are pushed, so there are now two identical pointers to the format string on the stack—one in *printf( )*'s stack frame and the other in *doprnt( )'s* stack frame. The second argument to the output function *(fputc( ))* is *stdout*, so *stdout* is pushed next. Finally, the pointer to the output function—the address of the first instruction in *fputc( )*—is pushed.

Note that *args* will always be at the same relative position in *printf( )*'s stack frame, regardless of how many actual arguments were passed to *printf( )*. That is, *args* is always at the same offset from the frame pointer. Any additional arguments will be below *args* on the stack (at a higher address). Arguments to subroutines are pushed in reverse order so that you always know where the first one is located in the stack frame. Without this knowledge, a subroutine with a variable number of arguments could not be written.

9.3. Macros used by doprnt( ).

The header portion of *doprnt( )* is shown in figure 9-3:

Two external routines are used: *ltos( )* and *dtos( )* (declared on lines 13 and 14). We'll talk about them shortly.

Two subroutine-like #**define**s follow the **extern** statements (on lines 26-30). One of the trade-offs made in writing *doprnt( )* was the traditional code size versus execution speed. Since most of a program's time is usually spent doing I/O, it seemed reasonable to optimize *printf( )* for speed. Therefore, the number of subroutine calls in *doprnt( )* were minimized because a subroutine call takes extra time to execute. On the other hand, the organization of a subroutine (making it a separate unit, apart from the routine in which it's called) makes a program more maintainable. I compromised by using subroutine-like macros. Care must be taken with these macros though—they have side effects.

For example, the (incorrect) macro invocation:

```
TOINT( p++, x );
```

will be expanded to:

```
while( '0' <= *p++ && *p++ <= '9' )   \
        x = (x * 10) + (*p++++ - '0')
```

The first two expansions of p have the undesirable side effect of incrementing p twice. The third expansion, $p{+}{+}{+}{+}$, is illegal. There's another problem. Even if *TOINT* is used correctly, p will be advanced past any scanned digits. A subroutine couldn't do this (at least not directly), so even when it's used properly, the macro has side effects. Another consideration is the back slash used to continue the macro to the next line. The code is more readable if it's correctly formatted. Nonetheless, some compilers don't support multiline macros; with these compilers you'll have to merge the definition onto a single line.

The next **#define** is on line 37:

```
#define INTMASK   (long)( (unsigned)(~0) )
```

INTMASK is used to truncate a **long** to the equivalent **int**. That is, given a 32-bit **long** and a 16-bit **int**

```
longvar &= INTMASK;
```

will clear (set to 0) the top 16 bits of the number. The expression

```
#define INTMASK   0xffff
```

won't work. The problem here is automatic type conversion. 0xffff is an **int**. Moreover, it's a negative number (-1). When an expression involves both a **long** and an **int**, the **int** is converted to **long** before the expression is evaluated. Because 0xffff is negative, it would be converted to 0xffffffff (because of sign extension). Thus *longvar &= 0xffff* is treated by the compiler as *longvar &= 0xffffffff*, which will do nothing. This problem can be circumvented by saying

```
#define INTMASK   0xffffL
```

The trailing L tells the compiler that 0xffff is a 32-bit long that has the bottom 16 bits set. This code isn't portable, however. We're assuming that an **int** is 16 bits wide. The expression:

```
#define INTMASK   (long)( (unsigned)(~0) )
```

is portable. It makes no assumptions about the size of an **int**. Here, ~0 is an **int**-sized object in which all the bits are set (to 1). We cast this number into an **unsigned** to avoid sign extension when it is used in an expression with a **long**. Finally, we cast it into a **long**.

Fig. 9-3: Doprnt.c: #defines, and so on

```
 1  /* DOPRNT / FDOPRNT
 2   *
 3   *      The actual formatting routine for printf, sprintf etc.
 4   *
 5   *      - #define FLOAT to support the %f conversion (this can be
 6   *              done from the command line w/ a -dFLOAT option.
 7   *              In this case, the compiled subroutine will be called
 8   *              fdoprnt( ) rather than doprnt( ).
 9   *
10   *      - The nonstandard conversion %b (binary) is supported.
11   */
12
13  extern char     *ltos(long,   char*, int);
14  extern char     *dtos(double, char*, int);
15
16  /*-------------------------------------------------------------------
17   *      Macros to save some code space below. If your compiler doesn't
18   *      accept multiline macros, remove the back slashes and merge the
19   *      entire definition onto one line.
20   *
21   *      PAD(fw)         outputs filchar, fw times. fw = 0.
22   *      TOINT(p,x)      works like "x = atoi(p);" except p
23   *                      is advanced past the number.
24   */
25
26  #define PAD(fw)         while( --fw >= 0 )                      \
27                              (*out)( filchar, o_param )
28
29  #define TOINT(p,x)   while( '0' <= *p  &&  *p <= '9' )   \
30                          x = (x * 10) + (*p++ - '0')
31
32  /*-------------------------------------------------------------------
33   *      INTMASK is a portable way to mask off the bottom N bits of a
34   *      long, where N is the width of an int in bits.
35   */
36
37  #define INTMASK         (long)( (unsigned)(~0) )
38
39  /*-------------------------------------------------------------------
40   * Many compilers don't accept this expression:
41   *
42   *                      int    *ap;
43   *                      x = *( (long *)ap )++;
44   *
45   *      Consequently, I've used the form:
46   *
47   *                      char *ap;
48   *                      x = *( (long *)ap );
49   *                      ap += sizeof(long);
50   *
51   *      Less elegant, but more portable.
52   */
53
54  #define NEXTARG(x, type)                        \
55          {                                       \
56                  x = *(type *)ap;                \
57                  ap += sizeof(type);     \
58          }
```

```
59
60  /*-----------------------------------------------------------------
61   *        Use fdoprnt as the subroutine name if FLOAT is #defined, else
62   *        use doprnt.
63   */
64
65  #ifdef  FLOAT
66  #define DOPRNT      fdoprnt
67  #else
68  #define DOPRNT      doprnt
69  #endif
70
```

We'll look at the *NEXTARG* **#define** in a moment. The next **#define**, on lines 65 through 69, determines the name of the final subroutine. If *FLOAT* is **#define**d, then the subroutine will be called *fdoprnt()*; else it will be called *doprnt()*. The same source code can thus be used to produce two versions of the same subroutine—one called *fdoprnt()* which supports floating point and another called *doprnt()* which doesn't.

9.4. Fetching Arguments off the Stack

We've already discussed the various arguments to *doprnt()* already. Note that *ap,* the pointer to the arguments (on the stack), is declared as a character pointer. This is necessary because we don't know the types of the arguments at compile time. We have to deduce these types at run time by analyzing the format string (%d and %c correspond to **int**-sized arguments, %f corresponds to a **double**-sized argument, and so on). When we advance *ap* from one argument to another, we'll have to add to it the size of the object-pointed-to, the size of one argument on the stack. By making *ap* a **char** pointer, we can simplify this addition; pointer arithmetic on a **char** pointer is just plain arithmetic. Adding 1 to a **char** pointer actually adds the number one to the contents of the pointer (because sizeof(char) == 1).

Let's look at how *ap* is used in *doprnt()*. A *printf()* call and the resulting stack frame are shown in figure 9-4. Here, *ap* is initialized to point to the first argument following the format string in printf (&args). To fetch the object-pointed-to by *ap*, we have to say the following:

```
int     x;

x = *( (int *)ap );
```

The cast is required because *ap* is **char** pointer. It says to treat *ap* as if it were a pointer to an **int**, rather than a pointer to a **char**. The expression

Fig. 9-4: Using the Argument Pointer

```
int      intvar;
long     longvar;
double   doublevar;

printf( "%d,%ld,%f" , intvar, longvar, doublevar );

          initializes ap as follows:

                      |            |  |
IN PRINTF'S           |            |  |          IN DOPRNT'S
STACK FRAME:          |            |  |          STACK FRAME:
                      |            |  |          ap:
                      |--------------|  |--------------|
intvar:    100:  |    |              |<------|--*  100       |
                      |--------------|  |--------------|
longvar:   102:  |    |              |
           104:  |    |              |
                      |--------------|
doublevar: 106:  |    |              |
           108:  |    |              |
           110:  |    |              |
           112:  |    |              |
                      |--------------|
                      |            |  |
```

```
x = *ap;
```

would fetch only one byte, rather than the 2 bytes used by an **int**. The expression *x=*((int *)ap);* says to fetch the object-pointed-to by *ap,* but that object is **int**-sized rather than **char**-sized, so fetch the entire **int**.

To advance *ap* past the the **int** to the next argument, we have to add the size of an **int** to it:

```
ap += sizeof( int );
```

Since *ap* is a **char** pointer, we will add 2 to *ap*. The new situation is shown in figure 9-5:

Fig. 9-5: Advancing the Argument Pointer

```
x = *( (int *)ap );
ap += sizeof(int);

does the following:
```

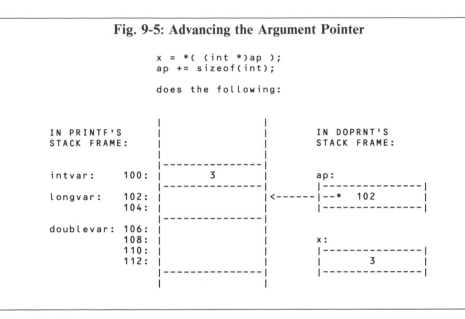

Ap is now pointing to the second argument on the stack, *longvar*. We can fetch this value using the same process as before, but with a different cast:

```
long    lx;

lx = *( (long *)ap );
ap += sizeof( long );
```

puts the **long**-sized object pointed to by *ap* into *lx,* and then advances *ap* to point to the **double** by adding 4 (the size of a **long**) to it. The new situation is shown in figure 9-6.

Fig. 9-6: Advancing the Argument Pointer Again

```
x = *( (long *)ap );
ap += sizeof(long);

does the following:
```

```
IN PRINTF'S        |         |         |         IN DOPRNT'S
STACK FRAME:       |         |         |         STACK FRAME:
                   |         |         |
                   |---------------|
intvar:    100:    |       3       |         ap:
                   |---------------|         |-------------|
longvar:   102:    |     70000     |    +---|--*   106     |
           104:    |               |    |    |-------------|
                   |---------------|    |
doublevar: 106:    |               |<--+
           108:    |               |         lx:
           110:    |               |         |-----------------------|
           112:    |               |         |          70000        |
                   |---------------|         |-----------------------|
                   |         |         |
```

A **double** can be fetched with

```
double   dx;

dx = *( (double *)ap );
ap += sizeof( double );
```

The *NEXTARG(x,type)* macro, which we mentioned earlier, fetches an argument of the indicated *type* and puts it into *x*. It then advances *ap* past the argument. *NEXTARG(lnum,long)* is expanded as follows:

```
{
        lnum = *(long *)ap;
        ap += sizeof(long);
}
```

Note that the body of *NEXTARG* is surrounded with braces (because it's composed of two statements). This way we can say

```
if( condition )
        NEXTARG( x, int );
```

A trailing **else**, however, will cause problems because of the close curly brace. Here the semicolon is interpreted as a null statement following the **if**, and the compiler won't find anything to connect the **else** to. To correct this problem, omit one of the semicolons:

```
if( condition )
        NEXTARG( x, int )              /* No ; */
else
        NEXTARG( x, long );
```

Be sure to comment the code when you do something like this, so that the missing semicolon doesn't look like an error.

Another way to handle the two-statements-in-a-macro problem is with the comma operator. We could have #**defined** *NEXTARG* as follows:

```
#define NEXTARG(x, type) x=*(type *)ap, ap += sizeof(type)
```

Here, though, we're counting on left-to-right evaluation of the comma operator. The expression is also harder to read (at least to me).

There are two other alternatives for *NEXTARG:*

```
#define NEXTARG(x,type)   x = *( (type *) p )++
```

should fetch the argument off the stack and advance the pointer in one operation. Many compilers won't accept this statement, however. The problem has to do with *rvalue*s, temporary variables used by the compiler. The value of a cast number is often put into an rvalue. That is, since a cast may change the size of the converted object, this object is often put into an anonymous temporary variable. If this is the case, the above expression is telling the compiler to increment the temporary variable, the rvalue, rather than *p* itself. Since incrementing an rvalue is meaningless, many compilers reject this statement.

The second alternative for *NEXTARG* is

```
#define NEXTARG(x,type)   x = ((type *)( p += sizeof(type) ))[-1]
```

Here, *p* must be a pointer to **char**. It is advanced past the object we want to fetch with the +=. We then reach backwards into the stack, indexing from the new position with a *[– 1]*. Note that all the parentheses in this expression are required because the cast operator is both higher precedence than += and lower precedence that [].

9.5. doprnt( ): The Code

The actual code for *doprnt()* is shown in figure 9-7. Simple cases of printing, in which no conversions have to be made, are all done in the code on lines 94 through 99. We scan through the format string, one character at a time, calling the output routine indirectly to print the characters. The remainder of the subroutine is in the **else** clause that takes care of % conversion. It starts on line 100 and goes to line 252.

The code on lines 102 through 120 treats the variables that keep track of the conversion modifiers. They are initialized to default values, and then modified as required. *Fldwth* is set to the field width, *lftjust* is set true if a minus sign follows the % character, and so forth. Note that the conversion

%*... is accepted. Here the * says to take the field width from the argument list. This way you can call *printf()* with

```
printf("%*d", width, x )
```

to print *x* in a field *width* characters wide. The notation "%*.*f" isn't supported, however. You have to use an explicit number as the precision specifier (to the right of the decimal point).

The conversions are carried out in the **switch** on lines 140-209. Arguments are fetched off the stack in the way we just discussed, using the *NEXT-ARG* macro. Remember that the *%c* argument has a character passed to it in an **int**, so an **int** is fetched from the stack. Similarly, arguments corresponding to %f are passed in a **double**. The **if** on line 192 is needed to prevent sign extension when we pass an integer sized object to *ltos()* and that integer isn't being printed in base 10. (We'll discuss *ltos()* in a moment.)

When we leave the switch, the conversion will have been performed, and an ASCII string representing the converted number will have been loaded into the string pointed to by *bp.* That buffer is printed on lines 242 through 249, along with any required padding.

9.6. Structured Programming Considerations

Doprnt() is not a model of a properly structured subroutine, though all the deviations from the rules presented in Chapter 5 were done for good reasons. First of all, *doprnt()* is longer than a subroutine should be, in order to improve its execution time. One of the undesirable results of this length is the size of the outermost **for** loop (which starts on line 94 and ends on line 252, several pages later) and the length of the **else** clause (which extends from line 101 to line 251). Note that the **if** associated with this **else** is structured to put the shortest action close to the **if** statement. If we had said:

```
if( *format == '%' )
```

the **if** clause would have been several pages long and then we would have encountered

```
        else
            (*out)( *format, o_param );
```

but we probably would have forgotten to which test the **else** was associated. Moving the short action to the top of the **if/else** makes the code easier to read.

Fig. 9-7: Doprnt.c Continued: doprnt( ) Itself

```
71  /*---------------------------------------------------------------*/
72
73  char *DOPRNT (out, o_param, format, ap)
74  int      (*out)( );              /* Output subroutine               */
75  int      o_param;                /* Second argument to pass to out( ) */
76  char     *format;               /* Pointer to format string        */
77  char     *ap;                   /* Pointer to arguments            */
78  {
79          char     filchar ;      /* Fill character used to pad fields */
80          char     nbuf[34];      /* Buffer used to hold converted #s  */
81          char     *bp     ;      /* Pointer to current output buffer  */
82          int      slen    ;      /* Length of string pointed to by bp */
83          int      base    ;      /* Current base (%x=16, %d=10, etc.) */
84          int      fldwth  ;      /* Field width as in %10x            */
85          int      prec    ;      /* Precision as in %10.10s or %10.3f */
86          int      lftjust ;      /* 1 = left justifying (eg. %-10d)   */
87          int      longf   ;      /* Doing long int (%lx or %ld, etc.) */
88          long     lnum    ;      /* Holds numeric arguments           */
89
90  #ifdef FLOAT
91          double   dnum    ;      /* used to hold double arguments     */
92  #endif
93
94          for(; *format; format++ )
95          {
96              if( *format != '%')            /* No conversion, just */
97              {                              /* print the next char. */
98                  (*out)(*format, o_param);
99              }
100             else                           /* Process a % conversion */
101             {
102                 bp           = nbuf  ;
103                 filchar      = ' '   ;
104                 fldwth       = 0     ;
105                 lftjust      = 0     ;
106                 longf        = 0     ;
107                 prec         = 0     ;
108                 slen         = 0     ;
109
110                 /* Interpret any modifiers that can precede a
111                  * conversion character. ( %04... , %-10.6.., etc).
112                  * If an * is present instead of a field width then
113                  * the width is taken from the argument list.
114                  */
115
116                 if( *++format == '-') { ++format ;  ++lftjust;     }
117                 if( *format   == '0') { ++format ;  filchar = '0'; }
118
119
120                 if( *format != '*' )
121                         TOINT( format, fldwth );
122                 else
123                 {
124                         format++;
125                         NEXTARG( fldwth, int );
126                 }
127
128                 if( *format == '.' ) { ++format; TOINT(format, prec);}
```

```
129                    if( *format == 'l' ) { ++format; ++longf ;              }
130
131
132                    /*
133                     *  By now we've picked off all the modifiers and
134                     *  *format is looking at the actual conversion
135                     *  character. Pick the appropriately sized argument
136                     *  off the stack and advance the pointer (ap) to
137                     *  point at the next argument.
138                     */
139
140                    switch( *format )
141                    {
142                    default:    *bp++ = *format ;
143                                break;
144
145                    case 'c':   NEXTARG( *bp++, int );
146                                break;
147
148                    case 's':   NEXTARG( bp, char *);
149                                break;
150 #ifdef FLOAT
151                    case 'f':
152
153                        NEXTARG( dnum, double );
154                        if( dnum < 0   &&  filchar == '0')
155                        {
156                                /* If we are zero filling then we have
157                                 * to print the - now so that we won't
158                                 * get "0000-5.2."
159                                 */
160
161                                (*out)( '-' ,o_param) ;
162                                --fldwth;
163                                dnum = -dnum ;
164                        }
165
166                        bp = dtos( dnum, bp, prec ? prec : 6 );
167                        break;
168 #endif
169                    case 'd':   base = 10 ;
170                                goto pnum ;
171
172                    case 'x':   base = 16 ;
173                                goto pnum ;
174
175                    case 'b':   base = 2 ;
176                                goto pnum ;
177
178                    case 'o':   base = 8 ;
179                                /* fall through */
180 pnum:
181                        /* Fetch a long or int-sized argument off the
182                         * stack as appropriate. If the fetched number
183                         * is not a base 10 int, then mask off the top
184                         * bits to prevent sign extension.
185                         */
186
187                        if( longf )
188                                NEXTARG( lnum, long )          /* No ; */
189                        else
190                        {
191                                NEXTARG( lnum, int );
192                                if( base != 10 )
```

```
193                                    lnum &= INTMASK;
194                   }
195
196                   if( lnum < 0L  &&  base == 10  && filchar == '0' )
197                   {
198                           /* Again, print a - to avoid "000-123."
199                            * Only decimal numbers get - signs.
200                            */
201
202                           (*out)( '-' ,o_param) ;
203                           --fldwth ;
204                           lnum = -lnum ;
205                   }
206
207                   bp    = ltos( lnum, bp, base );
208                   break;
209           }
210
211
212           /*   Terminate the string if necessary and compute
213            *   the string length (slen). Bp will point to the
214            *   beginning of the output string.
215            */
216
217           if (*format != 's')
218           {
219               *bp   = '\0';
220               slen = bp - nbuf;
221               bp    = nbuf;
222           }
223           else
224           {
225               slen = strlen(bp);
226               if( prec  &&  slen > prec )
227                       slen = prec;
228           }
229
230
231           /*   Adjust fldwth to be the amount of padding we need
232            *   to fill the buffer out to the specified field
233            *   width. Then print leading padding (if we aren't
234            *   left justifying), the buffer itself, and any
235            *   required trailing padding (if we are left
236            *   justifying).
237            */
238
239           if( (fldwth -= slen) < 0 )
240               fldwth = 0;
241
242           if (!lftjust)
243               PAD( fldwth );
244
245           while( --slen >= 0 )
246               (*out)(*bp++,o_param);
247
248           if ( lftjust)
249               PAD( fldwth );
250
251       }       /* end else                            */
252   }       /* end for(; *format; format++)   */
253 }
254
```

There are a few other dubious pieces of code which, again, make *doprnt()* faster. First, the body of the *case 'f':* statement (lines 152–168) should be in a subroutine to reduce the size of the **switch**. Similarly, the body of the *case 'o'* (lines 181–208) should be in a subroutine that is called in place of all the preceding **goto** statements. In other words, if the routine were structured properly, it would look like this:

```
do_int( ... , base )
{
        /* Old contents of the case 'o' go in here */
}

doprnt( ... )
{
        /*   ...   */

        case 'd':     do_int( ..., 10 );    break;
        case 'x':     do_int( ..., 16 );    break;
        case 'b':     do_int( ...,  2 );    break;
        case 'o':     do_int( ...,  8 );    break;

        /*   ...   */
}
```

The **goto**s allow us to avoid a subroutine call without adding the extra code that a subroutine-like macro would give us.

The final part of the doprnt.c file is a test routine that is only compiled if *DEBUG* has been **#define**d. This routine is shown in figure 9-8. We're using the name *printm()* on line 261 so that we can use the *printf()* that was supplied with the compiler for debugging. I always include a small test program in a file destined for inclusion in a library. This way I can test the library routine by compiling the file as an independent module, without creating a second file with a *main()* and then linking. If *DEBUG* isn't **#define**d, *main()* won't be compiled and *doprnt()* can be linked into a library.

9.7. ltos( )

Two more routines are needed to round out *doprnt(): ltos()*, which converts a **long** to an ASCII string, and *dtos()*, which converts a **double** to a string. The code for *ltos()* is in figure 9-9.

Fig. 9-8: Doprnt.c Continued: Test Routines

```
255 /*-----------------------------------------------------------------*/
256
257 #ifdef DEBUG
258
259 #include <stdio.h>
260
261 printm (format, args)
262 char    *format;
263 char    *args;
264 {
265         /*  A version of printf. Call it printm( ) so that we can
266          *  use the real printf for debugging.
267          */
268
269         extern int  fputc( );
270
271         DOPRNT( fputc, stdout, format, &args );
272 }
273
274 /*-----------------------------------------------------------------*/
275
276 main( )
277 {
278         printm("%d %x %o %ld %lx %lo %3.1f %c %s\n",
279                                 0, 1, 2, 3L, 4L, 5L, 6.7, '8', "9" );
280
281         printm("%s %s %c", "hello", "world", '\n'          );
282         printm("should see <string> : <%6.6s>\n", "string NO NO NO");
283         printm("should see <70000> : <%ld>\n", 70000L );
284         printm("should see <fffff> : <%lx>\n",0xfffffL);
285         printm("should see <ffff> : <%x>\n",       -1  );
286         printm("should see <-1>     : <%ld>\n",    -1L );
287         printm("should see <x>      : <%c>\n",     'x' );
288         printm("should see <a5>     : <%x>\n",     0xa5 );
289         printm("should see <765>    : <%o>\n",     0765 );
290         printm("should see <1010>   : <%b>\n",     0xa );
291         printm("should see <   123> : <%6d>\n",    123 );
292         printm("should see <   456> : <%*d>\n",  6,456 );
293         printm("should see <  -123> : <%6d>\n",   -123 );
294         printm("should see <123   > : <%-6d>\n",   123 );
295         printm("should see <-123  > : <%-6d>\n",  -123 );
296         printm("should see <-00123> : <%06d>\n",  -123 );
297
298 #ifdef FLOAT
299         printm("should see < 1.234> : <%6.3f>\n",   1.234 );
300         printm("should see <01.234> : <%06.3f>\n",  1.234 );
301         printm("should see <1.010 > : <%-6.3f>\n",  1.010 );
302         printm("should see <-1.3  > : <%-6.1f>\n", -1.26 );
303         printm("should see <  -1.2> : <%6.1f>\n",  -1.24 );
304         printf("should see <1.234567>: <%f>\n",    1.234567  );
305         printf("should see <1>       : <%1.0f>\n", 1.234567  );
306 #endif
307 }
308
309 #endif
```

Fig. 9-9: ltos.c - Convert Long to String

```
1  char     *ltos( n, buf, base )
2  unsigned long   n    ;
3  char            *buf ;
4  int             base ;
5  {
6          /*      Convert long to string. Prints in hex, decimal, octal,
7          *                                              or binary.
8          *       "n"    is the number to be converted.
9          *       "buf"  is the output buffer.
10         *       "base" is the base (16, 10, 8, or 2).
11         *
12         *       The output string is null terminated, and a pointer
13         *       to the null terminator is returned.
14         *
15         *       The number is put into an array one digit at a time
16         *       as it's translated. The array is filled with the digits
17         *       reversed (ie. the \0 goes in first, then the rightmost
18         *       digit, etc.) and then is reversed in place before
19         *       returning.
20         */
21
22         register char    *bp   = buf;
23         register int     minus = 0;
24         char             *endp;
25
26         if( base == 10 && (long)n < 0 ) /* If the number is negative */
27         {                               /* and we're in base 10, set */
28                 minus++ ;               /* minus to true and make it */
29                 n = -( (long)n );       /* positive.                 */
30         }
31
32         *bp = '\0' ;                    /* We have to put the null in now  */
33                                         /* because the array is being      */
34                                         /* filled in reverse order.        */
35         do {
36                 *++bp = "0123456789abcdef" [ n % base ];
37                 n /= base;
38
39         } while( n );
40
41         if( minus )
42                 *++bp = '-';
43
44         for( endp = bp; bp > buf ;)     /* Reverse string in place. */
45         {
46                 minus  = *bp;           /* Use minus for temporary  */
47                 *bp -- = *buf;          /* storage.                 */
48                 *buf++ = minus;
49         }
50
51         return endp;                    /* Return pointer to terminating null */
52  }
```

Ltos( ) is passed three arguments: *n* is the number to be converted, *buf* is a pointer to a buffer into which the converted string will be placed, and *base* is the conversion radix. *Base* is 2 for conversion to binary, 8 for octal, 10 for decimal, and 16 for hex. You can also use *ltos( )* to convert to an unusual base (like base seven) if you want, but *base* has to be in the range 2 to 16. Base ten numbers can be negative, and they will be printed with a leading minus sign when this is the case. Other bases are viewed as bit patterns so it's not meaningful to treat them as negative numbers.

The argument *n* is declared as an **unsigned long**, even though it's liable to be a signed number. This declaration makes the modulus mathematics on line 36 more reliable. However, we have to cast *n* into a normal (signed) **long** on line 26 in order to test for less than zero. There's an implicit type conversion here when *ltos( )* is called (from signed **long** to **unsigned long**). Since a **long** is the same size whether it's signed or unsigned, this implicit conversion has no unwanted side effects.

The converted digits are put into the buffer in reverse order (the least significant digit first). Consequently, the terminating '\0' is put into the string before any characters are added (on line 32). When the conversion is complete, the entire string is reversed in place (on lines 44-49).

The actual conversion, which is admittedly somewhat weird looking, is done with the **do** loop on lines 35 through 39. This code is explained in depth in Chapter 6. The expression *"0123456789abcdef"* evaluates to a character pointer and the square bracket operator can be applied to any character pointer. The expression *"0123456789abcdef"[5]* evaluates to the character '5.' Here we're doing a modulus division by the current base rather than the simple AND operation that was used in Chapter Six. (An AND would let us convert only to bases that are powers of two.) Note that modulus division can have unexpected results when one of the operands is negative. That's why *n* is declared **unsigned**. The following formula should be true in a modulus operation:

```
x == ((x / n) * n) + (x % n)
```

but you can't count on it.

9.8. dtos( )

The floating point equivalent of *ltos( )* is *dtos( )*, which does a **double** to ASCII conversion (see figure 9-10). Most of the actual conversion work done by *dtos( )* is actually done by *ltos( )*. Consequently, the main function of *dtos( )* is to convert a double into two **long**s—one for the integer part of the number and the second for the fractional part. These **long**s are then passed to *ltos( )* for conversion. The problem with this strategy is that the size of the number is limited to the size of a **long**, which is by necessity less than that of a **double**.

That is, you can represent a larger number in a 64-bit **double** than you can in a 32-bit **long**, so a **double** with a very large (or small) value will be truncated by *dtos( )*.

The integer part of the **double** is extracted by the cast on line 50 of *dtos( )*. Casting a **double** into a **long** does a floating point to integer conversion. It will truncate the fractional part of the number as part of the conversion. The integer part of the number is eliminated by the subtraction on line 51. After this subtraction, the integer part of the number is reduced to zero and the fractional part remains untouched.

The fractional part of *n* is extracted in the **if** clause on lines 53 through 84. The **for** loop on lines 60 and 61 multiplies the fraction we extracted earlier by 10 to the *precision* power. (*Precision* is the number of bits we want to the right of the decimal.) This multiply has the same effect as a decimal left shift of *precision* digits (or of moving the decimal point *precision* digits to the right). We've thus moved the part of the fraction in which we're interested into the integer part of the number. We now have to round the integer up or down, depending on what the remaining fraction is. Failing to do this will cause 0.9999999 to be printed instead of 1.0 and so on. The rounding is done on line 69. On line 71 we do two things. We convert the extracted fraction to a string using the same cast and call to *ltos( )* that we used earlier. At the same time, *i* is initialized to contain the number of zeros needed to fill out the number [leading zeros won't be printed by *ltos( )*]. Finally, we copy the decimal point, the leading zeros, and the converted fraction into the original buffer with the two **for** loops on lines 79 through 83.

9.9. Exercises

9-1 Using *doprnt(),* write *sprintf(). Sprintf()* is a standard library routine that works like *printf()* except that it writes to a string rather than to standard output. For example, the call:

```
char      buf[80];

sprintf( buf, "%d", n );
```

Converts n to an ASCII string and puts the string into *buf* (rather than printing it on the screen). If your solution is longer than about 15 lines of code, you're doing something seriously wrong.

9-2 Modify *doprnt()* so that it can accept an * instead of the precision portion of the field width specifier (currently, it only supports an * to the left of the decimal point). Also add the following conversions:

Fig. 9-10: dtos.c - Convert Double to String

```
 1 extern   char     *ltos   (long,     char*,    int       );
 2 extern   double   floor   (double              );
 3 extern   double   ceil    (double              );
 4
 5 #define MAXPREC    32                  /* Maximum number of digits    */
 6                                        /* permitted to the right of   */
 7                                        /* the decimal point.          */
 8 #define FRACT(n) ((n)-(long)(n))   /* Extract fractional part of n.*/
 9
10 #define min(a,b)  ((a) < (b) ? (a) : (b))
11
12 /*-----------------------------------------------------------*/
13
14 char     *dtos( num, buf, precision )
15 double   num  ;
16 char     *buf ;
17 int      precision ;
18 {
19          /*   Convert double to string. Only decimal conversion is
20           *           supported.
21           *   "num"   is the number to be converted.
22           *   "buf"   is the output buffer.
23           *   "precision" is the number of digits to the right of the
24           *           decimal. Maximum precision is 32. If precision is
25           *           zero, only the integer portion of the number is
26           *           converted.
27           *   The output string is null terminated and a pointer to
28           *   the null terminator is returned.
29           */
30
31          static   char     tbuf[MAXPREC+1];
32          int               i  ;
33          char              *bp ;
34          long              lnum;
35
36          precision = min(precision,MAXPREC); /* Truncate the preci-  */
37                                              /* sion if necessary.    */
38
39          if( num < 0.0 )                 /* Convert number to positive */
40          {                               /* and print the '-' sign if  */
41                  *buf++ = '-' ;          /* necessary.                 */
42                  num = -num;
43          }
44
45          /*   Strip off the integer part of the number and convert it
46           *   to an ASCII string using ltos. Then subtract the integer
47           *   part from the original number to isolate the fraction.
48           */
49
50          buf  = ltos( lnum = (long)num, buf, 10 );
51          num -= lnum ;
52
53          if( precision )
54          {
55                  /*   Print the fraction. First multiply it by 10
56                   *   to the precision power to move it into the
57                   *   integer part of the number.
58                   */
```

```
59
60                         for( i = precision; --i >= 0 ; )
61                                 num *= 10.0 ;
62
63                         /*   Round the resulting number up or down as approp-
64                          *   riate, and then compute the number of leading
65                          *   required zeros in the resulting number as we call
66                          *   ltos( ). (Ltos won't print the leading zeros.)
67                          */
68
69                         num = (FRACT(num)  >=  0.50) ? ceil(num) : floor(num);
70
71                         i = precision - ( ltos((long)num, tbuf, 10) - tbuf);
72
73
74                         /*   Finally transfer the decimal point, the leading
75                          *   zeros, and then the fractional part of the number,
76                          *   to the target buffer.
77                          */
78
79                         for( *buf++ = '.';   --i >= 0;   *buf++ = '0')
80                                 ;
81
82                         for( bp = tbuf; *bp ; *buf++ = *bp++ )
83                                 ;
84                 }
85
86         *buf = 0 ;
87         return( buf );
88 }
```

```
        %p - prints a pointer-sized object in hex.
        %u - prints an unsigned int in decimal.
        %X - like %x except that the letters are
             printed in upper case.
        %e - prints a double in engineering notation
             Use the form [-]m.nnnE[+|-]xx, where the
             length of the string of n's is specified
             by the precision (default is 6) and m
             is always one digit.
```

9-3   Modify *dtos()* so that it can print all possible values of a **double**, not just those **double**s whose integer values are representable in a **long**.

9-4   Write the input function *scanf()*. Use your own compiler's documentation as a specification. You need support only the following conversions: %d %c %o %x %f %s. If a * follows the %, you should remove the indicated object from the input stream and not put it anywhere.

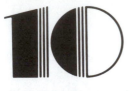

DEBUGGING

This chapter looks at many of the most common debugging problems and programming errors in C programs. Both problems and solutions are presented. Some of these problems are covered in greater depth elsewhere in the text but are mentioned again here so that all the debugging issues are concentrated in one place.

Stack-related and pointer-related problems are not addressed here; they're discussed in depth in Chapters 4, 6, and 7.

10.1. Using printf( ) for Debugging

Perhaps the most powerful debugging aid at your disposal is *printf( )*. If your program isn't working properly, liberally sprinkle the suspected areas of the code with *printf( )* statements that tell you the current contents of important variables, the number of iterations of a loop, and so forth. It usually takes much less time to insert a *printf( )* statement in the code than it does to use a debugger such as adb or symdeb. If you're developing your program in a structured manner (see Chapter Five), you should already have a good idea of the problem's location before you start adding diagnostics.

Debugging *printf( )* statements should always contain the name of the subroutine being debugged and something that identifies where in the code the *printf( )* statement can be found. For example:

```
printf("In oz( ), before while(away_the_hours): x = %d\n", x);
```

The **#define** mechanism can be used if you want to leave the debugging statements in the code but you want them to be inactive when they're not being used. (I always seem to erase a debugging diagnostic five minutes before I need it again.) Two good way to do this are shown in figure 10-1.

Fig. 10-1: Two Methods for Eliminating Diagnostics

```
#ifdef DEBUG
#define DIAG(x,y)    fprintf(stderr, x, y);
#define D(x)         x
#else
#define DIAG(x,y)
#define D(x)
#endif

fred()
{
        DIAG("This is only be printed if DEBUG is #defined\n", 0 );
        DIAG("fred(): At top of program, x = %d\n", x);

        D( printf("This will go away when DEBUG isn't #defined\n") );

        for( i = 0; i < it_should_be ; i++ )
        {
                DIAG("fred( ): Doing iteration %d of for loop\n", i );
        }
}
```

DIAG expands to a *printf( )* statement if *DEBUG* is **#define**d; otherwise it expands to a null string and its arguments are ignored. Using *DIAG* yields cleaner code than you'd get by putting #*ifdef DEBUG* statements all over the place. Since *DIAG* is a macro, you have to pass it two arguments even if the second argument isn't used. You can pass in a dummy second argument to the macro, however (the 0 in the example just cited).

The second method illustrated in figure 10-1 is the null macro, *D*. When *DEBUG* is **#define**d, *D* expands to its argument, in this case a *printf( )* statement. As before, when *DEBUG* isn't **#define**d, it expands to nothing.

There are a few caveats for the *D* macro. Some preprocessors won't accept it all, so it's not necessarily portable. Similarly, some preprocessors get hopelessly confused if there's a comma inside the argument to *D*. Be especially careful of the comma operator. Finally, the position of the semicolon can cause problems, best illustrated with an example. The code:

```
if( (2 * b) || !two_b )
        D( printf("That is the question\n");   )
else
        printf("slings and arrows\n");
```

will expand as follows if *DEBUG* isn't **#define**d:

```
if( (2 * b) || !two_b )
else
        printf("slings and arrows\n");
```

This is not legal C.

Another debugging aid is a subroutine's printing its own return address. You can compare the address from which a subroutine is called with a *link map*— a list, created by the linker, of the base addresses of all nonstatic subroutines—to trace subroutine execution. This is especially useful when you're trying to track down problems related to stack overflow. The procedure is explained in section 9-1.

A common problem with *printf()* diagnostics is the program's normal output getting mixed up with the error diagnostics in unpredictable ways. This is especially a problem if normal output is going to *stdout* and diagnostic output is going to *stderr.*

The MS-DOS and UNIX output mechanisms treat these two streams as completely independent output devices; consequently, the two streams will not necessarily be printed on the screen in the same order that the lines are output by the program. That is:

```
printf (           "First\n"  );
fprintf( stderr, "Second\n" );
```

may well appear on the screen as

```
Second
First
```

Though the lines are transposed, the characters within the lines won't be mixed together.

One way to circumvent this problem from inside a program is to call *fflush(stderr)* or *fflush(stdout)* after every *fprintf()* call. There are other work-arounds. You can log all output to the printer (with a SHIFT-PrtSc or ^P) and then redirect standard output (with *foo > outfile*) All text sent to standard error is printed on both the screen and the printer and all text sent to standard output will be in the indicated file. MS-DOS doesn't let you redirect both standard error and standard output, though there are UNIX-like shells that replace command.com, the standard command-line interpreter, that do allow redirection of both streams (see Bibliography).

In UNIX, *prog >& file* can be used to redirect both standard error and standard output to a file. Though UNIX systems don't rearrange *stderr* and *stdout* when they're both sent to the screen, the two streams will be mixed up when you use *>&* to redirect them. (On the system that I use, all the standard output is put into the file as a block, followed by all the standard error output.) You can put the standard error and standard output in different files by using the following on the command line:

```
( prog > file1 ) >& file2
```

All messages sent to *stdout* will be in file1, and messages sent to *stderr* will be in file2.

10.2. Comments Do Not Nest

Comments don't nest. That is, you can't put a comment inside another comment (see figure 10-2).

Fig. 10-2: Comments Don't Nest

```
        /*          /*      text    */      text     */
         |           |       |        |       |        |
         |           |       |        |       |        |
   This is the       |   This is the  |   This is an error
  start of comment.  |   end of comment.  | because there's no
                     |                |   matching open
                     |                |   comment.
                     |                |
    This is considered to be part     |
    of the comment and is ignored.   The compiler will try to
                                      compile this, probably
                                      generating an error.
```

Nested comments can cause several problems. The easiest one to find is an error message that's generated because the compiler is trying to process text that you intended to be part of a comment.

If you need to comment out a large block of code that contains comments use a **#ifdef** statement and never **#define** the associated macro name. For example:

```
#ifdef NEVER
        /* None of this code is compiled only if
         * NEVER hasn't been previously #defined.
         */
#endif
```

Just never say *NEVER*. **#ifdef**s do nest, so the following is legal:

```
#ifdef EMMA

        /* This code is compiled only if EMMA
         * has been #defined.
         */

#ifdef WOODHOUSE

        /* This code is compiled only if EMMA and
         * WOODHOUSE have both been #defined.
         */
#endif
        /* This code is compiled only if EMMA
         * has been #defined.
         */
#endif
```

Harder to find is code that is not compiled because of a missing close comment:

```
/* Here is a comment that
isn't closed properly the
following while loop is part
of the comment: /

while( condition )
        action( );

/* Here is another comment. The
start of comment is ignored but
the end of comment is not. */
```

generates no error messages, but the **while** loop is not compiled.

The best solution to this problem is to write your code in such a way that it's easy to find close comments. That is, always write your comments in one of these ways:

```
/*  Here you can find the close
 *  comment by looking down the
 *  line of asterisks.
 */

/*  Here the open and close comments    */
/*  are easy to find because they're    */
/*  in neat columns.                    */
```

10.3. Lvalue Required

One of the most common, but most difficult to understand, error messages is the *lvalue required* error. In order to see the problem more clearly, we should start by defining *lvalue*. Kernighan and Ritchie define it as follows:

An *object* is a manipulatable region of storage; an *lvalue* is an expression referring to an object. An obvious example of an lvalue is an identifier. There are operators that yield lvalues: for example if E is an expression of pointer type, then *E is an lvalue expression referring to the object to which E points. The name *lvalue* comes from the assignment expression *E1=E2* in which the left operand *E1* must be an lvalue expression.[1]

An lvalue is the place where the results of an expression evaluation are stored (or as Pooh said, "a useful pot to put things in"). That is, it's an address, a place where the result of an evaluation can be stored. An lvalue has to be a real place—a variable that's been declared somewhere or the place to which a pointer points.

The complementary concept to an lvalue is an *rvalue*. An rvalue represents the value of an lvalue. That is, if an lvalue is the address into which the result of an evaluation is put, an rvalue is the result itself, the number that is put into the lvalue. More precisely, an rvalue is an anonymous temporary variable, used during expression evaluation to hold intermediate results of the evaluation. Since you didn't declare this temporary variable, you can't access it directly. In

```
x = (y * z);
```

the result of *(y * z)* is put into an anonymous temporary by the compiler. The contents of this temporary rvalue are then copied to the lvalue, *x*. Note that in

```
x = y;
```

y is an rvalue because the contents of y may be copied to anonymous temporary and that temporary copied to *x*. This behavior is a side effect of the way that compilers work rather than planning on the part of the compiler writer. Most optimizers will remove the redundant copying. Nonetheless, *y* is still an rvalue.

Rvalues have very short life times. They are deleted once evaluation of the expression in which they're used is finished. Usually, but not always, the contents of an rvalue must be copied into an lvalue by the end of the evaluation process. We'll look at exceptions to this rule in a moment.

Only a few constructs generate an lvalue. These are shown in figure 10-3. All operators, unless they're part of a pointer or offset calculation, generate an rvalue, not an lvalue, and that rvalue must be stored in an lvalue. So

```
x++ = 5;
```

creates an "lvalue required" error message because x++ generates an rvalue (that contains the contents of x before the increment) but the rvalue is never

---

1. B. Kernighan and D. Ritchie, *The C Programming Language* (Englewood Cliffs, N. J.: Prentice-Hall, 1978), p. 183.

stored in an lvalue.[2] On the other hand,

$$*++ptr = 5;$$

is legal because even though the ++ creates an rvalue, the * converts the rvalue back into an lvalue.

Fig. 10-3: Expressions That Yield Lvalues

```
Identifiers:                       x = 5

Complete array references:         array[i] = 5
                                   array[i+j] = 5
                                   etc.

Structure member references:       structure.field = 5

Indirect member references:        struct_pointer->field = 5
                                   (struct_pointer + offset)->field = 5
                                   (struct_pointer ++)->field = 5
                                   etc.

Object-pointed-to:                 *pointer = 5
                                   *(pointer + offset) = 5;
                                   *(pointer++) = 5;
                                   etc.
```

Perhaps the reason for this is made clearer if you look at what the compiler does with the two constructs. Many compilers treat

```
char    *ptr;
*++ptr = 'a' ;
```

as follows:

(1) Fetch the contents of *ptr* and put it in a temporary variable.

(2) Increment the temporary variable and then store the resulting value in *ptr*.

(3) Move *a* into the address contained in the temporary variable.

Even though all three of these operations involve a a temporary variable, the temporaries used in steps 1 and 2 are rvalues (because they contain a value) but the temporary used in step 3 is an lvalue (because it holds an address and that address is used before evaluation is complete). Step 1 initializes the temporary variable, step 2 modifies and copies the temporary somewhere, and

---

2.   Note that the ++ and -- operators are unusual in that they both can generate an
     lvalue or an rvalue, depending on the context.

step 3 uses the temporary as a pointer (as an lvalue).

The incorrect statement:

```
int    x  ;
++x = 'a' ;
```

is processed as was just shown:

(1)   Fetch the contents of x and put it in a temporary variable

(2)   Increment this temporary variable and store the result in x.

(3)   Move *a* into a temporary variable.

Here, however, the temporary that was loaded in step 3 is never used. What point is there in moving *a* into a temporary if we don't eventually store it somewhere else? None. That's why the compiler generates an "lvalue required" error message in this situation.

There's another problem. The expression

```
x = --( y - z );
```

is also illegal. Here you'd think this was acceptable because even though you're modifying the rvalue [*(y-z)*], you're storing the modified value. Unfortunately, the -- operator *must* be applied to an lvalue, not an rvalue. This problem is something of a right-hand-not-knowing-what-the-left-hand-is-doing problem. The part of the compiler that generated the code to evaluate *y-z* put the result in a temporary, but the part of the compiler that's generating the code to do the -- doesn't know where that temporary is. In other words, the -- processing routine assumes that you're always going to tell it exactly what to decrement, but since you don't know where the temporary is in memory, you can't tell that to the -- processor.

How do you find out which operators require lvalues and which operators require rvalues? By consulting the grammar used by your compiler (or the one in the back of Kernighan and Ritchie (see Bibliography). There's a non-terminal called an lvalue in the grammar. That's one of the reasons we looked at grammars so closely in Chapter 8: so that you could use a grammar when you had to.

10.4. Operator-related Errors

10.4.1. Order-of-Precedence Errors

Be careful of the order of precedence of operators. I've enlarged a few copies of the C order-of-precedence chart and hung a copy next to every computer I'm likely to use. As we saw in Chapter 6, *++p* increments the pointer while *++*p* increments the object-pointed-to by *p* .

Other operators are more treacherous, especially the various assignment operators. For example, the test in

```
while( c = getchar( ) != EOF )
        something( c );
```

evaluates to

```
while( c = (getchar( ) != EOF) )
        something( c );
```

That is, *c* has the value 1 assigned to it if the character returned from *getchar()* is not *EOF*, otherwise *c* has 0 assigned to it. The character returned by *getchar()* is lost. The problem can be solved with parentheses:

```
while( (c = getchar( )) != EOF )
        something( c );
```

More insidious is the += operator and its cousins. It's very common to say something like this:

```
while( i++ < 10 )
        do_something( );
```

But what if you want to add 2 rather than 1? The temptation is to say

```
while( i += 2 < 10 )
        do_something( );
```

but the order of precedence chart tells us that < is higher precedence than +=. Consequently the expression parenthesizes to:

```
while( i += (2 < 10) )
        do_something( );
```

The *i* has 1 added to it if 2 is greater than 10, otherwise it has zero added to it. Since 2 is usually less than 10, *i* is always incremented. The loop is executed many more times than we intended. Again, the problem can be fixed with parentheses:

```
while( (i += 2)  < 10) )
        do_something( );
```

The moral here is to be careful. Don't think that you shouldn't use += because it's liable to cause problems, just be careful when you do use it.

There's another problem. Consider this expression:

```
x = a-----b;
```

that has five minus signs in a row. How does it parenthesize? Some possibilities are:

```
x = ( a-- ) - ( --b );
x = ( a-- ) --( -b  );
x = a  -  ( --( --b ));
```

Of these, only the first is legal syntactically. However, the decisions about whether an operator is a - or a -- are made by the early stages of the compiler (the lexical analyzer) in the easiest possible way, and these early stages don't know anything about C syntax. They just collect characters from input until they've collected the longest possible object that makes sense. The compiler will probably choose the middle of the three possibilities and give you an error message.

10.4.2. Order-of-Evaluation Errors

In C, as in most programming languages, the order in which two operators having the same precedence level are evaluated is not guaranteed.[3] This usually doesn't matter. For example, when we say

```
x = --y + --z ;
```

it doesn't matter whether y is decremented before or after z, as long as both are decremented before doing the addition. The expression

```
int     a = 4;

x = --a - --a;
```

is another matter. This is a legal expression in the language and is accepted without an error message by most compilers. Nevertheless, if the leftmost a is decremented first, the expression evaluates to

```
x = 3 - 2;
```

or 1. If the rightmost a is decremented first the the expression evaluates to

```
x = 2 - 3;
```

or -1; a is decremented twice before subtracting, but we don't know which a is decremented first.

Don't confuse associativity and order of precedence with order of evaluation. Associativity and precedence determine which of several possible operators are associated with a particular variable and how implied parentheses are inserted. Order of evaluation is the order in which expressions at the same level of parentheses nesting are evaluated.

Order of evaluation also causes problems in subroutine calls. The order in which arguments to a subroutine are evaluated is not defined. In the call

```
a = 4;
foo( a, a++ );
```

the problems we saw earlier still apply. If the left a is evaluated first, foo is

---

3.   The exceptions to this rule are the || and && operators, which evaluate left to right. Here evaluation is guaranteed to terminate when it can be decided whether the expression is true or false.

called with *foo(4,4);* if the right argument is evaluated first, foo is called with *foo(5,4).* Similarly, in the call

```
sit( spot( ), fido( ) );
```

you don't know whether *spot()* or *fido()* is called first. If the two subroutines interact via global variables, this can cause problems. (By the way, this problem is another reason to avoid using global variables if at all possible.)

A final order-of-evaluation problem is the addition operator. Some compilers assume that addition is both commutative and associative. Consequently, these compilers ignore parentheses in expressions that only use the + operator. For example

```
z = (a + b) + (c + d)
```

may be treated as

```
z = a + (b + c) + d
```

even though the parentheses are present in the expression. To guarantee order of evaluation you have to say.

```
x =   a + b;
y =   c + d;
z =   x + y;
```

This usually doesn't matter but it might if a, b, c, or d are subroutine calls.

10.4.3. Using the Wrong Operator

The obvious problem here is confusing = with ==, & with &&, and so forth. Be especially careful of

```
while( x = y )
```

when you really mean:

```
while( x == y )
```

The former evaluates to the contents of y, the latter to 1 or 0, depending on whether x equals y. There are operator-related problems that are harder to detect though. For example: in C, the statement

```
x + y;
```

alone on a line is perfectly legal. It doesn't do anything useful, but many compilers won't even kick out a warning message when they see it. This can be a problem if you meant to say

```
x += y;
```

By the same token, many compilers accept the statement

```
x >= y;
```

when you intended to say

```
            x >>= y;
```

The first statement does nothing while the second statement shifts x right by y bits.

Incidentally, you occasionally see statements like

```
            x && y++ ;
```

used instead of

```
            if( x )
                    y++;
```

Y won't be incremented in either statement unless *x* is non-zero. The former is difficult to read, however, and should be avoided. Similarly, the comma operator should be avoided everywhere except in a **for** statement. Don't use

```
            if( condition )
                    x++, y++ ;
```

instead of

```
            if( condition )
            {
                    x++;
                    y++;
            }
```

except possibly in a macro definition where the brackets would be inconvenient.

10.5. Control Flow

10.5.1. Unwanted Null statements, Unattached { }

A semicolon is a statement terminator in C, rather than a statement separator (as in Pascal). In practice, this means that a semicolon by itself is a legal statement in the language; it's called a *null statement* because it doesn't do anything. Sometimes the null statement is useful, as in a **for** loop that has no body. An example is shown in figure 10-4.

Fig 10-4: A For Loop with a Null Body

```
strlen( str )                      /* Return the length      */
char    *str;                      /* of the string in bytes */
{
        register char    *p;

        for( p = str; *p ; p++ )   /* Advance p to the end */
                ;                  /* of string            */

        return( p - str );
}
```

More often than not, the presence of a null statement is a bug. For example

```
while( condition );
        --condition;
```

says "while *condition* is non-zero do nothing (that's the null statement following the **while**) then decrement *condition*." The loop never terminates. The same thing can happen in an **if** statement:

```
if( condition );
        thing_1( );
else
        thing_2( );
```

Here the compiler rearranges the code as follows:

```
if( condition )
        ; /* Do nothing */

thing_1( );
else
        thing_2( );
```

"If condition is true, do nothing, then execute *thing_1()*." When the compiler tries to process the **else** clause, it won't find any preceding **if** and will print an error message to that effect.

Putting curly braces after the **if** doesn't help when a semicolon precedes the curly brace. Curly braces don't have to be attached to a **while**, **for**, **if**, or whatever. For example, the following is legal:

```
while( condition )
{
        {
                do_something( );
        }
}
```

The reason for this usage of the brace is to limit the scope of a variable that's declared within the body of (rather than at the top of) a subroutine. For example:

```
alice( )
{
        int     i = 1; <---------- This "i" is a different
                                   variable than this "i."
        {                                                  |
                int     i; <-------------------------------+

                for( i = MAXVAL; --i >= 0 ; )
                        action();
        }
}
```

Here, the second *i* exists only within the inner curly braces. It is a physically different variable than the first *i,* added to the stack frame when it's declared and deleted from the stack frame when the } is encountered. The situation is identical to that of a global variable and local variable having the same name. The local variable is used when inside the subroutine, but the global variable still exists, there's just no way to get at it directly from inside the subroutine.

This rather odd convention is occasionally useful in a macro, when you have to create a temporary variable but don't want to worry about a conflict with an already-existing variable having the same name. For example

```
#define SWAP_INT(a,b) {int temp; temp=(a); (a)=(b); (b)=temp;}
```

exchanges the contents of *a* and *b*. The variable *temp* only exists while the code between the curly braces is being executed. It doesn't matter if another variable in the subroutine is also called *temp* the *temp* inside the curly braces is a different variable.

10.5.2. If/else Binding Incorrectly

An **else** statement always binds to the closest preceding **if**. For example, the following is wrong:

```
if( condition )
        if( condition )
                action( );
else <--------------------------- WRONG
        action( );
```

Here the **else** binds to the second **if** statement, not the first one, as is implied by the incorrect indenting. The problem shows up most often in a series of **if/else**s, as follows:

```
if( ... )
        action( );
else if( ... )
        action( );
else if( ... )
        action( );
```

If you don't think and put a second **if** statement in any of the **else** clauses, everything starts binding incorrectly. For this reason you should always use braces with a series of **if/else**s:

```
if( ... )
{
        action( );
}
else if( ... )
{
        action( );
}
else if( ... )
{
        action( );
}
```

10.6. Macros

10.6.1. Macro Order of Precedence Problems

In most compilers, you can only depend on compile-time evaluation of constant expressions when the expression is fully parenthesized. For example, in

```
x = i * (1024 * 6);
```

the *1024 * 6* is evaluated at compile time, so code will be generated exactly as if you had said *x = i * 6144.* If the parentheses aren't included in the expression, compile-time evaluation is not usually guaranteed. In this case the compiler inserts implied parentheses based on the left-to-right associativity of the multiplication operator. That is

```
i * 1024 * 6
```

is parenthesized by the compiler to:

```
((i * 1024) * 6)
```

because * associates from left to right. The compiler then says to itself, "I can't evaluate *(i * 1024)* at compile time because the expression contains a variable; I can't evaluate *((i * 1024) * 6)* at compile time, either, because the subexpression *(i * 1024)* contains a variable." When you **#define** a compound constant inside a macro, parenthesize it:

```
#define  ARRAY_SIZE  (1024 * 6)
```

This behavior is compiler-dependent but you should use the parentheses for portability even if your compiler does the evaluation correctly.

There are more subtle problems that can arise from macro expansion, though. Consider the macro

```
#define  SQUARE(i)   i * i
```

which evaluates to i^2. The macro, when invoked with:

```
x = SQUARE(a + b);
```

is expanded to

```
x = a + b * a + b;
```

Since * is higher precedence than +, the compiler evaluates this expression as

```
x = a + (b * a) + b;
```

which is not what we want.

The preprocessor doesn't know C, all it can do is text substitution, and that in the stupidest possible way. The preprocessor doesn't know how you intend arguments in a macro to evaluate, it just makes the indicated text substitutions. The problem with the *SQUARE* macro can be fixed by #**defining** *SQUARE* so that explicit parentheses force evaluation in the intended way:

```
#define  SQUARE(i)   ((i) * (i))
```

Our earlier example is now expanded to

```
x = ((a + b) * (a + b));
```

To avoid these problems, fully parenthesize all expressions in macros and surround all macro arguments with parentheses.

10.6.2. Unexpected Macro Argument Substitution

Most C programmers know that a macro won't be expanded inside a quoted string. For example, in

```
#define  FOO  xxxx

printf("FOO");
```

FOO is printed, not *xxxx*. Most C programmers don't realize that many compilers will expand macro arguments into quoted strings that are part of the macro definition. For example, given:

```
#define HELLO(name) printf("Hello name\n");
```

the invocation:

```
                                HELLO( Jean );
```

is expanded to

```
                              printf("Hello Jean\n");
```

This can cause problems in macros like:

```
        #define PRINT(s)          printf("%s",       s);
                    |                      |          |
                    |                      |          |
          The string corresponding         |          |
             to this argument      is expanded      |
                                      here        and here.
```

This in-string expansion can be useful at times. For example, when

```
    PRINT_NUM(name,radix)   fprintf(stderr, "name = %radix\n", name );
```

when invoked with

```
        PRINT_NUM(sarah, x )   /* Print in hex      */
        PRINT_NUM(bill,  d )   /* Print in decimal */
```

PRINT_NUM expands to:

```
        fprintf(stderr, "sarah = %x\n", sarah );
        fprintf(stderr, "bill  = %d\n", bill  );
```

10.6.3. Macros with Side Effects

Macros can modify variables in unexpected ways. Consider the macro *max(x,y),* which evaluates to either x or y, whichever is greater:

```
        #define max(x,y)  ((x) > (y) ? (x) : (y))
```

When this macro is invoked with

```
        y = max( *ptr++, MAXNUM );
```

it is expanded to:

```
        y = ((*ptr++) > (MAXNUM) ? (*ptr++) : (MAXNUM))
```

Ptr is incremented twice if *ptr is larger than *MAXNUM*. (it's only incremented once if *ptr is less than or equal to *MAXNUM*.) This sort of behavior is called a *side effect*. Unfortunately, most of the macros in ctype.h (*isupper*, *toupper*, *isdigit*, and so on) can have side effects. Be careful with them.[4]

---

4.   The proposed ANSI C standard prohibits side effects in standard library macros (like those in ctype.h). You can't count on an absence of side effects, however.

10.7. An Int Is Not 16 Bits Wide

10.7.1. Precision

You can never be sure that an **int**, or any other type for that matter, is a particular size. I've never seen an **int** represented in fewer than 16 bits. However, both 16-bit and 32-bit **ints** are common. This is a consideration in mathematical computation. If you assume that an **int** is 32 bits wide, numbers may be truncated when you try to move the code to a machine that uses a 16-bit **int**. If you need 32 bits of precision, put the variable into a **long** rather than an **int**. (A subroutine for computing the size of an **int** was given in Fig. 5-13).

10.7.2. Incomplete Statments in a Macro

A final macro-related problem is a macro that contains an **if** statement. For example

```
#define ERR(e,s)    if(e) printf(s)

if( condition )
        ERR( e, "error" );
else
        printf("something else");
```

doesn't work as expected. The **else** statement will bind to the closest preceding **if**, which happens to be part of the *ERR* macro. The above code incorrectly expands to the following:

```
if( condition )
{
        if( e )
                printf( "error" );
        else
                printf("something else");
}
```

The problem can be fixed by taking advantage of the null statement that caused problems earlier. A semicolon by itself is a legal statement in C (it does nothing, but it's legal). The *ERR* macro can be redefined as follows:

```
#define ERR(e,s)    if(e) printf(s); else
```

The **if** now has an associated **else** clause whose body will be the single semicolon supplied when we invoke the macro using

```
ERR(e,s);
```

10.7.3. Masks

An **int**'s size also is important in explicit masks with which we modify the top or bottom bits of a word. figure 10-5 is a chart of some of the most common of these masks presented in both portable and nonportable forms.

The left column shows explicit masks that assume that we're using a 16-bit-wide **int**. The middle column holds equivalent expressions that don't assume anything about the size of an **int**. The right columns describe the functions of the masks in AND and OR operations. Note that all of the complex expressions in figure 10-5 should be evaluated at *compile* time (not at run time) because the expressions are composed of nothing but constants, though this is compiler-dependent.

Fig. 10-5: Portable Bit Masks

```
nonport-
able:     portable:              X &= MASK:               X |= MASK:

0xffff    ~0                     Set all bits to 1.       Does nothing
0xfffe    ~1                     Clear rightmost bit.     Set all but rightmost
0xfff0    ~0xf                   Clear bottom 4 bits.     Set all but bottom 4
0x7fff    ((unsigned)(~0) >>1)   Clear top bit.           Set all but top bot.
0x8000    ~((unsigned)(~0) >>1)  Clear all but top bit.   Set top bit.
```

10.7.4. A Constant is an Int

A simple numeric constant is of type **int**. This can cause problems when a constant is passed to a subroutine that expects a noninteger argument. Consider this:

```
foo( x )
long    x;
{
}

foo( 10 );      /*    WRONG    */
foo( 10L );     /*    Correct  */
```

Here, the first call to *foo()* is incorrect. Since *10* is an **int**, the compiler pushes an **int**-sized object onto the stack. *Foo()*, however, expects a **long**-sized object. (This problem was discussed in depth in Chapter 3.) The second call to *foo()*, where the *10* is followed by an *L* fixes the problem. Constants followed by *L* are of type **long**.

A similar problem is encountered when constants are too long. For example, the largest number that can be contained in a 16 bit **int** is 32,767. You can say:

```
int x = 40000;
```

and most compilers won't print an error. Nevertheless, 40,000 decimal can't be represented in a 16 bit signed number, (though it can be represented in a 16 bit unsigned). 40,000 is 0x9c40. Since the top bit is set, 0x9c40 is a negative number (-25536 decimal). The expression *x = 40000* initializes *x* to -25536. Saying 40000L won't help because the number is still truncated when the assignment is made. The only way to fix the problem is to declare *x* **unsigned** or **long**.

10.8. Automatic type conversion problems

Automatic type conversion is active in every expression evaluation. In particular, all **char**s are *always* converted to **int**; all **float**s are *always* converted to **double**. Thereafter the numbers in the expression are converted to the largest possible type. For example, if the expression involves an **int** and a **long**, the **int** is converted to **long** before it's used. If an expression involves a **long** and a **double**, the **long** is converted to **double** before it's used. If one operand is an **int** and the other is an **unsigned**, the **int** is converted to **unsigned**. The conversions are done one or two operands at a time, as the expression is evaluated.

Since a **return** statement takes an expression as its argument, it's impossible to return a **char**-sized object. The automatic type conversion converts the **char** to an **int** before the **return** is executed. Similarly, the arguments to a subroutine are all expressions, thus you can't pass a **char** or a **float** to a subroutine because they are converted to an **int** or **double** before the routine is called.[5]

Because it's impossible to use a variable without its being part of an expression, and type conversion happens in all expressions, there's nothing to be saved by storing variables in **char**s or **float**s (unless space is really tight or you're using an array of them). That is, an array of **char** makes sense; a single **char**-sized variable does not. Use an **int**. The space savings are illusory because code is required to do the type conversion. You may save 1 byte in the data area by storing a number in a **char** rather than an **int**, but you add 20 bytes in type-conversion code at the same time. It takes longer to multiply 2 **float**s together than it does to multiply 2 **double**s (because the **float**s are converted to **double**s before they are used).

There are other problems that are caused by automatic type conversion. The test in the loop

```
unsigned x;

for( x = VAL; x > -1 ; --x )
        action( );
```

is always false, regardless of the value of *x*. Here -1 (represented by the bit

---

5.   You can declare an argument to be type **char**, but this practice usually has no
     effect.

pattern 0xffff) is treated as if it were an unsigned number. Though -1 is an **int**, the automatic type conversion turns it into an **unsigned**. 0x0ffff has the value 65535, the largest possible number that can be represented in a 16-bit **unsigned int**. X can never be larger than the largest possible number that you can represent, so the test is always false.

You can't use

```
long    x;
x &= 0xffff;
```

to clear all but the bottom 16 bits of a 32-bit **long**. 0xffff is not only an **int**, it's also negative (having the value -1). Since x is a **long**, the constant 0xffff (-1) is converted to **long** before it's used. When converted to a 32 bit number, -1 has the value 0xffffffff. Consequently, the above expression is treated like:

```
x &= 0xffffffff;
```

an expression that does nothing. Here the problem can be solved by saying 0xffffL .

There's another type-conversion problem. An expression is evaluated two terms at a time, and the intermediate result is put into an anonymous temporary variable that has the same type as the two terms. Moreover, the automatic type conversion rules are also applied to the two terms as they're evaluated. For example, in

```
int     a = 10, b = 20 ;

d = a * b ;
```

a and b are multiplied, and the result is put into an anonymous temporary variable. Since a and b are both of type **int**, no type conversion is necessary. The contents of the temporary are copied to d. Again, since the type of the anonymous temporary and d are both **int**, no type conversion is necessary. If the expression were more complicated, either there would be more temporaries or the temporaries would be used in more complex ways.

Now consider the following:

```
int     a = 32767, b = 10 ;
long    d;

d = a * b ;
```

The number 32,767 can be represented in a 16-bit **int** but 327,670 can not. So we decide to put the result into a **long**. The expression still will not evaluate correctly, however, because the type of the anonymous temporary is the same as that of the operands. That is, a and b are both of type **int**, so no type conversion is performed. The compiler can't know at compile time what the contents of a and b are going to be at run time. All it knows is the types of the operands. Consequently, 32,767 will be multiplied by 10, but the result will be put into an **int** sized temporary variable. Since 327,670 (0x4fff6) can't fit into an **int**, it will be truncated to -10 (0xfff6). The compiler will now look at the types of the temporary variable and of *d.* Since *d* is of type **long**, type conversion is performed on the temporary (it's converted to **long**) and the value -10 is assigned to *d.*

The problem can be fixed by forcing a type conversion on one or both of the operands, thereby also changing the type of the anonymous temporary too. This is done with a cast:

```
d = (long)a * (long)b ;
```

Note that even though only one cast is necessary in this example, it's often a good idea to cast all operands in a complicated expression, just to be sure that all the evaluations will work correctly. Remember that the order of evaluation is not guaranteed in C and that the type conversions are done as the expression is evaluated.

10.9. Missing or Implied Extern Statements

Another type-related problem is the return value of an external subroutine. If the compiler hasn't seen an explicit declaration for a subroutine (either by seeing the actual subroutine definition or by seeing a preceding **extern** statement), it assumes that the subroutine returns an **int**.

This assumption can cause problems when a subroutine is used in a file before it is declared. When the compiler sees an unknown subroutine being used, it creates a symbol table entry for that routine, showing a return value of **int**. If the compiler then encounters the actual definition of the subroutine, and that definition says that the subroutine returns something other than an **int**, the compiler thinks that you've declared two subroutines with the same name but returning values of different types. It complains with a "type mismatch" error message.

C provides a mechanism to circumvent this problem—the **extern** storage class. **Extern** doesn't really mean "external." Rather it's a directive to the compiler to put a variable (or subroutine) name into its symbol table as having a particular type. The compiler lets the *linker* find out where the variable (or subroutine) actually is in memory (at link time, not at compiler time). In other words, **extern** is a *declaration,* not a *definition.* A variable declaration just tells the compiler to put an entry in the symbol table; a definition actually causes space to be reserved for the variable and creates the symbol table entry too.

External declarations for subroutines take the following form:

```
long      john_silver( );  /* Returns a long           */
char      *capn_flint( );  /* Returns a pointer to char */
double    billy_bones( );  /* Returns a double          */
```

I usually group all my **extern** statements together at the top of the file.

Another problem caused by a missing **extern** statement is return value truncation. If a subroutine actually returns a **long** or a pointer, but the compiler thinks that it returns an **int**, the return value is truncated to the size of an **int** before it's used. To prevent this truncation, precede the first use of the subroutine with an **extern** statement that declares the subroutine as returning a type other than **int**.

Don't use a cast instead of an **extern** statement. The reason for this prohibition is exemplified in the following:

```
char     *ptr;
ptr = (char *) malloc( ARRAY_SIZE );
```

There is no preceding declaration for *malloc()*. Here you're telling the compiler that *malloc()* returns an **int** (because there's no **extern** statement telling it otherwise) and that the returned **int** should be converted to a character pointer before it's used. If a pointer is 32 bits wide and an **int** is 16 bits wide, problems result. Since the compiler thinks that *malloc()* returns an **int**, it truncates *malloc()*'s return value to 16 bits. The compiler then processes the cast, converting the truncated number to a 32-bit pointer. However, once the number is truncated, the top 16 bits are lost. The conversion to pointer won't restore them; instead the conversion will probably fill the most significant bytes with zeros. In any event, the pointer won't be pointing to anything meaningful.

The same problem results when a subroutine returns a **long** and you try to use

```
long    x;
x = (long) foo( );          /* foo returns a long */
```

instead of

```
long            x;
extern  long    foo( );

x = foo( );
```

Again, when the **extern** statement is missing, the compiler assumes that *foo()* returns an **int**. It truncates the top 16 bits from the value returned from *foo()*, and then converts the truncated number to **long**. Here sign extension is active as part of the type conversion. Not only are the top 16 bits of *foo()*'s return value lost, but the return value might be converted into a negative number as well (if the top bit of the bottom word happened to be 1).[6]

10.10. I/O

10.10.1. Scanf()

Don't use *scanf()* unless your program is reading a file that was created by another program. *Scanf()* was never intended to interact with a human being. If you have to use the *scanf()* conversion functions, get the input string with *gets()* or *fgets()* and then use the *sscanf()* function to extract the required information from the string.

Scanf() ignores white space and a newline ('\n') is white space. Thus, if you expect the input file to contain three numbers on a line, but one line has only two numbers on it, scanf() goes to the next line to get the third number. You're now out of synch with with the input from that line until the end of file.

Remember that *all* the arguments to *scanf()* have to be *pointers.* Disaster results if you forget an ampersand:

```
scanf("%x", num );
```

Here *scanf()* is passed the contents of num and it treats that number as if it were a pointer into which the number will be placed. If the value of *num* is 0, then the *scanf()* puts the converted number into memory location 0. This example should read as follows:

```
scanf("%x", &num );
```

Be very careful when mixing *scanf()* calls with other input functions, especially when *scanf()* is used along with *gets()* or *fgets().* Consider the following code:

```
int      num;
char     buf[128];

scanf("%d", &num );       /* Get a number */
gets( buf );              /* Now get a string */
```

If you type a number, followed by a newline, followed by a string, the following actions are performed:

(1) *Scanf()* reads characters, skipping any white space, until it encounters a digit.

(2) *Scanf()* then reads digits, converting them to an integer, until it sees a nondigit (the newline).

---

6.   Even though the keyword **extern** is actually optional in this sort of declaration, it's considered good programming style to use it.

(3)   *Scanf()* pushes the nondigit back onto the input stream with a *ungetc()* call and then returns.

(4)   *Gets()* is called; it reads the newline that *scanf()* pushed back, treats that as the end of string, and returns immediately. *Buf* contains a single '\0' as its first and only character.

The situation can be corrected by using either

```
gets( buf );
num = atoi( buf );
gets( buf );
```

or

```
gets  ( buf );
sscanf( buf, "%d", &num );
gets  ( buf );
```

10.10.2. Getc is a Buffered Function

Getc() is a buffered input function [as is *getchar()*, which is a macro that calls *getc()*]. This means that the first time *getc()* is called, it reads in an entire line of input , and puts that line into a buffer. *Getc()* then returns the first character in the buffer. The second time *getc()* is called it returns the second character in the buffer. *Getc()* won't go out to the keyboard again until there are no more characters in the buffer, whereupon it gets another whole line. Don't press a single key and expect immediate action from your program if that program uses *getc()* as its input function. Nothing happens until you type an entire line along with a terminating carriage return.

Some compilers get around this problem by supplying a second, "direct," input function—usually called *getch())*— that doesn't buffer the input line. Other compilers support a function that lets you change the way that keyboard input is handled. UNIX calls this subroutine *ioctl()*. UNIX also has a system call *(stty)* that can be executed before you execute your program (from within a shell script, for instance). Typing *stty raw* puts your terminal into unbuffered input mode; *stty cooked* puts it back into buffered mode. The low-level I/O function, *read()*, shouldn't buffer its input, so in theory, you can get a single character with:

```
int     c;

read( fileno(stdin), &c, 1 );
```

Not all compilers support this use of read( ), however. Lacking any of the above, you'll have to write a routine that communicates directly with your operating system.

10.10.3. Translated Versus Untranslated I/O

A related problem, found on CP/M and MS-DOS systems, is translated versus untranslated I/O. C uses a single character to represent end-of-line ('\n'). CP/M and DOS, however, use the two-character sequence CR-LF (0x0d-0x0a). (UNIX uses a single LF.) Consequently, the input functions usually translate the CR-LF sequence into a single '\n' for you on input and translate '\n' back into CR-LF on output. This behavior can present problems when you're reading binary data. Most compilers have a way to disable I/O translation. The most common method is to use:

```
fp = fopen( "file", "r" );
```

to open a file for translated reading while

```
fp = fopen( "file", "rb" );
```

opens the same file for untranslated, *binary mode,* input. If you need untranslated input from the keyboard, you can often communicate directly with the device. Consult your compiler's documentation for more details.

In DOS, you can create another FILE pointer for the console with all of the following:

```
fp = fopen( "con",      "rb" );
fp = fopen( "con:",     "rb" );
fp = fopen( "/dev/con", "rb" );
```

Figure 10-6 shows how to write directly to the printer using this mechanism.

Fig 10-6: Writing Directly to the Printer under MS-DOS

```
#include <stdio.h>

main( )
{
    FILE     *lpr;

    if( !(lpr = fopen("/dev/prn", "wb")) )
        printf("Can't open printer\n");
    else
        fprintf(lpr, "Quo usque tandem abutere...patientia nostra\n");
}
```

In UNIX, you have to say

```
fp = fopen( "/dev/ttyNN", "r" );
```

to talk directly to a terminal. The *NN* is replaced by the tty number of your own terminal (use the *who* or *whoami* command to get this number).

The /dev directory is used by UNIX to access all hardware devices; /dev is a dummy directory maintained by the operating system (rather than your compiler's I/O library). The files in it are actually devices in the I/O system.

DOS recognizes the filename *con* as special, however; the directory in which *con* is found is immaterial. That is, you could say */foo/con*. Strictly speaking, you should use *con:*, *con*, *CON*, or *CON:* when writing to the DOS device. Some compilers won't accept lower-case, others require lower case, Some compilers require a trailing colon (as in con:), still others won't accept a colon. All compilers that I know of accept */dev/con* because DOS itself accepts it; so */dev/con* would seem to be more portable.

10.11. Optimizers discarding operations

Even when the C code you write is perfectly reasonable, the compiler may change the code into garbage as it optimizes. Most optimizer-related problems can be circumvented simply by not optimizing a subroutine when it's compiled. Optimization can usually be suppressed with either a command-line switch or by just not executing a pass of the compiler.

Let's look at some examples. You might try the following code to clear (set to 0) the high bit of a number:

```
unsigned x;
x = (x << 1) >> 1;
```

However the optimizer might think that a left shift followed by a right shift doesn't do anything, however, and it will ignore the line. Of course, it's better to say

```
x &= (unsigned)(-1) >> 1;
```

There are more realistic problems that surface when you're interfacing to memory-mapped hardware (see Chapter 7). Hardware events are sometimes initiated by writing to an output port. The hardware doesn't care what you actually write to the port, it just waits for the port to be addressed. Thus, in a situation like

```
hardware.register = 1;

for( i = DELAY ; --i >= 0 ; )
          ;

hardware.register = 1;
```

the optimizer can see that 1 has been written to hardware.register. When it processes the second write, it notices that hardware.register has not been modified by any intervening code, so it optimizes out the second instruction (doesn't execute it). Here is a related problem:

```
c1 = uart.data
c2 = uart.data
```

This may be translated by the optimizer into

```
temp = uart.data
c1 = temp;
c2 = temp;
```

Similarly, when you say

```
uart.data = c;
uart.data = e;
```

the optimizer may discard the first assignment because uart.data isn't used before being reinitialized. This problem is common when an analog-to-digital is being used. You write to the converter to start the conversion process, and then read the result of the conversion back immediately:

```
char *atod = (char *) 0x1000;

*atod = 1;
c = *atod;
```

Writing 1 to *atod starts the conversion; the next statement reads in the result. Since *atod isn't modified or used between the two statements, the optimizer may translate the above into

```
*atod = 1;
c     = 1;
```

10.12. Exercises

10-1 Rewrite the max(x,y) macro and the two macros in exercise 10-3 so that they don't have side effects. You may not turn any of these macros into subroutines.

10-2 What's wrong with this program?

```
#include <stdio.h>
#define PRINT(d)          printf("Got %d lines\n", d );

main( )
{
        char    *buf;
        int     c, count ;

        for(count = 0 ; c ; count++);
        {
                if( gets(buf) != EOF )
                        if( c = *buf == 0 )
                                printf("Got <%s>\n", buf );
                else
                        PRINT( count );
        }
}
```

10-3   What does the following program print? Why?

```
#define islower(c)        ('a' <= (c) && (c) <= 'z')
#define toupper(c)        (islower(c) ? (c) - ('a'-'A') : (c))

main( )
{
        char    *p = "masonic dozens DEIfy forelock too ..";

        while( *p )
                printf("%c", toupper(*p++) );
}
```

BIBLIOGRAPHY

References and Textbooks

The classic book on C is:

> Brian Kernighan and Dennis Ritchie. *The C Programming Language*. Englewood Cliffs, N.J.: Prentice-Hall, 1978.

Usually called "K&R," this book is definitely for the experienced programmer; it's terse in places, and nothing is ever said twice. Nonetheless, Kernighan and Ritchie present the entire language in a clear, brief manner that I personally like quite a bit. You should supplement it with:

> Samuel P. Harbison and Guy L. Steele Jr. *C: A Reference Manual.* Englewood Cliffs, N.J.: Prentice-Hall, 1984.

This book is the best C reference I know of. It's coverage is comprehensive. The language, including many recent extensions, is fully described. This is not a text book, though, it's a reference. The definitive description of C is the emerging ANSI standard (X3J11). At this writing it's in the working draft stage. Copies are available from the X3 Secretariat: Computer and Business Equipment Manufacturers Association, 311 First Street, N. W., Suite 500, Washington, DC 20001-2178.

Also worth having is:

> *The Unix Programmer's Manual (Revised and Expanded Version).* New York: Holt, Rinehart & Winston, 1979.

Volume 1 has documentation for all the subroutines in the UNIX, ver. 7, standard library; it's useful for comparing with your own compiler's documentation to see just how standard your compiler is. If you live near a University, you can probably get a more recent edition of the manual there. Call the university library or Computer Science department.

There are several good introductions to C that are more useful to the average reader than K&R. My current favorite is

> Bryan Costales. *C from A to Z.* Englewood Cliffs, N.J.: Prentice-Hall, 1985.

The book is readable and complete in its discussions of the language. Another good alternative is:

> Alan R. Feuer. *The C Trainer.* Englewood Cliffs, N.J.: Prentice-Hall, 1986.

This book is meant to be used along with a C interpreter. It teaches the language in an interactive way, writing some code and then seeing how that code works. The interpreter itself is available for many computers (including the IBM, the Mac and several main frames). The book assumes a certain amount of programming experience and is expensive when you include the cost of the interpreter.

Two excellent study aids are available:

> Alan R. Feuer. *The C Puzzle Book: Puzzles for the C Programming Language*. Englewood Cliffs, N.J.: Prentice-Hall, 1982.

> Clovis L. Tondo and Scott E. Gimple. *The C Answer Book.* Englewood Cliffs, N.J.: Prentice-Hall, 1986.

The C Puzzle Book is a book of exercises and detailed solutions to each exercise. This is an invaluable book. I could have saved myself several days of debugging time had this book been available when I was learning the language. The exercises are designed to teach you how to find obscure but prevalent bugs in C programs. *The C Answer Book* provides detailed answers to all the questions in Kernighan and Ritchie. The answers assume no knowledge of C other than what you'd get from reading K&R up to the point where the exercises are assigned.

It's also useful to look at examples of actual C programs. Good resources are:

> *The Dr. Dobb's Toolbook of C.* New York: Brady Communications, 1986.

> Ted J. Biggerstaff. *Systems Software Tools.* Englewood Cliffs, N.J.: Prentice-Hall, 1986.

> Joe Campbell. *Crafting C Tools for the IBM PCs.* Englewood Cliffs, N.J.: Prentice-Hall, 1986.

> Douglas Comer. *Operating System Design, The XINU Approach.* Englewood Cliffs, N.J.: Prentice-Hall, 1984.

> William James Hunt. *The C Toolbox: Serious C Programming for the IBM PC.* Reading, Mass.: Addison-Wesley, 1985.

The *Toolbook* contains 700 pages of C source code, including a version of Grep, a complete line-oriented editor, and a compiler. While on the subject, *Dr. Dobb's Journal* is a pretty good source for C code in general; it has published more C programs than any other computer magazine. A one-year subscription is $29.95 from Dr. Dobb's Journal, P. O. Box 27809, San Diego, California 92128.

Systems Software Tools and *Operating System Design* both contain the complete source for a multi-tasking operating system. Comer presents a complete UNIX-like operating system for the LSI-11. Just the operating system itself is presented, the user interface or *shell* is not. Comer's book includes the source for a low-level disk driver, however. Biggerstaff describes a multi-tasking system that runs on the IBM-PC family. It supports windows and provides a user interface, but it just uses MS-DOS to access the disk. Biggerstaff covers the basics of operating system design in a more accessible fashion than Comer but Comer covers the low-level disk interface details better.

Crafting C Tools is about low-level IBM PC programming in C (as compared to assembler) It's very complete and has lots of useful subroutines. *The C Toolbox*, title not withstanding, has little to do with the IBM PC. It's more about applications programming. It contains several significant programs, such as a BTREE data-base manager.

Math & Computer Science

All programmers need a certain amount of math, Boolean algebra, basic probability, a little graph theory, and so on. A good introduction to these topics is:

> Romualdas Skvarcius and William Robinson. *Discrete Mathematics with Computer Science Applications*. Menlo Park, Calif.: Benjamin/Cummings, 1986.

Structured programming is covered in:

> Kirk Hansen. *Data Structured Program Design*. Englewood Cliffs, N.J.: Prentice-Hall, 1986.

> Brian Kernighan and P. J. Plauger *The Elements of Programming Style* Englewood Cliffs, N.J.: Prentice-Hall, 1978.

Hansen's book teaches the Warnier/Orr methodology for program design. *The Elements of Programming Style* is very useful if you're comming to C from FORTRAN and need a good introduction to structured design. All of its examples are in FORTRAN.

Two excellent books on data structures are

> Robert L. Kruse. *Data Structures and Program Design*. Englewood Cliffs, N.J.: Prentice-Hall, 1984.

Aaron M. Tenenbaum and Moshe J. Augenstein. *Data Structures Using Pascal*. 2d ed. Englewood Cliffs, N.J.: Prentice-Hall, 1986.

Kruse's explanations are clearer than Tenenbaum and Augenstein's. The latter is more complete, however. All examples in both books are in Pascal.

Assembly Language

Though the 8086 is a miserable machine from the assembly language programmer's perspective, you'll want to learn it if you own an IBM-PC. Fortunately, if you program in C you won't have to go to 8086 assembler very often, but if the need should arise you might want to consult the following:

John Angermeyer and Kevin Jaeger. *MS-DOS Developer's Guide*. Indianapolis, Ind.: Howard W. Sams & Co., 1986.

Robert Lafore. *Assembly Language Primer for the IBM PC and XT*. New York: Plume/Waite, 1984.

Christopher Morgan. *Bluebook of Assembly Routines for the IBM PC & XT*. New York: Plume/Waite, 1984.

The MS-DOS Developer's Guide Is actually about IBM PC systems programming. It's loaded with good practical examples of how assembler is used, however. Lafore's book is a good introduction to 8086 Assembly Language programming. It's easy to read and very complete. Morgan is a book of small 8086 Assembly Languages subroutines. It doesn't teach you assembler; rather, it provides good examples. If you buy your assembler from IBM, you'll get a language reference along with the assembler. On the other hand, the Microsoft Macro Assembler is a better assembler (Microsoft is usually a few releases ahead of IBM), but the Microsoft assembler doesn't come with a reference. A good reference is:

Russell Rector and George Alexy. *The 8086 Book*. Berkeley: Osborne/McGraw-Hill, 1980.

You can't learn 8086 assembler from this book; it's a reference and nothing more. Also of interest for Z-80 programmers is:

Daniel N. Ozick, *Structured Assembly Language Programming for the Z80*. Hasbrouck Heights, N.J.: Hayden Book Co., 1985.

It not only teaches the language, but also teaches you how to write assembler in an readable, maintainable fashion.

Compiler Design and Construction

A simple grammar for the C language is contained in Kernighan & Ritchie, pages 214 through 219. A better grammar (one that can actually be used by a real compiler) is contained in Harbison and Steele. Of course, there's a grammar in the ANSI standard as well. A good, short, description of table-driven parsing techniques can be found in:

> Henry A. Seymour, "An Introduction to Parsing," *Dr. Dobb's Journal,* 98 (December, 1984) pp. 78–86.

A more in-depth look at the subject, and at compiler design in general, can be found in:

> Alfred V. Aho, Ravi Sethi and Jeffrey D. Ullman. *Compilers: Principles, Techniques and Tools*. Reading, Mass.: Addison-Wesley, 1986.

This book is a rewrite of the "dragon book" *(Principles of Compiler Design)* so called because of a dragon on the cover. This is the definitive book on the subject of compiler design. Unfortunately, like most math books, it's not very readable. It explains simple concepts in unnecessarily complex ways, and the book contains almost no real programming examples. A more readable, but less comprehensive, book is:

> P.M.Lewis, D.J.Rosenkrantz, and R.E.Stearns. *Compiler Design Theory*. Reading, Mass.: Addison-Wesley, 1976.

Finally, a book with an entirely practical orientation is

> Per Brinch Hansen. *Brinch Hansen on Pascal Compilers*. Englewood Cliffs, N.J.: Prentice-Hall, 1985.

YACC and LEX are programs that take as input a grammar and a description of a token set, and output the C source code for a parser and a lexical analyzer. Perhaps The best description of how to use Yacc and Lex that I know of is:

> Axel T. Schreiner and H. George Friedman, Jr. *Introduction to Compiler Construction with UNIX*. Englewood Cliffs, N.J.: Prentice-Hall, 1985.

A topic related topic to compilers is the root or startup module. There's an example of how to modify the Aztec CII root module to support Unix-like redirection, pipes, and wild-card expansion in

> Allen Holub, "C-Chest," *Dr. Dobb's Journal of Software Tools*, 101 (March, 1985) pp. 10–28.

Tools

Several useful UNIX tools and programs are available for the IBM-PC too:

SH, a scaled-down version of the UNIX C shell that runs under MS-DOS, is available from Dr. Dobb's Catalog (M&T Publishing, 501 Galveston Drive, Redwood City, Calif. 94063 (800/528-6050). A package of UNIX-like utilities (called /util) that includes a version of *grep.* is also available from the same source. Both packages come with the complete C source code as well as the executable programs on disk. They are useful programs in their own right and are also good examples of C programs of a realistic size. M&T also distributes machine readable versions of several of the programs in *The Dr. Dobb's Toolbook,* (the small C compiler and assembler, a set of text-processing tools, and so on) all with the complete C source code included.

Versions of the *make* utility are available from Polytron Software (P. O. Box 787, Hillsboro, OR 97123; 503/648-8595) and from Lattice Inc. (P. O. Box 3072, Glen Ellyn, Ill. 60138; 312/858-7950). The Polytron version, called Polymake, is more UNIX compatible. The Lattice version, called LMK, is a little more expensive but it occupies considerably less memory when it runs. Versions of make are also supplied with several compilers (at this writing Microsoft C, Aztec C, and Datalight C all include a make). The source code for a bare-bones make was printed in the July, 1985 C-Chest (*Dr. Dobb's Journal*, 105, p.20f).

A good version of lint is PC-Lint, available from Gimple Software, 3207 Hogarth Lane, Collegville, PA, 19426; (215) 584-4261.

I've avoided talking about compilers because they change so often that discussing of them here would be almost meaningless. If you're in the market for a compiler you should read reviews in recent issues of technical computer magazines. *Dr. Dobb's Journal*, the *PC Tech Journal*, and *Computer Language Magazine* publish reviews.

APPENDIX A

C Order of Precedence		
Associativity	Operator	Notes
left to right	() [] -> .	structure member
right to left	++ -- (type) sizeof ! - ~ * &	NOT, Unary minus, one's complement, pointed-to, address-of
left to right	* / %	multiply, divide, modulus
left to right	- +	binary minus and plus
left to right	<< >>	left and right shift
left to right	< <= > >=	logical test
left to right	== !=	logical equality
left to right	&	bitwise AND
left to right	^	bitwise XOR
left to right	|	bitwise OR
left to right	&&	logical AND
left to right	||	logical OR
right to left	$e\,?\,t:f$	conditional: if e then t else f
right to left	= += -= /= %= >>= &= etc.	assignment
left to right	,	sequence operator
Operators on the same line have the same precedence. Operators on lower lines are lower precedence.		

ASCII Character Set								
	0	*1*	*2*	*3*	*4*	*5*	*6*	*7*
0	\0	DLE	*space*	0	@	P	`	p
1	SOH	DC1	!	1	A	Q	a	q
2	STX	DC2	"	2	B	R	b	r
3	ETX	DC3	#	3	C	S	c	s
4	EOT	DC4	$	4	D	T	d	t
5	ENQ	NAK	%	5	E	U	e	u
6	ACK	SYN	&	6	F	V	f	v
7	BEL	ETB	'	7	G	W	g	w
8	\b	CAN	(	8	H	X	h	x
9	\t	EM	)	9	I	Y	i	y
a	\n	SUB	*	:	J	Z	j	z
b	\v	ESC	+	;	K	[	k	{
c	\f	FS	,	<	L	\	l	|
d	\r	GS	–	=	M	]	m	}
e	SO	RS	.	>	N	^	n	~
f	SI	US	/	?	O	_	o	DEL

APPENDIX B

Shell Sort

I thought for years that Shell sort was named after a shell game. Anyone who's tried to figure out the sort routine in Kernighan and Ritchie's book can understand how I reached this conclusion. As it turns out, the algorithm is named after its inventor, Donald Shell, who developed it in 1959. Shell sort works by breaking up the sorting problem into a series of smaller problems. For example, a set of eight objects to be sorted is broken up into 4 subsets of 2 objects, each of which is sorted separately. The eight objects are then re-organized as 2 sets of 4 objects, again each sorted separately. Finally, the set is sorted as one set of 8 objects. The rationale behind this breaking up into smaller sets is that you will get the more out-of-order parts of the original set into order very quickly. The array will then be easier to sort on the next pass. What makes a Shell sort a Shell sort is the reorganization into smaller sets. The algorithm used to actually sort the items in each subset is immaterial, except that the behavior of this algorithm should get better as the set it's working on gets closer to being in order. A bubble sort has this behavior. In fact, you can look at Shell sort as an improved bubble sort.

A concrete example may clarify the process. Let's start with a set of 8 objects:

```
{9, 2, 1, 7, 3, 8, 5, 4}
```

We'll break this up into four subsets consisting of the pairs {9,3}, {2,8}, {1,5} and {7,4}:

```
9 2  1 7  3 8  5 4
| |  | |  | |  | |
+-------+ | | |
  +-------+ | |
    +-------+ |
      +-------+
```

Then we'll sort each pair separately:

```
3 2  1 4  9 8  5 7
| |  | |  | |  | |
+-------+ | | |
  +-------+ | |
    +-------+ |
      +-------+
```

Next we'll break up the set into two subsets of four elements ({3,1,9,5} and {2,4,8,7})

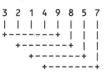

```
3 2  1 4  9 8  5 7
| |  | |  | |  | |
+---+---+---+ |
    |   |   |   |
    +---+---+---+
```

and sort these separately, yielding:

```
1 2  3 4  5 7  9 8
| |  | |  | |  | |
+---+---+---+ |
    |   |   |   |
    +---+---+---+
```

Finally, we'll treat the input as one set of eight elements and just sort it, yielding

```
1 2  3 4  5 7  8 9
| |  | |  | |  | |
+-+-+-+-+-+-+-+
```

Let's compare this process to the program in the text (Figure 7-16). The outermost **for** loop (on line 11) determines how many elements will be in each subset. *Gap* is the distance in the array between two elements of the same subset. In the foregoing example, the distance between the 9 and 3 (which compose the first subset) is 4; this would be the initial value of *gap*. Each time through this first **for** loop, we divide *gap* by 2, which effectively doubles the number of elements in a subset.

The second and third **for** loops (lines 12 and 13) are the actual sort routine. The algorithm is essentially a bubble sort, though the situation is complicated by sorting all the subsets at the same time. You can best see how the sort works by reducing the algorithm to handle only the last case (a gap of 1) and reversing the sense of the compare, thereby creating a bubble sort:

```
for( i = 1 ; i < argc ; i++ )
     for( j = i - 1; j >= 0 ; --j )
          if( strcmp( argv[j], argv[j+1] > 0)
                    exch( argv[j], argv[j+1] )
```

In the innermost loop, bubble sort scans along the unsorted array look-ing for two adjacent out-of-order elements. When it finds these elements, it exchanges them. Thus an out-of-order element will tend to "bubble" up to its correct place in the array. You have to do a bunch of comparisons and exchanges to get it there, though (worst case is an array already sorted, but in reverse order; you have to make N-1 exchanges to get an out-of-place element from the right end of an N element array all the way to the left end). This inner loop has to be executed enough times to guarantee that all out-of-order elements will find their way to the proper position in the array; so bubble sort will *always* use $O(N^2)$ comparisons. In worst case, it will need almost as many exchanges. It's no wonder that bubble sort is slow.

You can now see how the Shell sort strategy helps bubble sort. It will take that pathologically out-of-place element and move it to the front of the array in $O(\log N)$ exchanges, rather than N-1 exchanges. The behavior of Shell sort can be improved by fiddling with the increments between elements. This lets the various passes interact with each other in a more productive fashion. The increments should not be even multiples of each other, powers of 2 are actually among the worst choice of increments. Knuth has, by means of magic, determined that 1, 4, 13, 40, 121, $((121 * 3) + 1)$, ... is a good choice of increments He also says that the sequence 1, 3, 7, 15, 31 ... 2^n-1 works well. Using the latter sequence of increments, Shell sort will sort an N element array in $O(N^{1.2})$time—much better than the $O(N^2)$ time required for bubble sort. If you're interested, the gory details of this analysis are in Donald E. Knuth, *The Art of Computer Programming,* vol 3. (Reading, Mass.: Addison-Wesley, 1973) p. 84f.

INDEX

TEAR OUT THIS PAGE TO ORDER THESE OTHER HIGH QUALITY C LANGUAGE AND UNIX* SYSTEM TITLES FROM THE WORLD'S PREMIER C/UNIX PUBLISHER— PRENTICE-HALL

Quantity		Title/Author	ISBN	Price	Total $
_____	1.	The C Programming Language; Kernighan/Ritchie	013-110163-3	$24.95 paper	_____
_____	2.	The C Answer Book; Tondo/Gimpel	013-109877-2	$17.95 paper	_____
_____	3.	The UNIX* Programming Environment; Kernighan/Pike	013-937699-2	$26.95 cloth	_____
_____	4.	The C Puzzle Book; Feuer	013-109934-5	$21.95 cloth	_____
_____	5.	C: A Reference Manual, 2/e; Harbison/Steele	013-109810-1	$28.95 cloth	_____
_____	6.	The Design of the UNIX* Operating System; Bach	013-201799-7	$31.95 cloth	_____
_____	7.	Advanced UNIX* Programming; Rochkind	013-011818-4	$32.95 cloth	_____
_____	8.	System Software Tools; Biggerstaff	013-881772-3	$28.95 cloth	_____
_____	9.	Crafting C Tools for the IBM PC; Campbell	013-188418-2	$21.95 paper	_____
_____	10.	The UNIX* System User's Handbook; AT&T	013-937764-6	$16.95 paper	_____
_____	11.	The Vi User's Handbook; AT&T	013-941733-8	$16.95 paper	_____
_____	12.	The C Programmer's Handbook; AT&T	013-110073-4	$16.95 paper	_____
_____	13.	AT&T Computer Software Catalog: MS DOS; AT&T	0-8359-9278-0	$19.95 paper	_____
_____	14.	AT&T Computer Software Catalog: UNIX* System V; AT&T	0-8359-9279-0	$19.95 paper	_____
_____	15.	The UNIX* C Shell/Field Guide; Anderson/Anderson	013-937468-X	$23.95 paper	_____
_____	16.	DOS/UNIX*: Becoming A Super User; Seyer/Mills	013-218645-4	$21.95 paper	_____
_____	17.	UNIX* RefGuide; McNulty Development, Inc.	013-938952-0	$24.95 paper	_____
_____	18.	Preparing Documents With UNIX*; Brown	013-699976-X	$21.95 cloth	_____
_____	19.	Learning to Program in C; Plum	013-527854-6	$34.95 cloth	_____
				Subtotal $	_____

OVER PLEASE ▶

Quantity		Title/Author	ISBN	Price	Total $
				Subtotal $	
				(from previous page)	
_____	20.	Programming in C With a Bit of UNIX*; Moore	013-730094-8	$22.95 paper	_____
_____	21.	The C Companion; Holub	013-109786-5	$19.95 paper	_____
_____	22.	The C Trainer; Feuer	013-109752-0	$22.95 paper	_____
_____	23.	UNIX® Ada* Programming; Gehani	013-938325-5	$24.95 paper	
				Total $	_____
				— discount (if appropriate)	_____
				Sales Tax	_____
				(where applicable)	
				New Total $	_____

AND TAKE ADVANTAGE OF THESE SPECIAL OFFERS!

(a) When ordering 3 or 4 copies (of the same or different titles), take 10% off the total list price (excluding sales tax, where applicable).

(b) When ordering 5 to 20 copies (of the same or different titles), take 15% off the total list price (excluding sales tax, where applicable).

(c) To receive a greater discount when ordering 20 or more copies, call or write:

Special Sales Department
College Marketing
Prentice-Hall
Englewood Cliffs, NJ 07632
201-592-2498

SAVE!
If payment accompanies order, plus your state's sales tax where applicable, Prentice-Hall pays postage and handling charges. Same return privilege refund guaranteed. Please do not mail in cash.

☐ **PAYMENT ENCLOSED**—shipping and handling to be paid by publisher (please include your state's tax where applicable).

☐ **SEND BOOKS ON 15-DAY TRIAL BASIS** & bill me (with small charge for shipping and handling).

Name _____

Address _____

City _____ State _____ Zip _____

I prefer to charge my ☐Visa   ☐MasterCard

Card Number _____ Expiration Date _____

Signature _____

All prices listed are subject to change without notice.

Mail your order to: Prentice-Hall, Book Distribution Center, Route 59 at Brook Hill Drive, West Nyack, NY 10994

Dept. 1

D–TMAR–LR(7)

TEAR OUT THIS PAGE TO ORDER THESE OTHER HIGH QUALITY C LANGUAGE AND UNIX* SYSTEM TITLES FROM THE WORLD'S PREMIER C/UNIX PUBLISHER— PRENTICE-HALL

Quantity		Title/Author	ISBN	Price	Total $
_____	1.	The C Programming Language; Kernighan/ Ritchie	013-110163-3	$24.95 paper	_____
_____	2.	The C Answer Book; Tondo/Gimpel	013-109877-2	$17.95 paper	_____
_____	3.	The UNIX* Programming Environment; Kernighan/ Pike	013-937699-2	$26.95 cloth	_____
_____	4.	The C Puzzle Book; Feuer	013-109934-5	$21.95 cloth	_____
_____	5.	C: A Reference Manual, 2/e; Harbison/Steele	013-109810-1	$28.95 cloth	_____
_____	6.	The Design of the UNIX* Operating System; Bach	013-201799-7	$31.95 cloth	_____
_____	7.	Advanced UNIX* Programming; Rochkind	013-011818-4	$32.95 cloth	_____
_____	8.	System Software Tools; Biggerstaff	013-881772-3	$28.95 cloth	_____
_____	9.	Crafting C Tools for the IBM PC; Campbell	013-188418-2	$21.95 paper	_____
_____	10.	The UNIX* System User's Handbook; AT&T	013-937764-6	$16.95 paper	_____
_____	11.	The Vi User's Handbook; AT&T	013-941733-8	$16.95 paper	_____
_____	12.	The C Programmer's Handbook; AT&T	013-110073-4	$16.95 paper	_____
_____	13.	AT&T Computer Software Catalog: MS DOS; AT&T	0-8359-9278-0	$19.95 paper	_____
_____	14.	AT&T Computer Software Catalog: UNIX* System V; AT&T	0-8359-9279-0	$19.95 paper	_____
_____	15.	The UNIX* C Shell/Field Guide; Anderson/ Anderson	013-937468-X	$23.95 paper	_____
_____	16.	DOS/UNIX*: Becoming A Super User; Seyer/Mills	013-218645-4	$21.95 paper	_____
_____	17.	UNIX* RefGuide; McNulty Development, Inc.	013-938952-0	$24.95 paper	_____
_____	18.	Preparing Documents With UNIX*; Brown	013-699976-X	$21.95 cloth	_____
_____	19.	Learning to Program in C; Plum	013-527854-6	$34.95 cloth	_____

Subtotal $ _____

OVER PLEASE ◗

Quantity		Title/Author	ISBN	Price	Total $
				Subtotal $	
				(from previous page)	
_____	20.	Programming in C With a Bit of UNIX*; Moore	013-730094-8	$22.95 paper	_____
_____	21.	The C Companion; Holub	013-109786-5	$19.95 paper	_____
_____	22.	The C Trainer; Feuer	013-109752-0	$22.95 paper	_____
_____	23.	UNIX® Ada* Programming; Gehani	013-938325-5	$24.95 paper	_____
				Total $	_____
			— discount (if appropriate)		_____
				Sales Tax	_____
			(where applicable)		
				New Total $	_____

AND TAKE ADVANTAGE OF THESE SPECIAL OFFERS!

(a) When ordering 3 or 4 copies (of the same or different titles), take 10% off the total list price (excluding sales tax, where applicable).

(b) When ordering 5 to 20 copies (of the same or different titles), take 15% off the total list price (excluding sales tax, where applicable).

(c) To receive a greater discount when ordering 20 or more copies, call or write:

Special Sales Department
College Marketing
Prentice-Hall
Englewood Cliffs, NJ 07632
201-592-2498

SAVE!
If payment accompanies order, plus your state's sales tax where applicable, Prentice-Hall pays postage and handling charges. Same return privilege refund guaranteed. Please do not mail in cash.

☐ **PAYMENT ENCLOSED**—shipping and handling to be paid by publisher (please include your state's tax where applicable).

☐ **SEND BOOKS ON 15-DAY TRIAL BASIS** & bill me (with small charge for shipping and handling).

Name _____

Address _____

City _____ State _____ Zip _____

I prefer to charge my ☐Visa   ☐MasterCard

Card Number _____ Expiration Date _____

Signature _____

All prices listed are subject to change without notice.

Mail your order to: Prentice-Hall, Book Distribution Center, Route 59 at Brook Hill Drive, West Nyack, NY 10994

Dept. 1   D–TMAR–LR(7)